Continued to Back Cover

Logging Railroads
in
Skagit County

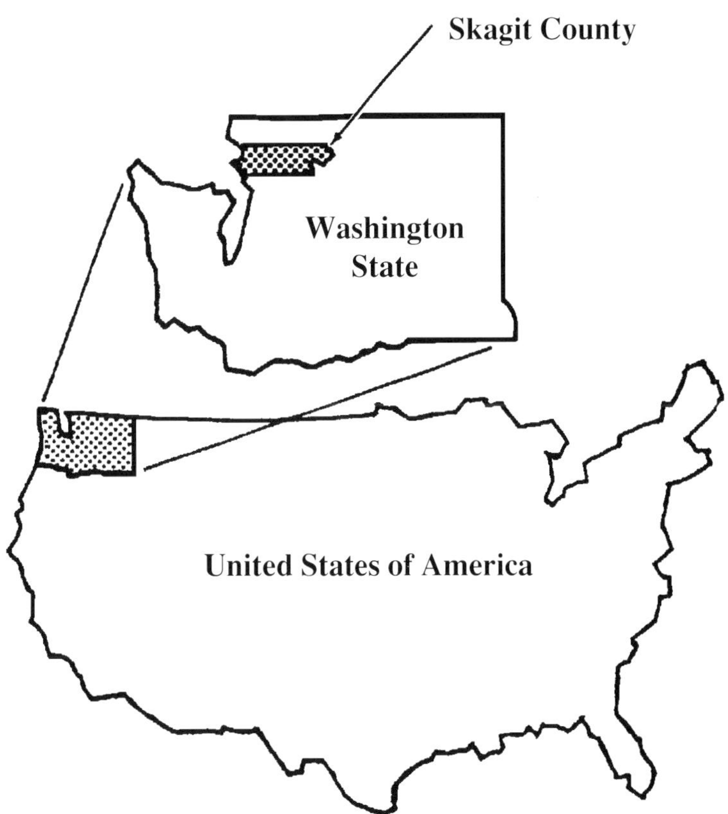

Logging Railroads in Skagit County

The First Comprehensive History of the Logging Railroads in Skagit County, Washington, USA

by

Dennis Blake Thompson

Illustrations by E. L. Hauff

Cartography by R. Dale Jost, M.D.

NORTHWEST SHORT LINE
Seattle, Washington
1989

Published by NorthWest Short Line
Box 423 Seattle WA 98111-0423 USA
SAN 693-2037

Book Concept by Dennis Blake Thompson
Book Design and Typography by NWSL Publications
Cartography by R. Dale Jost, M.D.
Editors: F. Raoul Martin, Sheryl P. Martin, Larry D. Richards
Created with Ventura Publisher
Typeset by Seattle Imagesetting
Manufactured in the United States of America

Second Edition
1996

Library of Congress Cataloging in Publication Data
Thompson, Dennis Blake 1943-
Logging Railroads in Skagit County: The first comprehensive history of the logging railroads in Skagit County, Washington, USA/by Dennis Blake Thompson; illustrations by E. L. Hauff; cartography by R. Dale Jost
Includes index.
ISBN 0-915370-06-9:(hardcover)
1. Logging railroads--Washington (State)--Skagit County
I. Hauff, E. L. II. Title
TF24.W2T47 1989
385'.54'0979772-dc20 89-23113

- Endpapers - Railroad map of Skagit County depicting topography and logging railroad grades. *R. D. Jost MD*
- Frontispiece - Puget Sound Sawmills and Shingle Company 3-truck Climax crossing the Baker River Bridge prior to flooding by the Baker River hydroelectric project. *D. Kinsey, Whatcom Museum of History and Art*

TABLE OF CONTENTS

Dedication

To my wife, NONA
For Her Encouragement and Patience

PHOTOGRAPH CONTRIBUTORS

We are greatly indebted to these persons and organizations for taking, collecting, identifying, cataloging, preserving and/or providing the photographic glimpses of the past provided in this book to bring enjoyment and understanding of the way it was. This book and your enjoyment of it has been made possible by the generosity of these persons and organizations. Many of the photographs are from family albums or collections, some regrettably in poor condition (such as the photograph on page 218 that shows the results of being folded) and/or of poor quality (such as on page 140 with stains and spots) but nevertheless very valuable in that they provide a scene otherwise unavailable and lost to time. Too often, such scenes are lost forever when "worthless old snapshots" are discarded in hasty cleanup efforts. Many scenes were captured by Darius Kinsey and other professional photographers who chronicled these times for us in their daily efforts to capture scenes that could be sold. This is why so many scenes included the workmen of the day - all potential customers for a print. And while many Kinsey negatives have survived in various collections, many prints have been obtained from the persons, or their descendents, who purchased the print with their hard earned (as shown) money.

The author, a historian by avocation, has done a superb job of collecting these old scenes and restoring them in his darkroom so we can enjoy another momentary window to the past.

The photo credit form used herein is that the final name in italics is the person or organization which made the photograph available. The photographer, if known, is the first name in italics.

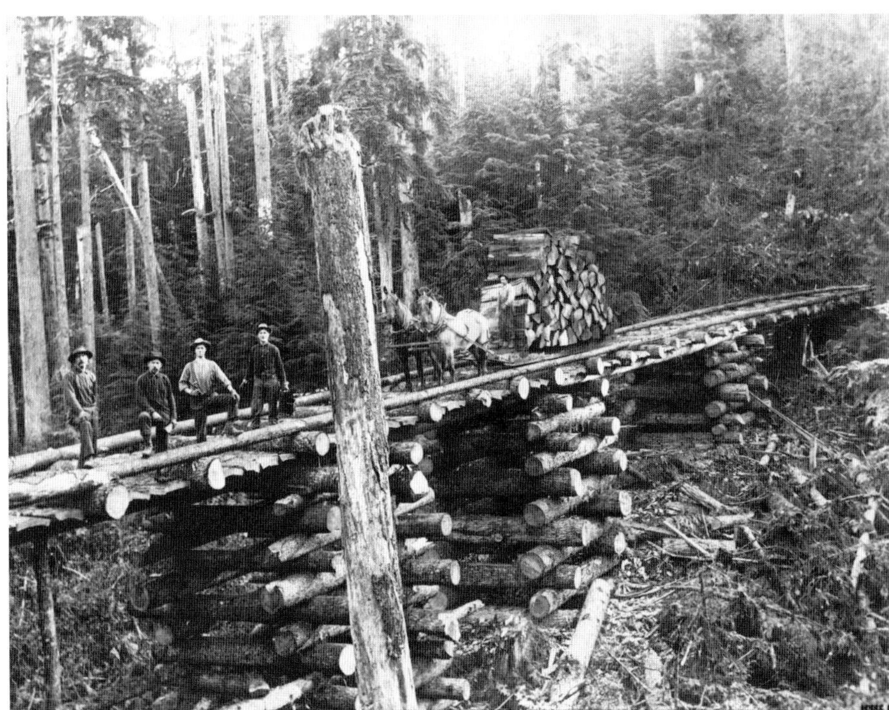

EARLY POWER. Horse team, shingle bolts sled and skid road. A scene repeated countless times throughout the Pacific Northwest. *Bert Kellogg*

ACKNOWLEDGEMENTS

There are a few things I would like the reader to know: I began this project, in a serious fashion, in 1971, following a long standing curiosity about what logging railroads had once existed in Skagit County. To a large degree it has been a frustrating project because the pieces of this historical "puzzle" have been quite difficult to locate and assemble. While some logging railroads in other parts of the western United States have been effectively documented, their counterparts in Skagit County have just as effectively disappeared from record. Sources of information have been, and indeed still are, perpetually evasive and perpetually fragmented.

Fortunately much has come to light through the years, which I respectively offer in this volume. Without the assistance of scores of wonderful people and institutions, this book would not be possible. I have interviewed countless loggers, trainmen and pioneers - this book is their story.

I would like to thank Mr. E. L. Hauff for the pen and ink sketches appearing in this book. Each sketch represents a scene known to have once existed in Skagit County but not recorded by a reproducable photograph, or not recorded by any image at all. I am very pleased that he was so able to create pleasing illustrations from my verbal requests.

Cartographics herein are the work of R. Dale Jost, M.D. I first met Dr. Jost at a time when I had accumulated a large amount of resource material from which maps were to be created for this volume. I discovered here a man with boundless energy and dedication to maps of Western America logging railroads. It occurred to me that the quality of the book might be enhanced by Dr. Jost's singular devotion to that subject, and he kindly agreed to prepare the maps. The result has been excellent. He has scrutinized documents for every square foot of Skagit County in search of abandoned grades. He has contributed substantial material of his own discovery. While it is impossible to claim that every grade built is now recorded, the result I believe is one of the best county maps yet prepared. And, additions or corrections are certainly invited. My deepest appreciation to Dr. Jost for his work.

The following organizations and institutions were of great value in preparing this book: Alco Historic Photos, Allen County (Ohio) Historical Society; Burlington (Washington) Public Library; Carstens Publications, Inc.; Everett (Wash.) Public Library; Georgia-Pacific Corporation; Library of Congress; Railroad Museum of Pennsylvania; Railway and Locomotive Historical Society; Scott Paper Company; Seattle Public Library; Skagit County Historical Society; Skagit-LTV Energy Products; University of Washington; Washington State Archives; Washington State Department of Natural Resources; Washington State Historical Society; Western Washington University and the Whatcom Museum of History and Art.

For technical assistance in the darkroom and for sharing their personal photograph collections, I owe a great deal to Galen Biery, Steve Hauff, Bert Kellogg and Rod Slemmons.

John Labbe has been good enough to open his extensive files to my constant questions, year after year.

John Pinelli, past employee of the Lyman Timber Company, provided long term insights to "up-river" logging in the early days. And the warm friendship that has ensued occupies a special place in my life.

D. S. Richter has provided many missing pieces to the still incomplete Locomotive Rosters.

Dale W. Thompson maintained a constant vigil for information throughout the life of this project. His many contributions clarified a multitude of obscure details throughout this work.

In addition I would like to thank the following for their contributions: John Abenroth, Rich Allen, Magnus (Maggie) Anderson, Millard Anderson, Genevieve Ball, John Ball (I sure miss him), Alfred Bandazy, Arthur Barringer, Mary Bates, Mrs. Denny Beeman, Mervin Benham, Roy Benham, Dave Bohn, Roger Boyd, Pete Brandt, John Bratnober, Bob Britten, Mrs. Frederick G. Brown, Roy Buckner, Charles W. Bullock, Ina Burkhart, Lawrence Burmaster, Fred Butler, Stanley Butler, Keith Campbell, Walter C. Casler, Mrs. Ras Chambers, George and Tillie Coble, Leo Coffman, Dan Cozine, Rod Crossley, Bob Culp, Frank Culp, Joel Dahlin, Orman Darby, Eunice Darvill, Alice Deierlein, Denny DeMeyer, John J. Dempsey Jr., Stan Dexter, Reynold Dickhaus, Dave Dilgard, Charles Dinsmore, Mollie Dowdle, Ted Dubenic, Naomi Ecret, Rex Everett, Inez Farmer, Albert Farrow, First American Title Insurance of Skagit County, Bill Fisher, Hiram Fosnaugh, Ruth Foster, Roger Fox, Al Frisell, Jim Futrelle, Cecil Gahan, Roy Gascon, Fred Gemmer, James Gertz, Lloyd Graham, James Graves, Frank Green, R. E. Gray, Fern Gross, Earnest A. Guthrie, Gary Haack, Lewellyn "Lew" Hall, Dudley Hansen, Claire Harvie, Peter Heffelfinger, Charles Herz, Al Hodgin, Josephine Hoffman, Fred Holder, Hob Hollyfield, Jack Holst, Bob Howard, Charlie Howard, Elsie Ingersoll, Mrs. B. B. Jenkins, Arne Johnson, Eunice Jonasson, Dr. J. A. Jonasson, Ray Jordan, Al Karr, Tommy Kell, Ed Kittila, Michael Koch, Louis LaMar, Dave and Fern Larrabee, Thomas Lawson, Jr., Mary Larsen, John Lewis, Earl Lind, Andy Loft, George Lomsdalan, Frank Maddox, Victor Maddox, Darlene Maloy, Ed Marlow, Charles Marquart, Fred Martin, Alfred McBee, Bill Martin, Harley McCalib, Blaine H. McGillicuddy, Dave McLaughlin, Marlin Miller, John Milnor, Joe Moe, Harold Mong, James D. Moore, June N. Moore, Chester Morrell, Herbert Neises, Art Nelson, Reid Nelson, Fred Nielson, George Nesset, Ingeborg Nesset, Tom Nesset, Carl Olin, Ruth Olsen, Harry Osborne, Bruce Paddock, Hazel Parker, Stan Parker, P. E. Percy, Lawrence Perrigo, Joe Pizzuto, Catherine Pulsipher, Bill Pulver, Myron Preston, Peter Replinger, Louis H Requa, Wilfred Richmeyer, Bill Rivord, Duane Riddle, Emery J. Roberts, Ralph Robertson, Dave Robinson, Bill Roy, Ernest Rothrock, Marie Royer, Gest Ruthford, Lud Sande, Harold Sandstrom, Frank Sanford, John Satushek, Ken Schell, L.P. Schrenk, Frank Scott, Dr. James W. Scott, Mary Scott, Sedro Woolley Courier Times, Robert Sherwood, Skagit Argus, Skagit Valley Herald, Charles Sleicher, Maurice "Pappy" Splane, Fred Spurrell, John Taubeneck, Walter Taubeneck, Tug Thomas, Blake R. Thompson, Jr., Blake R. Thompson, Sr., Thomas G. Thompson, Francis Todd, Tony Tronsdal, Jack Turner, Jackie Turner, Richard Vanderway, David Vanmeer, Bob Vose, Marvin Wahlgren, John S. Walter, Bert Ward, Winton Wefer, Dick Welch, Walter Welch, John Wells, El White, Ernie White, Margaret Willis, Gil Wold, Homer Wood and Andrea Xaver.

Finally, my interest in Skagit County logging railroads does not end with this volume. Additional information or corrections will be happily received by me and recorded.

Dennis Blake Thompson
Sedro Woolley Washington
August 1988

The young hands were known as punks, or high school loggers. They went to work lured by the high pay. They had a code which ran: 'If it isn't risky, it's no fun for us guys.' They tried to stay with it and sometimes came out on a flat car, under a tarp. Of one young man I wrote:

'They took him out beneath a tarp,
　　and the flat was cold and slick.
Soon the side was running sharp,
　　but a lot of the boys felt sick.
Now there is a tombstone there,
　　in the cemetery cold -
But I see a lad with curly hair.
　　He had turned nineteen years old.'

Catherine Pulsipher

INTRODUCTION

Puget Sound was the last corner of the United States to be developed. The heavily timbered shores held little attraction for early settlers. But with the discovery of gold in California in 1848 the picture changed. The flood of settlers that followed brought with it a demand for all the amenities of civilization. Few of these were available in the West, and cargoes from the East Coast had to be carried around Cape Horn in sailing vessels. Most of these sailed out of New England ports, and since most of the commerce was carried outbound, there was a great demand for cargo for the return trip. This problem had faced the early colonists in New England and they had developed an eager market for the products of their forests, a market that was still providing cargo nearly a hundred and fifty years later. So it was not surprising that these skippers found room in their holds for sawmill machinery for the West Coast. Wherever timber and water met there was a potential mill sight, and both were free for the taking on the Sound. Much of the lumber found a ready market in the boom towns to the south. Much more was carried to Hawaii, Australia, and the Far East to be traded for silk and spices, or bartered along the South American shoreline on the trip home. The first cargo mills on Puget Sound were built in the early 1850s. Henry Yesler built his mill at Seattle in 1852, and the following year Captain William Renton built a mill at Alki Point, while the Puget Mill Company at Port Gamble also began cutting for export. As the business grew and the demand for logs increased, the mills soon were forced to look beyond the shoreline for their timber. Few rivers provide adequate access to the interior from the Sound, the Skagit and the Snohomish being the most promising, and it was here that much of the early development centered. In 1881 the Blackman Brothers designed, and had built, the first locomotive to be constructed in the state. It was a crude affair that made use of poles for rails to carry logs to the Snohomish River replacing the horse that had provided the original power. This first machine proved too light for the job on the Snohomish and was replaced by a somewhat larger locomotive. The original machine was sold to William Gage in 1883, who put it to work hauling logs to the Skagit River. For the next seventy years the railroads carried logs down to the Sound from the remotest corners of Northwest Washington. There was scarcely a "forty" that didn't shudder to the passing of the trains or echo to their whistles. And today the diesel trucks are still following those early grades with their loads of logs.

John Labbe

CHAPTER 1

ENGLISH LUMBER COMPANY

The Skagit Valley Railroad

Undoubtedly the most famous logger in Skagit County history was an Irishman by the name of Edward G. English. He was one of the founding fathers of the city of Mount Vernon and involved in so many aspects of the Skagit lumber industry that the historian has considerable difficulty finding very many local logging operations that were not influenced by his business or civic interests.

E. G. English was born in the state of Maine in 1850, shortly after his parents arrived from Ireland. As an infant he traveled with his family to settle in Arcadia, Wisconsin, where he was raised on a farm. Following his education he taught one term of school and then started westward, coming to Washington Territory by way of California and Oregon.

Catherine Pulsipher speaks of English's early life in Skagit County with these words:

> *Ed came out from the East, just out of school. He was looking for work and went up the Skagit Valley, but found none. On his way back, he stopped at Minkler Landing (now Birdsview). My father was running a sawmill there, at the time. There was no work for Ed in the woods, but father did need a bookkeeper, and put him on the payroll. Ed had very little and only one white shirt. Mother said she used to wash it, dry it beside the fireplace, iron it and have it ready to wear again the next day. For this he paid her 25 cents. Ed stayed on for a while, but an older man came along and after talking to him, asked if he would like to go on to what is now Mount Vernon to start a business there. Ed did. For years Clothier and English ran a store there. Then Ed began to look over the timber prospects. Eventually he rose to wealth from his logging enterprises.*

In 1877, Harrison Clothier and E. G. English purchased ten acres of land from Jasper Gates and laid out a new town site. This city, which was to become the county seat, was named Mount Vernon. When the Ruby Creek gold rush sprang up in 1877, Clothier and English established a branch store at Goedell's Landing, near which the city of Seattle's Skagit River power plant is now situated. The new firm poled all their supplies up the many miles of the Skagit in canoes with Indian canoemen. English always spoke with pride of the faithfulness of these employees.

FIRST NEW SHAY LOCOMOTIVE for English was put to work at the old Tyee Camp just east of Sedro Woolley where this photograph and the full train scene on page 5 were probably taken on the same day. Grover Welch on gangway, Louis Huff, engineer, in window. *D. Kinsey courtesy of Whatcom Museum of History and Art*

2

TWO CYLINDER SHAY involved in one of Ed English's very early and undocumented logging ventures. A marvelous little pot - her air tank seems as big as her boiler. Ed Wilton, engineer, standing with oil can. *Photo courtesy Ed Wilton's daughter, Madge Ewing*

THE MUD LAKE CAMP of Ed English. This was nearly the end of the days for oxen. These two facing photographs are the only known record of this early operation, and represent the difficulty of tracing Mr. English's early ventures. *Nina McDonald*

The mercantile trade did not dominate the men's interests long for they almost immediately began a venture into the logging business. The result was Clothier and English Logging Company operating at Barney Lake on the Nookachamps and at Samish in 1882.

English was named a member of the board of directors for the Skagit Sawmill and Manufacturing Company in 1887, and a year later the company sold out to Clothier and English and Ed English was made president. Four years later English himself purchased the interests of his partner, Harrison Clothier. Perhaps due to his advancing age, Clothier's prominence in local affairs thereafter diminished.

By 1894, Ed was operating with another logger, this time under the name of English and McCaffery Logging Company. This firm was incorporated February 12, 1896, with a capital stock of $15,000, by E. G.English,

Thomas McCaffery and E. C. Million.

March 1899 found English and McCaffery building a logging camp near Lyman, and by May 25 employed seventy-five to one hundred men there. The same year English completed a fine new home on South Second Street in Mount Vernon.

Between 1877 and 1900, Ed English participated in logging operations near Camano City, Silvana and Lakewood - all in Snohomish County. To this day a location sign on the Burlington Northern Railroad near Lakewood proclaims: **ENGLISH**.

In Skagit County his efforts were felt in Lyman, Hamilton, Clear Lake, Sedro Woolley, Conway and Mount Vernon. His logging in the Lyman-Hamilton area was to last for many years.

LITTLE TWO CYLINDER SHAY shows her left side with single-stage air pump blocked up on running board. *Madge Ewing*

His early activities were so numerous that the historian is bewildered by lack of documentation and vague media reporting such as the following item quoted fully from the **Skagit County Times** of February 23, 1899: *E. G. English was in town Monday looking over the land where he wants to put a railroad into the north of the town he is interested in and expects to put in a camp there.*

On April 5, 1901, a company was formed in Seattle, which was to become a household word in Skagit County for over half a century. E. G. English, W. H. McEwan, A. F. McEwan and E. C. Million formed the English Lumber Company on a capital stock of $10,000. The new firm purchased the English and McCaffery Logging Company, its "logging outfit" and 1,700 acres of timber-

SKID ROAD MEETS RAILROAD at Mud Lake, adjacent to the present community of Clear Lake. This scene shows an isolated tract logged by English in the late 1890s. This *log rollway* was the method by which logs were loaded onto railroad cars. *Nina McDonald* 3

THE RIVERBOAT *Black Prince* prepares to pick up a log tow. She traveled the Skagit River for many years, these scenes were very common in early days. *Bert Kellogg*

railway was projected running east into English Lumber timber holdings.

The Tyee Logging Company, another English enterprise, was running a camp in Sedro Woolley near the Northern Pacific Railway with a spur track and one old rod locomotive. During the summer of 1902, the Tyee locomotive was transferred to Fir to use on the new railroad construction. A new 40-ton Shay was delivered lettered **English Lumber Company No. 1** and put to work at the Tyee camp.

Through the summer Ed was still traveling and making deals for he procured yet another locomotive that year. This time a used machine that had seen extensive service on the Oregon Railway & Navigation Company as their No. 39. She was a high-drivered 4-4-0 passenger engine. Dudley Hansen, during his days on the train crews with veteran English engineer Tom Paine, recalls Tom speaking of Ed's old rod engines: "...had drivers taller than a man but couldn't pull the hat off your head."

The winter of 1902-03 found about three miles of railroad completed from Fir east to Conway Hill where

lands located four miles east of Fir (Conway). The McEwans were involved in the Seattle Cedar Lumber Company and E. C. Million appears to have been a financial backer.

The founding of the English Lumber Company marked the beginning of one of Skagit County's most extensive logging railroads. The location chosen for a log dump was just south of Fir on Tom Moore Slough adjacent to the Great Northern Railway. From that point a logging

THE FIRST LOCOMOTIVE ENGLISH GOT AFTER OXEN DAYS, OR SO THE STORY GOES. Showing her Seattle, Lake Shore and Eastern ancestry, No. 5 strikes a pose with her admirers. *D.Kinsey, Bill Mason*

SHAY LOCOMOTIVE No. 1 new in the summer of 1902 probably near the old Tyee Camp. Taken at same time and location as chapter lead photo. Engineer is Louis Huff, Grover Welch in gangway. *D.Kinsey, courtesy Whatcom Museum of History and Art*

camp buildings and railroad shops were built. This was Camp No.1 of English Lumber Company, the area that later became widely known as "English Headquarters."

In later years, Ed English reminisced about those days in the **TheTimberman** magazine: *"In 1903 and 1904,"* *said Uncle Ed, "the output of logs on Skagit River was about 63,000,000 feet. There were probably 25 logging firms engaged in putting in these logs. Prices ran about $2.50 per thousand for No. 3, $4.50 for No. 2 and $5.50 for No. 1, and mill paper had to be taken, in some cases, payable any old time, but we got along. Up to this time we had used manila rope exclusively for logging, and in wet weather it was hard to handle. I remember of being at Vancouver, British Columbia, in 1906, with a raft of logs, and speaking with the captain of the schooner Kennedy. He said, 'Why don't you use wire rope?' At his suggestion I bought 200 feet of three-quarter inch line from Hunt & Moffet, in Vancouver, had the line shackled in three parts, took it home and the company tried it out. It worked first-rate and from that time we ceased using manila rope."*

By 1905, English Lumber Company had extended their railroad east and south of Headquarters and another new Shay was purchased. The Sedro Woolley Tyee Camp had been closed and its name reused for a new camp of the Tyee Logging Company southeast of Headquarters on what was called the *Oscar Rose farm*. Oscar was foreman of the camp and owned some land there.

A very classic locomotive was in use at this time by the railroad. She was No. 3 on the English roster and came from the well-known Nevada shortline, the Virginia & Truckee Railroad. She had been built by Baldwin in 1871, with 4-foot drivers and a 2-6-0 wheel arrangement. She tipped the scales at a mere 27-$^{1}/_{2}$ tons. Oregon Railway & Navigation Company purchased her in 1881, for $9,500, and operated her for a time before she came to English Lumber Company. After English was finished with her she went on to Mason County and continued to work in the lumber industry.

English Camp 2 was built two miles east of Headquarters about 1905. Camp 3 followed, built high on the slopes of McMurray hill where the woods lines incorporated the use of no fewer than fourteen switchbacks.

The railroad mainline built slowly south of the Tyee Camp through Blue Valley in the area of the present Starbird Road. It served a mill at Child's Spur and another small operator at Sjolander Spurs No. 1 and No. 2.

The railroad then entered Snohomish County and looped through an area known today as Victoria Heights where Tyee Camp 3, or Victoria Mill, was established about 1909.

Statistics for the Company in 1908 were: twenty-four miles of railroad; three geared locomotives; sixty sets of disconnected trucks; ten flat cars; eight donkeys. Ed English was now receiving his railroad equipment lettered **Skagit Valley Railroad**, reflecting the diverse locations of his railroad interests.

The point adjacent to the Tom Moore Slough dump where English Lumber Company crossed the Great Northern Railway became known officially in G N timetables as Skagit Crossing. The name remained for many years.

6 On October 18, 1906, Ed English's old business partner, Harrison Clothier, died at the age of 66.

Ed made the front page of the **Skagit News-Herald** on October 26, 1908, with these headlines:

ENGLISH IS KIDNAPPED!

This Monday evening as he was coming from his logging camp at Conway, Mr. English was accosted below the Cedardale road, and made to drive to a lonesome place near Little Mountain, and write a note to his wife, for a ransom for his release.

When the destination had been reached, the stranger produced a pen, ink and paper, and after Mr. English did as he was bid, he was secured by a chain, which was fastened to a tree, and the man left for town to deliver the message.

Mr. English succeeded in loosening himself from the bond by a fortunate kink in the chain, and crawled a long way until he was above the settlement at Gay's mill, when he broke into a run down hill and informed Mr. Gay of the occurrence, and the telephone wires were put to work.

A rather slender man, pretending to carry his arm in a sling, stopped Ernest Hueston near the bridge and gave the following note to him, requesting him to deliver it immediately to Mrs. English, as Mr. English was injured by a fall from the buggy: "Mrs. E. G. English:"

"Dear Wife - I am kidnapped for $5,000. Don't attempt to resist, as I am threatened with having my ears cut off if it is not forthcoming by tomorrow noon. For God's sake make all haste. Show this to Mr. Hannay and solicit his aid."

"E. G. English"

Below is a verbatim copy of the note attached by the highwayman to that of Mr. English to his wife;

"Walk toward Burlington on track with five thousand dollars in gold (and it must be the yellow metal gold $5,000).

"Come in haste to the place as described. First small trestle north of Skagit River. You must walk alone. Under the first water barrel on the south end of this trestle remove stone and find further orders in bottle. Burn these after reading them. Try to realize you are watched incessantly. Adhere strictly to instructions and avoid the

AT THE DUMP on Tom Moore Slough, the 3-spot Mogul waits to return empties to the woods. In this 1903 view three brakemen pose on the footboard. Holding oilcan is Bert Taylor, engineer, while fireman Matt Snider stands on running board. *Matt Snider / Lawrence Perrigo*

7

MULLIGAN CAR AND SHAY No. 4 at Victoria Mill about 1908. *D. Kinsey, Knute Husby*

strange sensation of mutilation for all we ask is direct obedience.

"And now by the blackest curse that human anatomy can endure we faithfully promise to 'express' our captive's ears to his nearest relatives if the ransom is not forthcoming by tomorrow noon, 12:00, at first trestle. XXXO"

Mr. English describes the man as medium height and heavy set, but the man with the note was slender and tall.

The note at the trestle above town was found as directed but the culprit is still at large.

The following month more news appeared in the November 16, edition of the **Skagit News-Herald:**

Leo Bezeman, the bold kidnapper, was captured the first of the week in one of the small suburbs of Seattle, while asleep. He was brought to Mount Vernon under a heavy guard and lodged in jail. He was brought in on the Tuesday evening flyer and nearly all the population was at the train to get a glimpse. Duncan Boyd is also under arrest under suspicion of being an accomplice and the officers are busy making connecting links in the evidence. His trial will take place at the next jury term.

Bezeman evidently pleaded guilty but insane and was convicted.

The English Lumber Company continued to grow and purchased another new Shay locomotive in 1910. She was numbered "6" and added to the roster. Company operations were described in the **TheTimberman** of that year:

The English Lumber Company of Mount Vernon, Wash., are operating about 30 miles of track, four Shay locomotives, eight donkeys and a Lidgerwood skidder. About 250,000 feet of logs are being put in the water daily. The company operates two camps-the Tyee and English camps on its road. In addition to handling its own timber, the company hauls the output of the Florence Logging Company, which is operated by the Port Blakely Mill Company. The line of the Florence Logging Company, connecting with that of the English road. The total output over the road will approximate about 400,000 feet daily. The character of the country is very rough and mountainous and it required the exercise of exceptionally high grade logging engineering skill to first locate the road upon such grades as can be successfully operated, and next to log the timber profitably after the roads are into the timber. Ed English is a first class

8

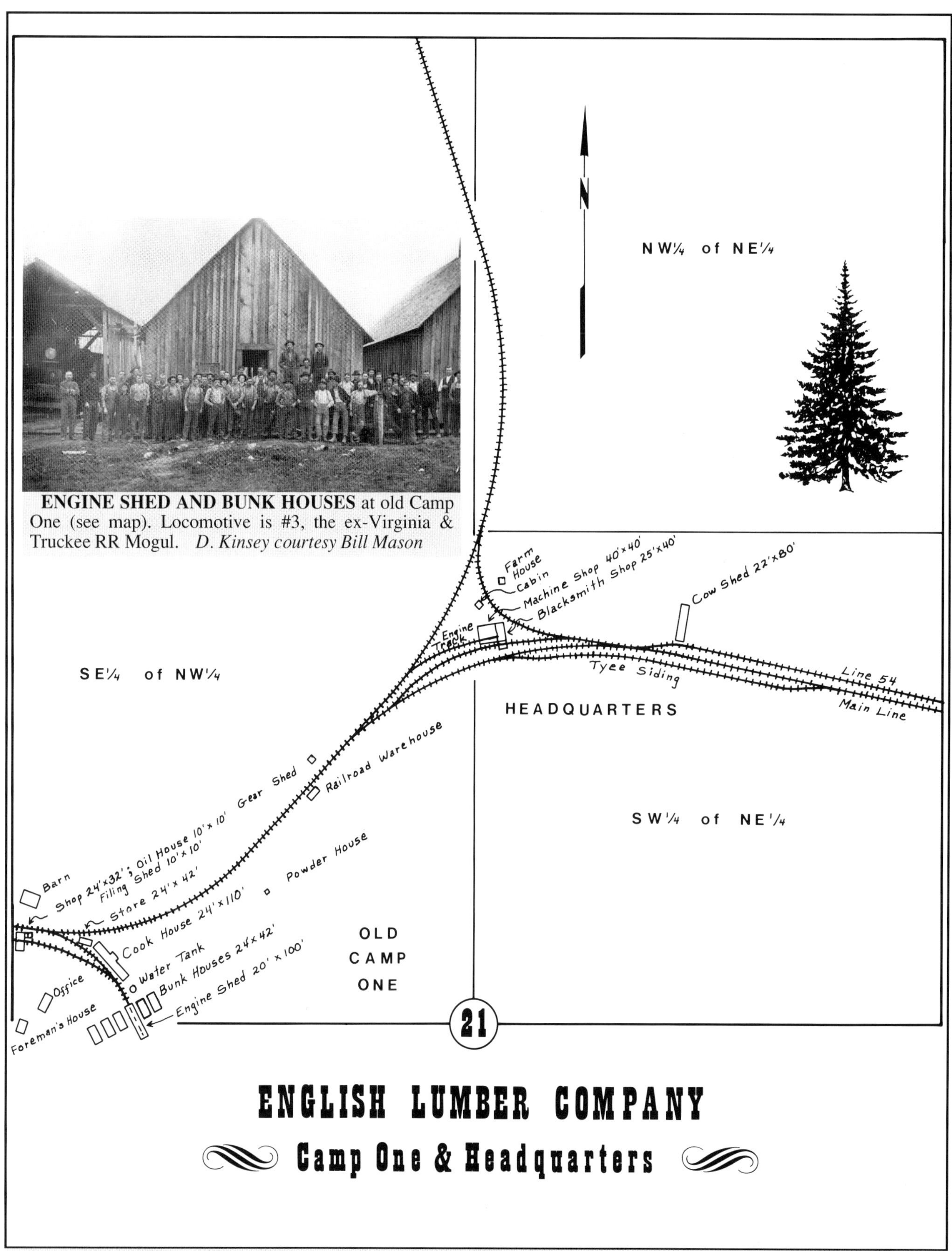

ENGINE SHED AND BUNK HOUSES at old Camp One (see map). Locomotive is #3, the ex-Virginia & Truckee RR Mogul. *D. Kinsey courtesy Bill Mason*

A complete map showing all English Lumber Company trackage over the years will be found at the end of this book following the index. The map folds out to fully display the extensive operations of this company and shows major existing roads to assist you in visualizing this extensive operation and locating the old grades.

logger, and associated with him in the management of his operations is James O'Hearne, the logging engineer and superintendent. The details and working plans of the English Lumber Company are as carefully prepared as those of a trans-continental railroad. There is no guess work. The day of a "shot in the brush" in locating roads has long been passed by Mr. O'Hearne. Despite the fact that he is a comparatively young man, his training and experience has eminently fitted him for the position he occupies. Oscar Rose is the foreman of the Tyee Camp and William Malone foreman of the English Camp. The company is using a Lidgerwood skidder with good success. The main or standing line is 1-1/4 inch, and is usually about 900 feet long. The logs are yarded from 75 to 100 feet to the main line. The wear and tear is light, and it is estimated that 20,000,000 feet can be transported by this cable before its efficiency has been impaired. The company is working the Lidgerwood skidder on the hard shows, lifting logs out of canyons 100 feet and over in depth. Fourteen men put in and load on the cars about 50,000 feet per day. A full crew consists of 15 men: skidding leverman, loading leverman, fireman, wood cutter, three loaders, four riggers, two tong hookers, signalman and tong shaker. At present, the cost of operation per day is $48.

Logs were put in the water at the Tom Moore Slough through the use of a pair of 40-foot tilting dumps. They worked very successfully and by the year 1911, plans were made to construct a new 50-foot tilting dump which would allow the three to be used together to handle 110-foot long loads.

The Daughters of the American Revolution in Mount Vernon were given a two hundred foot long flag pole by E. G. English for the 1912, Fourth of July. It was destined for the Lincoln School grounds and was reported to be the largest flag pole in the state. Ed also donated a flag pole to the Conway School in later years. He was also involved in fraternal organizations and was the first secretary for the Mount Baker Lodge No. 36, Free and Accepted Masons, of Mount Vernon. Hugh Sessoms, his associate, was a member of the same lodge.

English purchased a controlling interest in the Washington Tug Boat Company in January 1913. The buy included the steamers *Black Prince* and *T. C. Reed.* The *Black Prince* had been built in Everett in the winter of 1900-1901 for Elwell and Wright. She had been towing many of English's rafts out of Tom Moore Slough since then. Ed now owned his own river boats.

SKAGIT VALLEY RAILROAD No. 3 displays her graceful lines and Virginia & Truckee heritage. She was used for some time on the railroad that became Hamilton Logging Company and later Lyman Timber because Ed English was quite involved in those operations. She is shown here during that time. Bert Taylor with oil can, Matt Snider in cab and "old Rancher" from "up river" sitting on running board. *Matt Snider / Lawrence Perrigo*

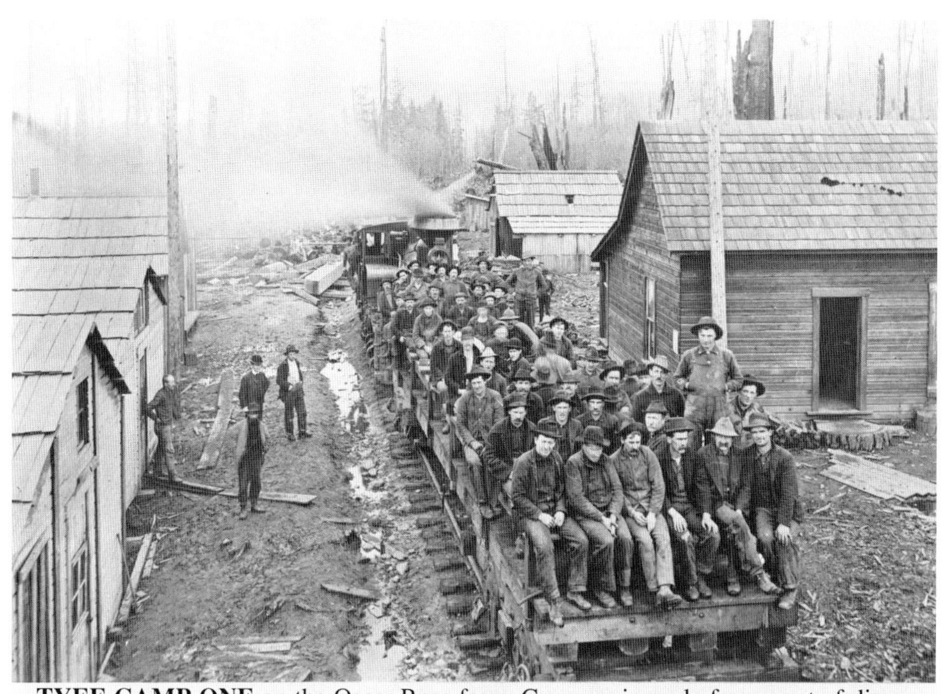

TYEE CAMP ONE on the Oscar Rose farm. Crew car is made from a set of disconnected logging trucks with a frame and benches providing the connecting span and forming a car. *Bill Mason*

When Tyee Camp 3 closed in 1913, steel was picked up around McMurray Hill, and the Blue Valley mainline continued to push south into Snohomish County. There, by 1917, Camp 6 would open as the southernmost logging camp of English Lumber Company.

Camp 4 opened in 1912, and also Shay No. 7 was added to the roster the same year.

Six miles of new railroad were built to provide access to Camp 4, which was located northeast of Lake 16. The new line included a continuous grade of six percent for one mile and curvatures to forty-two degrees. **The Timberman** states: *In some instances the grade is constructed by drifting one end of the stringers into the rock wall and placing piling for the outer support. Numerous trestle bridges are necessary. The road is built along the upper rim of the canyon.*

At the end of September 1913, a spark from a donkey caused a fire at Camp 4 which burned fourteen bunkhouses, four family houses with practically all the contents and 25,000 feet of logs. Five hundred acres of scrubby timber was burned and total damage estimated at $3,000. It was only after a hard fight that the remaining buildings in the

FLORENCE LOGGING COMPANY Ten-Wheeler No. 4 poses for the camera with company officials. This venerable 4-6-0 was born in 1889, and went to the Puget Sound and Grays Harbor Railroad where she bore the name *Captain Gray*. She came to Florence in the summer of 1920. The company logged timberlands near English Lumber Company for some time. Florence logging trains operated frequently over English mainline unloading logs in common waters with English at the Tom Moore Slough. *C. Kinsey, Steve Hauff*

camp were saved.

Camp 4 operated about three years during which time the only other major activity of the Company was beginning of a branch line north of Headquarters toward Mount Vernon. **The Timberman** comments: *English Lumber Company, Mount Vernon, is contemplating the construction of a five-mile branch on the Carpenter Creek. This road will have a maximum of 1% adverse grade and a 3% grade in favor of the load. The company recently purchased a Marion steam shovel for their logging operations. James O'Hearne is logging superintendent of the Company and C. R. Pope is his right-hand man. Mr. Pope has taken a two-year's course in logging engineering at the University of Washington and is making good. Jim still remains a bachelor. Above his bunk one finds the following bachelor's reverie: "The bachelor - created by God for the consolation of the widows and the hope of the maidens."*

CAMP HOME of Oscar Rose, foreman, here at Tyee Camp One. He also owned a farm at the same location. Blue Valley mainline passes by at the right of the house. l to r: Oscar Rose, Mrs. Oscar (Nora) Rose, Mrs. Claus Rose; children l to r: Claire, Eddie and Florence (Flossie). *D. Kinsey, Bill Mason*

When the new branch was finished, Camp 4 closed and moved to a point just east of Little Mountain on Carpenter Creek. It opened as Camp 5 in late 1914. From this camp logging was carried out on Little Mountain, north to what is now Mountain View Road and east to the hill overlooking Big Lake.

The most spectacular feature of Camp 5 was a trestle on the railroad. Spanning Sandy Creek, between the Camp and Headquarters, the structure was of single pile construction one hundred and nineteen feet high. It was claimed as the highest pile bridge on any logging railroad in the United States at that time. C. R. Pope speaks of building the trestle in **The Timberman**:

In construction we were handicapped on account of the canyon walls being hardpan and consequently not a very easy driving proposition even for a bridge within the

FLORENCE LOGGING COMPANY No. 4 shown here neatly lettered and with airbrakes and electric headlight added provides some elegance in the timber. *D. Kinsey, Tony Tronsdal*

ordinary pile limit. We found it necessary to loosen this up in order to secure sufficient penetration. To do this each pile required drilling and shooting; this preliminary work cost $500. Handling and driving 125-foot piling was a task regarding which we had neither experience nor data by which to be guided. Mistakes were made and delays occurred before the crew could be organized and become familiar enough with the work to carry it on to the best advantage. Piles up to 80 feet in length were raised direct by the pile line. All of greater length were first placed by a yarding donkey with the top end away from the driver, and by using one block purchase they were easily up-ended. For raising the latter, four snubbing lines were used, two near the butt to keep the pile from slipping and two near the top to prevent side swing. No more difficulty was experienced in raising the 125-foot piles than in those 80 or 90 feet in length. A 2,800-pound hammer was used in driving, and it was feared that the vibration of the long pile might prove an obstacle in the operation. No difficulty was experienced from this source, however. Piles exceeding 50 feet in length were sharpened and driven butt down. Practically the same penetration was secured on the longest piles as on those of shorter length. More distance was given between braces than is usually allowed. This was considered permissible on account of the size of the piling, as they were considerably larger than those generally used. As vibration from a 60-ton locomotive crossing the bridge can scarcely be detected, we feel satisfied that the bracing is sufficient.

SANDY CREEK TRESTLE under construction in 1914. At 119 feet in height, this bridge attracted considerable attention at the time and was considered the highest pile bridge of the period. Timber from Little Mountain and south Mount Vernon was removed over this line. *D. Kinsey, Bill Mason*

The piling used was largely fir, a few shorter lengths being cedar. The average butt diameter was 24-inches, average top diameter, 14-inches. The stringers were 16-inches thick and from 32 to 96-feet in length and all braces were 4 x 10 inch sawed timbers.

The Sandy Creek bridge stood for many years after the railroad was abandoned high on the hill east of the Cedardale district.

The fall of 1915 was a time of activity for some local bandits; the **Skagit County Times** of October 28, 1915, shares this news:

ANOTHER HOLD-UP AT LOGGING CAMP - The gentlemen now engaged in the 'Hold-Up' business seem at present to be about the only class who are not anxious to retire and who are not afraid of the sheriff. In fact they

12

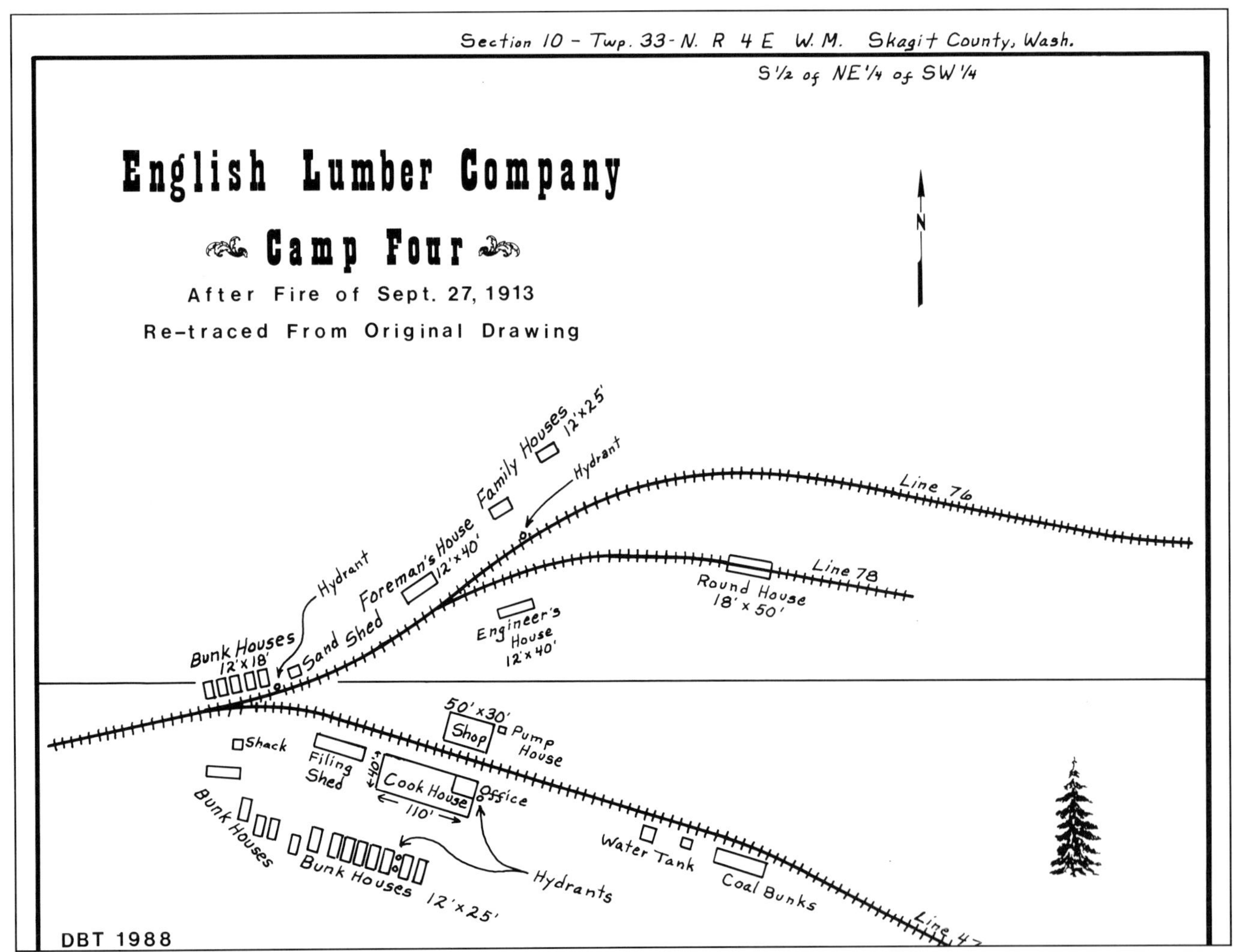

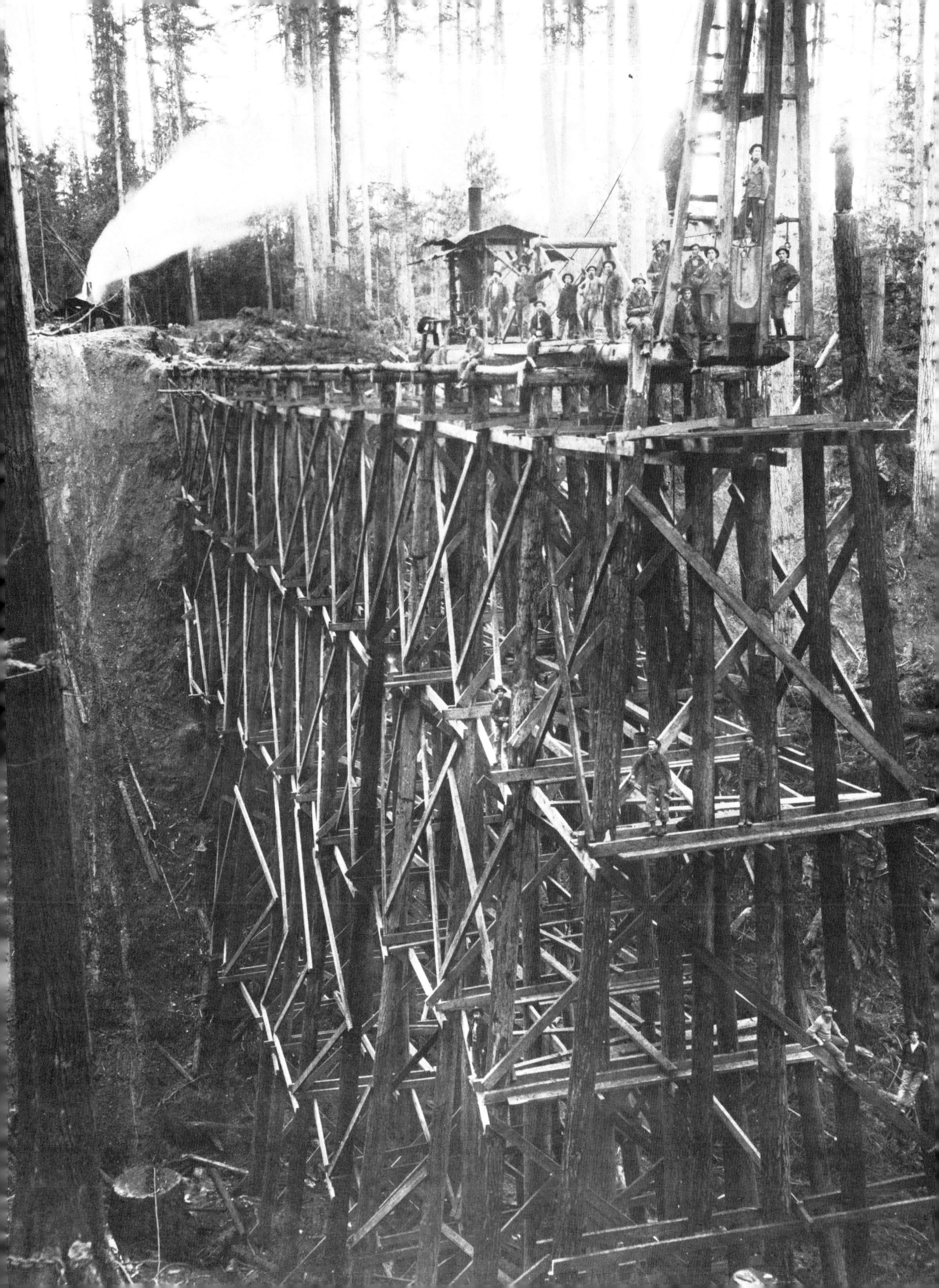

WOODS CREW and yarding donkey. *Bill Mason*

are apparently about the only class who possess the faculty of making prosperity come their way and pushing
14 *business to the limit. English's Camp 5 was last Saturday night the scene of the latest activities of urgent solicitation on the part of two men who are adding much to the hold-up activities of the season. At about 11 o'clock of the above named evening while the men in the bunk house were lining up for rest, a revolver shot outside the shack apprised them that other lineups were imminent. The shots outside were followed quickly by the appearance of two masked men inside the room and their abrupt demand upon the assembly for proper observance of the rules of the game. A bullet, said to have been fired from outside of the bunk house at the inception of the raid, struck Gilber Silbein, one of the logging crew, in the left breast, entering his lung and inflicting a painful and dangerous wound. The firing of the shots outside and the result to Silbein caused hasty action on the part of the other loggers for the reception of the impromptu visitors. All the preparedness hurried to was not toward resistance, but to the shunting of money and valuables into hiding. The result was that the robbers only got away with about $30, also, they have, so far, gotten away from the officers. The shooting of Silbein did not spare him from further molestation. A little thing like a bullet in his lung and the impression it made upon the other victims, did not deter the holdups from taking what money he had. Silbein's condition is said to be critical.*

If these hold-ups, which seem to have become a popular criminal diversion of late, continue, about the first aid woodsmen will need in the future will be a police force.

Later newspapers fail to disclose whether or not the woods bandits were ever caught.

The locomotives most often used at Camp 5 were Shays No. 4 and 5 and Heisler No. 8. The 8-spot Heisler was one of the most interesting and rare machines in

BUCKING A LOG with Walling Brothers gasoline drag saw, manufactured in Bellingham, Washington. Visable letters *S E & E P* on saw frame stand for *Sure Easy and Economical Power*. A steam donkey in the woods was often fired with wood cut in this manner by hired hands. *Bert Kellogg*

SHAY NUMBER TWO is seen with Ed Wilton at the throttle. She was built in 1907 as construction number 1878. *Madge Ewing*

Skagit County because she was a saddle-tank engine. Where Uncle Ed got her is not known, but Johnson-Deane Lumber Company of Robe, Washington, had one just like her and as rare as they were they could have been the same locomotive.

The saddle-tank was a Heisler factory option. It added water capacity for the boiler and traction for the engine because of the increased weight. The combination became somewhat popular in the Southern states but never in Washington.

At Camp 5 the Heisler's engineer was Phil Minor. About 1916-1917 Phil was running her on a woods line between the camp and Big Lake. The track crossed a "side-fill" at one spot: the rail near the hill was on solid ground and the outer rail was laid on fill material. It looked soft on the outside to Phil so he stopped the locomotive and sent his fireman on across to wait for the engine. Phil set the throttle for slow ahead and climbed down from the cab - the fireman would catch the unattended Heisler when she made it across. The locomotive did not make it. On the soft spot the track sagged on the outside and the sixty- ton machine rolled off the track.

After the accident it is not known what happened to the unfortunate 8-spot. 15

The lifestyle in Camp 5 was a little brighter in 1916, as the **Skagit County Times** of December 7 discloses:

Nothing but bones remained from 360 pounds of turkey, while an empty platter whereon a ninety-pound plum pudding had reposed an hour previous, testified to the excellence of the mammoth Thanksgiving dinner served

CAMP LIFE often revolved around the operation of the logging railroad, as evidenced here at Victoria Mill. Women and children, as well as the loggers, identified with the machinery of the period. The locomotives themselves contributed, adding their fire, smoke, smells, sounds and motion to these lives and times. Lokie is Shay No. 2. *Knute Husby, Bill Mason*

STEAM DONKEY just off-loaded from moving car. Machine is anchored to stump to the right of the scene. *Mrs. Dave Robinson*

NEAR LITTLE MOUNTAIN about 1915, cars are being loaded on the Camp 5 line. Common to the time, the men stood atop logs to be photographed. *Clark Kinsey, University of Washington*

by E. G. English, Skagit County's pioneer timber king, to the men and their families in his employ at Camp No. 5 and to the men from headquarters camp. It was undoubtedly this county's largest dinner Thanksgiving day, as more than 400 were seated at the tables. Special trains were run for the accommodation of those attending. The guests were the employees and their families and no host at a private dinner in his own home could have taken more pains to entertain a large party at dinner than was pleasingly exemplified at the Camp 5 dinner.

The long dining room was most attractively decorated with festoons of fir boughs and sword ferns. Overhead was a pretty, fragrant canopy formed of fir and cedar boughs and festoons of purple and white crepe paper.

The menu served was as follows: Oyster soup, roast turkey and dressing, cranberry sauce, mashed

16

potatoes, green peas, corn, olives, celery, lobster salad, mince pie, plum pudding with sauce, fruits, candy and nuts, coffee and cheese.

Bill Inglis is first cook and Edward Sopermier second cook. Both are artists in their line.

Prior to the dinner Superintendent James O'Hearne entertained the company with moving pictures. Afterward the tables were removed and the happy crowd danced for several hours with violin and banjo accompaniment. In fact, it was a day long to be remembered as one of genuine enjoyment. Camp No. 5, English Lumber Company, is only 4-1/2 miles south of here and is a veritable revelation to those who visit it. There is no large bunk house for the men, but neat cottages instead, occupied by six men each. Electric lights are installed and each little home has a shower bath for the men. At 5 o'clock in the morning the night watchman enters each cottage and starts the fires, thus giving the men the combined accommodation of heat and warm water when they arise. The entire grounds are beautifully kept, with rosebushes for borders and grass closely mowed. Another feature is the reading room, where the late papers and magazines are kept and where a roaring fire makes it most inviting. Few country homes anywhere have more advantages than E. G. English provides for the employees of Camp No. 5.

While Camp 5 was still operating, Camp 6 was opened southeast of Victoria Mill in Snohomish County and accessed via the old Blue Valley route. At Camp 6 was located the finest timber stands ever logged by English Lumber Company.

Again, Uncle Ed was expanding in several directions at once.

The year 1917 is significant in that English went into partnership with Fred J. Wood, president of the E. K. Wood Lumber Company. Together, the two men founded the Nimpkish Timber Company on the north end of Vancouver Island in Canada. The new British Columbia firm immediately built a railroad and began hauling logs with two geared locomotives.

REST BREAK at the landing. This log of 30 feet circumference waits shipment. Picture dates from about 1902. *Bill Mason*

In Skagit County, new camp buildings were erected for Camp 6 in 1919. Permanent buildings were constructed 18 x 46 feet divided into three rooms, accommodating eight men, four men in each room. A sitting room was provided 12 x 14 feet, well lighted and ventilated. Each man was provided a 4 x 5 foot locker and ceilings were

17

TOO BIG FOR THE RAILROAD was the opinion of many about English's 10-spot. Her rigid wheelbase was the major difficulty and several sharp curves had a guard rail spiked to each side of the running rail to allow her blind drivers to slide from rail to rail. These *six rail curves* kept her on her feet most of the time. In spite of her shortcomings she held down the run to the log dump for several years until the company went back to using Shays for the mainline haul. l to r: Dudley Hansen, Ed Wilton, Mike Griffin and Virgil Kell. *D.Kinsey, Bill Mason*

SHAY NUMBER FIVE stops in Camp 5 about 1916. Men are unidentified. *Madge Ewing*

18 **BUILDING RAILROAD GRADE** was handled often by this Model 21 Marion Steam Shovel. The hearty machine continued to earn her keep well into the 1940s. Here she is building grade near the Finn Settlement. l to r: George Betteger, Ed Jarvis, John Lind and Fred Jarvis. The year is 1922. *Bill Mason*

8 feet high. The portable buildings (or camp cars) were 14 x 46 feet.

At some time during the late teens or early 1920s, Ed English left his home in Mount Vernon and built a fine new residence in Seattle. It is said he transported Skagit Valley topsoil to Seattle and thus had the greenest lawn in the neighborhood. The new home even boasted an upstairs ballroom.

In 1919, the remaining timber holdings belonging to English Lumber Company were all east of McMurray. They included all of the Lake Cavanaugh country north to Day Lake and south just beyond the Skagit/Snohomish county line. A railroad extension into this large tract was begun in 1919 and finished as far as Camp 7 in 1921.

The route chosen was directly east of Headquarters to the town of McMurray. The local cemetery at McMurray was on the projected route and a portion of the cemetery was sold to English for right-of-way. English crossed over the Northern Pacific just south of Lake McMurray on a ninty-bend trestle, curved at each end. As the new railroad reached the hill east of the Northern Pacific a stiff grade was encountered on to the top of the hill where a camp for section crews was established and known as *Camp O.*

The Timberman for July 1921, announced the new extension:

> *When Ed English, president of the English Lumber Company, Mount Vernon, Washington, christens his*

ED WILTON oils around Shay No. 7 while the rest of the crew poses in a more relaxed manner. Purchased new in 1912, the Seven worked out her life on the English line. *Madge Ewing*

railroad, which is now about 50 miles in length all told, he has decided to call the young lady the Skagit Valley Railroad. The new section of his road connects with the Great Northern at Skagit Crossing, and later will connect with the Northern Pacific at McMurray. The new 17-mile Lake Cavanaugh extension is in operation. The line has a maximum grade of two-eights per cent favorable to the load, and 75/100 adverse, with a maximum curvature of 18 degrees. The track is laid with 60-pound steel and is rock ballasted throughout. There are 39 bridges on the line with varying heights from 50 to 75

ENGLISH CAMP 5 about 1915. Located just east of Little Mountain, this camp thrived from 1914 to 1920. During the winter of 1916, this camp hosted the Company Thanksgiving Day dinner feeding turkey to over 400 guests. *John Ball*

feet. The character of the country traversed by the road is comparatively free from slides, and should be easily maintained. In accordance with the Washington safety rules a turnout is provided on the bridges every 250 feet where the bridges are 400 feet or over, so the unwary traveler may be safe in case of meeting a train on the bridges. A Nordby tracklayer was employed, which gave excellent service; also a Marion 35-J one-yard steam shovel.

The new line will tap over one and a half billion feet of timber. The tract carries a large percentage of cedar of excellent quality and very fine grain. The fir is also of good quality, not overly large but long-bodied, with a small percentage of spruce and hemlock. The road will ultimately be extended into the Washington National Forest a distance of some 20 miles, tapping timber practically the entire distance. The line commands an outlet to probably four billion feet of timber. At Camp 7, now operating, the timber will run about 40 per cent cedar, 2 per cent spruce and 4 per cent hemlock, balance fir. Two sides are being operated since first of July. Knute Husby is logging foreman. Camp 6, in Snohomish County, is operating two sides with Oscar Rose in charge. The camp is putting in about 175,000 feet daily.

The first unit of the permanent camp buildings has been

HEISLER No. 8 at Camp 5 about 1914. Perhaps the most mysterious locomotive on the English roster, her lineage has eluded the historian. Saddle tanks for Heislers were a factory option but rare in the Pacific Northwest. However, she is identical to a machine built new for Johnson-Deane Lumber Company (see below) in Snohomish County and could be the same locomotive. In this picture Phil Minor is holding the oil can. *D. Kinsey photo, Roger Fox, Elsie Ingersoll, Felix Minor*

JOHNSON-DEANE LUMBER COMPANY No. 101operated in their logging operations east and north of Granite Falls. It was very likely the locomotive that went on to become English No. 8. *Peter Replinger*

IDLER flat car used to provide space between loads and locomotive. A sudden shift in logs will then be less likely to do damage. *Madge Ewing*

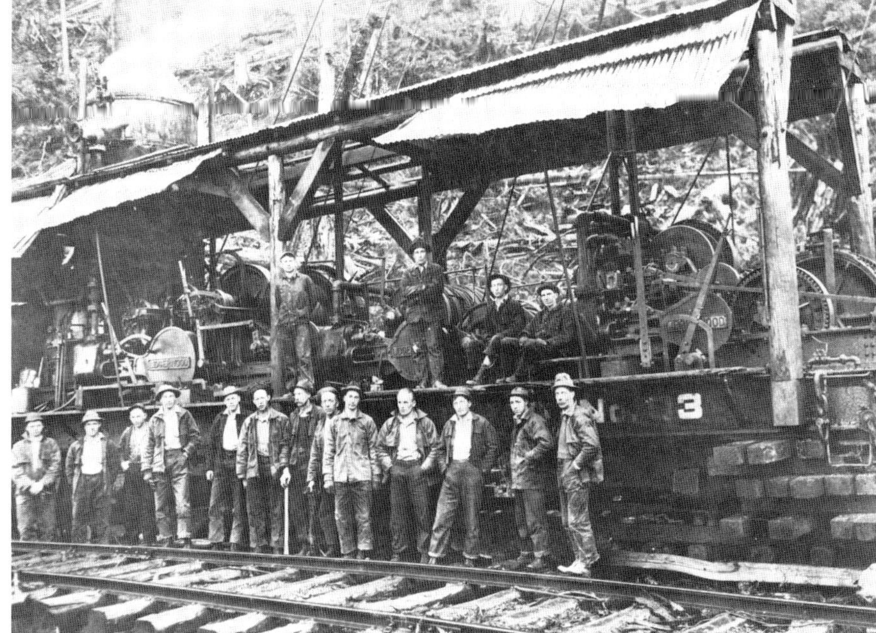

LIDGERWOOD tree-rigged skidder No. 3 taken at a Camp 10 setting. *D. Kinsey, Ed Marlow*

erected at the terminus of the line and five acres of land cleared.

By 1922, English was found running two camps, four sides, fifteen donkey engines, three hundred men and producing 225,000 feet per day. The railroad operated five Shay locomotives.

Two noteworthy events took place in 1922: First, English took delivery on a new Baldwin 2-8-2 rod locomotive and numbered her "10." She held the main-line duty from the dump to Camp 7.

Second, Parker-Bell Lumber Company sold out to English. Parker-Bell had a large mill in the town of Pilchuck and a railroad that ran up Pilchuck Creek almost to the English mainline at the Finn Settlement. English now opened up Camp 8 at the point where they could tie the two railroads together for the purpose of getting equipment moved between the two railroads and logging the remaining timber. In the deal, English got two more locomotives, each a 3-truck Climax. The two machines were numbered 4 and 5 on the Parker-Bell roster and renumbered to 11 and 12, respectively, on the English line. The No. 11 was sent to Camp 6 for switching duty, but was only kept about a year, then sold. The No. 12, an almost brand new locomotive, remained on the English railroad for many years.

The mill at Pilchuck was scrapped and English picked up the steel on the old Parker-Bell railroad.

The location where English crossed the Northern Pacific was known as Day's Spur. About 1921, on the west side of the Northern Pacific, a branch line was built by English extending south to connect to the railroad

BUILDING TRESTLE near headquarters in 1914. *D. Kinsey, Bill Mason*

22

A TREE RIGGED SKIDDER can reach out quite a distance to yard logs. The crew in the foreground of this picture are sending logs by skyline across the canyon to the spar uree highlighted by the smoke from the car mounted skidder. Location is Camp 11. *D.Kinsey, Bill Mason*

(To the right) - **WASHINGTON IRON WORKS car mounted skidder** (the skidder making the smoke in scene above) at English Lumber Company Camp 11 operation. *D. Kinsey, courtesy Whatcom Museum of History and Art.*

already operating at Camp 6. The new branch was shorter and more favorable to the loads and as soon as it was completed the old Blue Valley line was abandoned and the steel picked up and reused on the Lake Cavanaugh line.

The English Lumber Company railroad continued building slowly eastward and crossed Bear Creek on a bridge 54-feet long and 75-feet high. The goal was always fresh timber.

The last locomotive purchased new by English was delivered in 1923. She was a 90-ton Shay and the biggest geared engine on the line. She came equipped as an oil burner and it signified the beginning of the Company's conversion from coal fuel to oil. A large tank was purchased as salvage from the battleship Minnesota and installed at Headquarters as an oil tank for the locomotives.

The mainline crossed Pilchuck Creek in 1923, on an "A" frame bridge eighty feet long *(see drawing in Appendix D)*. The railroad continued east, southeast until it reached the shore of Lake Cavanaugh where Camp 9 was built. Camp 8 moved to Camp 9 in 1924.

English had purchased 170 skeleton logging cars by this time from Pacific Car and Foundry in Seattle. There were still some 25 disconnected trucks (or "rattlers" as the boys called them) on hand, however, the built-in train air brakes on the new skeletons made them the most desirable car to use.

The length of the railroad now exceeded 56 miles.

In 1924, a change was made in Ed English's Canadian venture. The Nimpkish Timber Company was renamed Wood and English Logging Company reflecting the names of the two principal owners. It was because of this new company name that a small town on the north end of Vancouver Island became known as **Englewood**.

At Headquarters, the English Lumber Company's permanent car and locomotive shops were busy rebuilding logging cars and maintaining motive power. And yet another geared locomotive was on its way to the English roster.

The story of Shay No. 14 rides the tide of good and

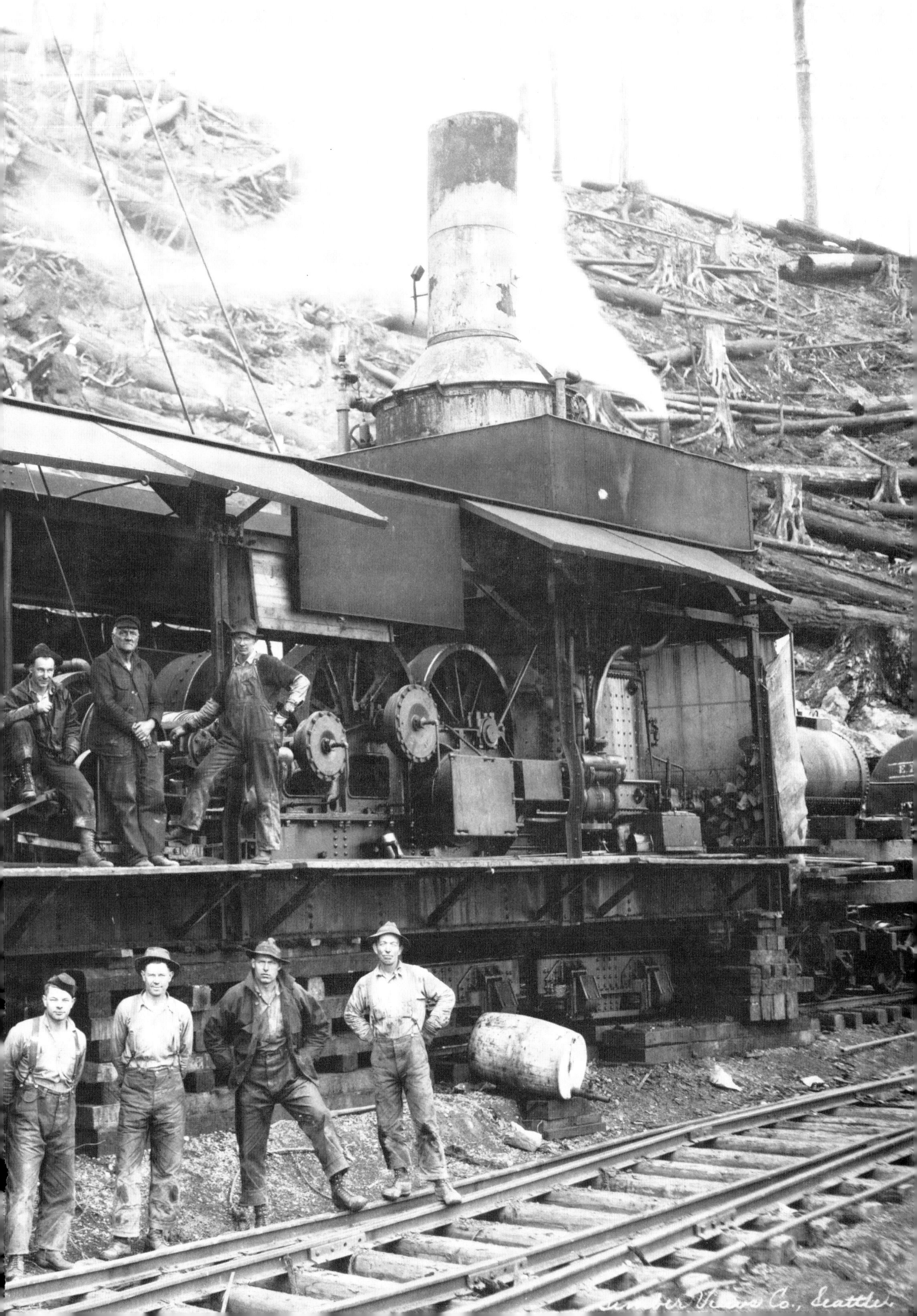
Co., Seattle

DINGBUSTER ALBUM

During the course of her career at English Lumber Company, Shay No. 4 acquired the nickname *Dingbuster*. It appears this happened in later years when her then smaller size removed her from the mainline and into lesser tasks. These "Bull Cook" duties included hauling a few logs one day, gravel cars the next or taking the crew to noon meals then back to the woods.

The 4-spot was built new in 1905 to Lima erecting plan No. 889 and bore the following vital statistics:

shipped from factory: January 5, 1905 — **destination** - Fir, Washington — **construction no.** 945
fuel: coal and/or wood — **water capacity:** 1750 gals. — **fuel capacity:** 3-1/4 tons coal or 2 cords wood
boiler pressure: 180 lbs. — **cylinders:** 11 x 12 inches — **gear ratio:** 1to 2.21 (19-42 tooth gears)
wheelbase: 28 feet 4 inches — **drivers:** 32 inches — **max. tractive effort:** 20,300 lbs.
steam and air brakes — **avg wt in working order:** 94,000 lbs — shipped with 12 inch diamond stack
built and lettered for Skagit Valley Railroad

26

Views of the Dingbuster: *(upper left)* -SHAY NUMBER FOUR and "Mulligan" or crew car. L to r: Lud Sande, Melvin White, Johny Mason. *Above photographs: Bill Mason; Below: Madge Ewing*

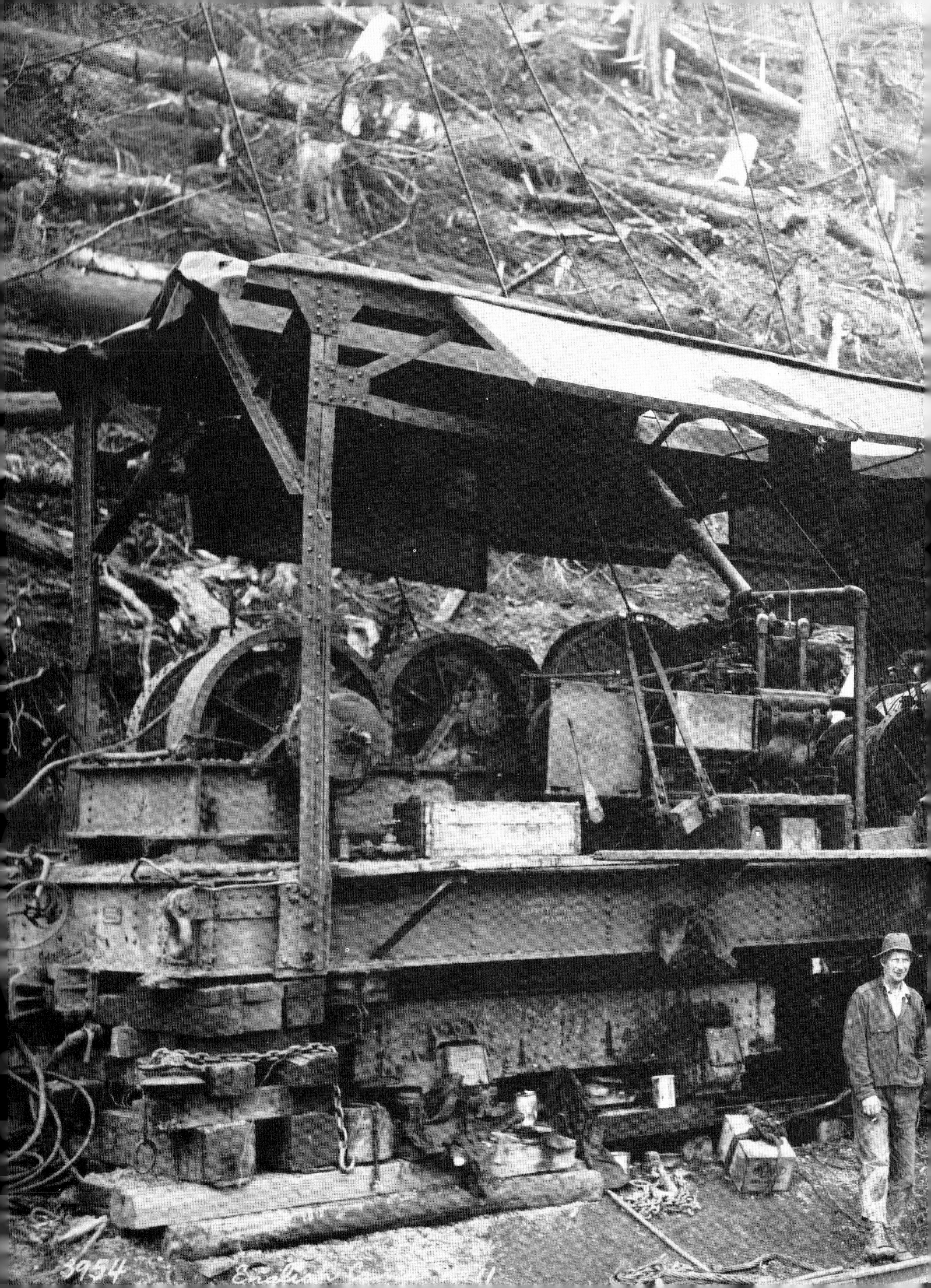
UNITED STATES
STANDARD
3954

PUSH PADS bolted to a reinforced foot board supplied several early English Lumber Company locomotives with the ability to push logs down the track between the rails. Logs could also be pulled by cable along the track in a similar manner which was called "trailing." This made the railroad a kind of "skid road" but was a bit hard on ties. The extended link and pin coupler pocket and "drop-in" knuckle coupler make for interesting details...with this equipment and the logger's ingenuity, the old 4-spot could be lashed up to just about anything. "Dutch" Walters is seen here holding his brake stick. *D. Kinsey, Madge Ewing*

(Below) - Another view of No. 4

TRAILING LOG between the rails with Shay locomotive. It was hard on the track and seldom done for long. *Bill Mason*

bad fortune. It begins with the arrival of the locomotive in the winter of 1924-1925, purchased secondhand, from Alabama. Local old timers say she came "stinking of Alabama mud!!" She was rumored to have a history of some accidents and was not popular here. Joe Moe recalls the No. 14s early condition at English, *...everything was wrong with it - just everything! No kidding. It had been wrecked and patched up in other words; so there was a lot of things out of alignment on it and you had bearing trouble with it and you stand out there after dark and try to change a bearing on a Shay with a jack, for a couple hours with the rain coming down...*

The 80-ton locomotive was ten years old when Uncle Ed bought her and brought her to Skagit County. For two years she steamed along Skagit rails and in 1926, was operated under the steady hand of Art Barringer, her engineer.

Art was running the No. 14 out of Camp 7 when a gypo

A COLD DAY as Shay No. 7 allows her portrait to be taken. Third man from left is Lud Sande. *D. Kinsey courtesy Whatcom Museum of History and Art.*

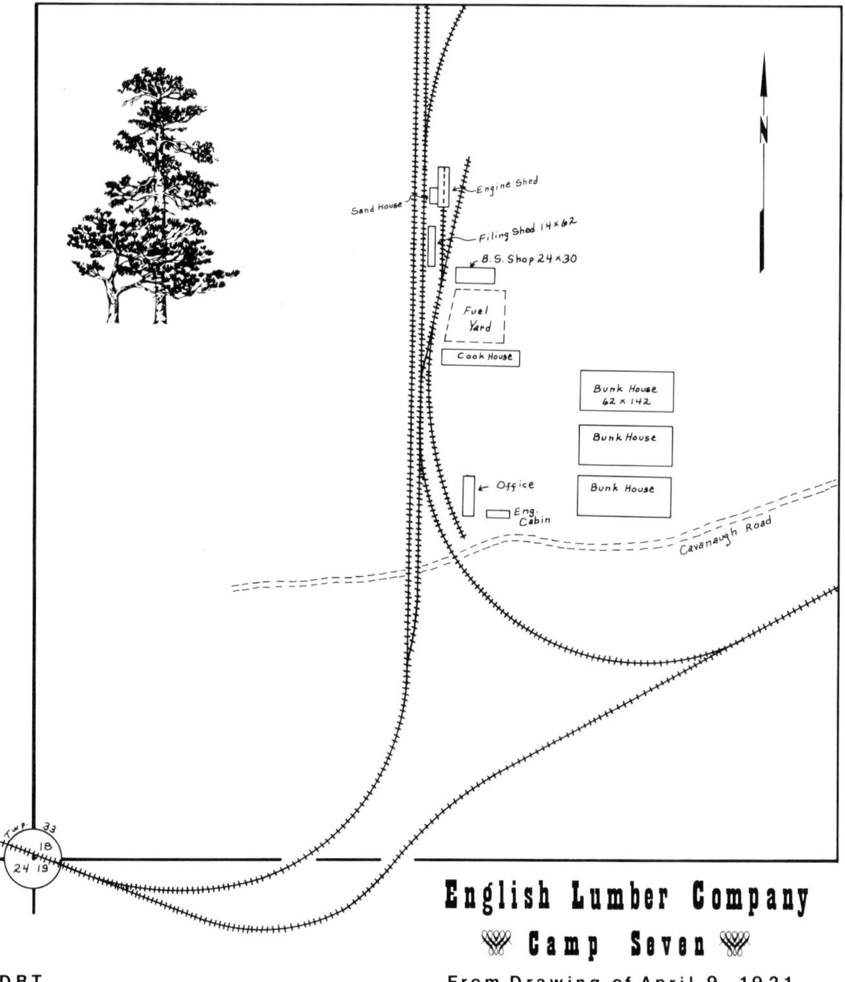

PUMPING WATER up to a steam donkey or for other purposes was often done using an early gasoline engine. Here the power is furnished by a Fairbanks-Morse single-cylinder, hopper cooled engine. Water supply pipe can be traced down the track and out of sight. *D. Kinsey, courtesy Whatcom Museum of History and Art.*

CHERRY PICKER assembled by the company machine shop pauses for the camera during a day's work in the woods. Innovative design was a trademark of the loggers where equipment was "designed" on the spot for the particular need. *Bill Mason*

29

AN OLD SKIDDER turned into yarder and loader at Camp 5. *C. Kinsey, Steve Hauff*

logger arranged with English Lumber to cut some telephone poles north of Camp. To get into the area it was necessary to use an old spur track that had been out of service for some three years. On the spur was at least one trestle of questionable condition. The track was deemed usable and Art tells the rest of the story: *We moved the gypos up there; there was a team of horses, hay, some tents, fixtures...for getting out telephone poles. They loaded one flat. Well, we went up and got that load. We were in and out of there four times. On Friday, September 10, 1926, we left to go back up there running*

ENGLISH CAMP SIX near Bryant was the southern-most major camp for the company. It was the terminus for the *Blue Valley* railroad line from Headquarters and a base of operations for logging in a portion of Snohomish County. The camp closed about 1927. *D. Kinsey, Mrs. Dave Robinson*

30

A FOREST FIRE NEAR THE FINN SETTLEMENT resulted in sprinklers being hurriedly installed in this trestle. The men seen here are looking after the important bridge. *Dale Thompson, Harry Osborne.*

light. We were on the bridge when Jack Knoppi, my fireman, was scooping coal into the firebox. He had about four scoops in when 'crunch' she broke through the bridge decking; it seemed like she hesitated, then she dropped. As we fell through the trestle the fireman hollered. The water tank jackknifed throwing Jack to the deck and he was hit in the head by a shaker bar.

When the engine hit the ground a one-fourth inch pipe on the lubricator broke and covered my head with valve oil, and I said "by golly I've got a chance to get out of this thing yet." (The cab was filled with scalding steam.) So out the window I went! You couldn't see nothin! There was a split in the firebox on that boiler with two hundred pounds pressure. And it was like a terrific fog bank; like a white sheet. Didn't last long; the steam died.

I turned around and climbed back into the cab. There was nothing I could do. I walked a mile and a half to camp for help. They put me in the hospital for a month.

Art recovered from severe burns. Jack died in the wreck. He was laid to rest in a picturesque little cemetery just up the hill from Milltown.

The No. 14 was removed from the ravine in pieces and hauled away in gondola cars. She was completely rebuilt with changes and improvements including a compound air pump. She gained popularity among the crews as though her ill reputation died in the wreck, and continued to run until the last days of English Lumber Company. Ernie Guthrie, veteran English trainman, recalls a conversation with Jim O'Hearne about Art Barringer and the wreck of the No. 14. Jim had said, *That man got no fear in him at all.* Ernie added, *Even after being burned so bad that engine didn't scare him.*

The locomotives all had personalities. The old 4-spot, affectionately called the *Dingbuster* by Millard Ander-

FLOATING HOME OF OSCAR ROSE on Lake Cavanaugh during Oscar's career as camp foreman at English Lbr. *Bill Mason*

SHAY No. 14 leaving fuel dock after setting out tank car of fuel oil at Camp 12. *Pete Brandt*

son and others, became an "odd jobs" engine. Of course those duties were never described in that manner, but rather the loggers referred to her as a "bull-cook" or "tramp" engine. She would take the crews to camp with the *Mulligan* car (crew car). She would work gravel trains, construction jobs and other miscellaneous errands suitable to a "tramp."

Shay No. 6 was removed from most of her work at the dump when the 10-spot began running the mainline. In later years the No. 10 and the No. 13 shared running mainline trains. The big Baldwin would take twenty-five empties out and the No. 13 would take thirty. Three trains per day were dumped at the Tom Moore Slough.

The No. 9 was light for a 3-truck Shay, only weighing about seventy tons. She seemed to be a well liked locomotive but she had such small gears she broke pinions frequently. In later years when the 4-spot had been sold, the No. 9 became the tramp engine.

The No. 10 ran well but had some trouble with the track. She had blind center drivers and some curves had six rails laid to allow for side movement without derailment.

The No. 12, being the only Climax to remain on the roster any length of time, was an engine that some of the crew did not like because she was rough riding and they had trouble running her. On the contrary, others just thought she was great and praised the big machine as the best woods engine on the railroad. Joe Moe was an engineer for English, and his feelings about the 12-spot were these: *Actually, that Climax was the most trouble free locomotive I've ever been on. If you had the right kind of railroad the Shays*

CLIMAX No. 12 rests at Headquarters enginehouse with several of the old hands: Top, l to r: George Betteger, car shop foreman; Al Karr, loco fireman; George Lower, air brake repairman; Pat O'Hearne, clean-up man; Louis Statelen, machinist; On Ground: Jim Miller, machinist helper; Tom Mills, car builder; Joe Tausher, boiler makers' helper; Stanley Reed, boiler maker; Mr. Bulson, car builder; John Reay, head air brake repairman. *D. Kinsey, Dudley Hansen*

ONE LOG CARRIED BETWEEN TWO SKELETON CARS ... a product of the Camp 11 crews. *D. Kinsey, Mrs. Naomi Ecret*

CAMP SEVEN with baseball field showing between buildings. Locomotive is Shay No. 9. *D. Kinsey, Pete Brandt*

were fine, and real nice riding - like a Pullman car almost. But if you had excessive curvature and steep grades then you'd come to a Climax or Heisler. They're better hill climbers. Millard Anderson, another English engineer, adds his comments about the Climax: *On this one you got the power; more flexible; will stay on the track best. That Climax would out pull anything on the railroad.*

Concerning the Shays, there was feeling that the driveline being on one side caused tremendous pressure to be placed on the sliding sleeve couplings during hard pulls up winding track. Again Joe Moe comments: *I've walked the center truck right off the track on a hard uphill curve. In later years that's where the 13 got into trouble on the Camp 11 hill. Denny Beeman, the foreman, said, "you keep that engine down below and*

A QUIET AFTERNOON AT HEADQUARTERS finds Shay No. 7 resting with her workmates in the enginehouse. *Albert Farrow*

ON THE GROUND, Shay No. 7 receives attention from Ed Wilton, left, and Will O'Hearne. A large screw jack has been inserted under the frame to assist in rerailing the engine. Note major repairs being carried out in open engine shed on right...or possibly an old engine being scavenged for parts to keep others running - the track is disconnected. *Madge Ewing*

SHAY NUMBER NINE in front of the enginehouse at Camp 7. L to r: Chris Nederlee, Pete Brandt in gangway, Art Barringer in window, Lud Sande and Tommy Clevenger on boiler. *D. Kinsey, Pete Brandt*

don't ever send her up here." The Climax worked the Camp 11 hill.

Impressive statistics for English Lumber Company in 1927 are: E. G. English, president and general manager; James O'Hearne, superintendent; H. G. Mercer, purchasing agent; Louis Statelen, master mechanic. The Company operated six sides, putting 350,000 feet per day in the Tom Moore Slough. Five hundred men were on the job working twelve donkey engines, one Washington high lead, one Lidgerwood 33
skidder, on sixty miles of railroad laid with seventy pound steel. In addition to the 10-spot, seven geared locomotives were in service, numbers 6, 7, 9, 12, 13, 14, and 15. The railroad maintained two hundred skeleton logging cars, six flat cars, one all-steel moving car for donkey engines, six tank cars and three speeders. This was high-ball logging.

NEW MACHINE - NEW SLED This Washington Duplex Loader is almost ready for work. *Bill Mason*

ENGLISH CAMP 10 on the shore of Lake Cavanaugh. Certainly one of the more pleasant locations for a logging camp. Shay No. 7 is working the camp this day. *Bill Mason*

CAMP ELEVEN near Lake Cavanaugh was one of the better known English logging camps of the 1930s. Camp layout, logging operations and grades are all evident in this Kinsey photograph taken looking south. *D. Kinsey, Mrs. Denny Beeman*

OSCAR ROSE standing on the far right shows off his Davis automobile which he converted for use on the railroad. It made many week-end "trips to town." *Bill Mason*

M.A.C. SPEEDER built by Skagit Steel and Iron Works, Sedro Woolley, was used to shuttle people and supplies to and from camp. *Fred Holder, Skagit Corp.*

THE ILL-FATED 14-Spot poses for the camera not long after her arrival from Alabama. Her fuel bunker is filled with coal and she is waiting at Camp 7. L to r: Art Barringer, Lorie Knoppi, Albert Vandenberg and Lud Sande. *D. Kinsey courtesy Whatcom Museum of History and Art*

Camp 11 had opened up in 1925, above Camp 9. This made available the timber in the Frailey and Stimson Mountain area.

Camp 6 was closed in 1928, and Millard Anderson spent all that fall with Shay No. 6 pulling out the steel from the Day's Spur branch to Camp 6. That camp moved to the newly opened railroad on the east end of Lake Cavanaugh and there opened as Camp 10.

Edward G. English died on February 23, 1920, at the age of 79. George M. Cornwall wrote an article in the March 1930 **The Timberman,** entitled:

HE HAULED HIS LAST LOG:

THE COVER REMOVED FROM HER STEAM DOME, No. 14 receives a tune-up in Camp 7. L to r: Gerhard Sande, Lud Sande, Jack Knoppi, Art Barringer. *Pete Brandt*

36

VIEWS AT THE FATAL SCENE showing the Fourteen at the bottom of the ravine. She was disassembled on the spot, removed and finally rebuilt to serve the woods lines again. The left side of the cab received the most damage and was where the fireman, Jack Knoppi, lost his life. *Art Barringer and Roger Fox*

37

THE ONLY KNOWN PHOTOGRAPH of Climax No. 11 after she came to work for English. She came with the purchase of Parker-Bell Lumber Company and was put to work switching Camp 6. After about a year she was sold. L to r: Art Barringer, fireman, "Cy" Perkins, engineer. *Photo courtesy Art Barringer's daughter, Josephine Hoffman*

CONSIDERED ONE OF THE BEST MOUNTAIN LOCOMOTIVES in the company, Climax No. 12 began her career at Pilchuck, Washington, just south of Lake McMurray. She was delivered there in 1921, to the Parker-Bell Lumber Company. Traveling with the new engine all the way from the factory in Corry, Pennsylvania, was Walt Casler, who cared for the big machine while in transit and then remained at Pilchuck long enough to set her up and insure her good operation. Parker-Bell sold out to English Lumber Company and the locomotive is shown in this photograph while working for English in the Lake Cavanaugh country. L to R: Art Barringer, engineer; Louis Statelen, fireman; Ernie Guthrie, head brakeman; and Alfred Peterson, second brakeman. *D. Kinsey, Whatcom Museum of History and Art*

CAMP 9 on Lake Cavanaugh. *D. Kinsey*

Edward G. English, "Uncle Ed," as he was affectionately known for the past half a century to the logging industry of the Pacific Greater West, slipped into the land of dreams at his home in Seattle February 23. "Uncle Ed" had lived more than the allotted three score and ten years - nearly four score. His life was a busy, constructive and helpful one. His men believed in him.

Mr. English was engaged in the logging and lumber business on Puget Sound for about half a century. A few years ago he entered the British Columbia field, and despite his advancing years was active in his business to the last. He literally died in his calked shoes, just as he wished it might be - a thought he often expressed.

Mr. English, at the time of his death, was president of English Lumber Company, Mount Vernon, Washington; president Lyman Timber Company, Lyman, Washington and vice-president Wood & English, Ltd., Vancouver, British Columbia.

"Uncle Ed" was one of the founders of the Pacific Logging Congress, and in this connection intimately contacted the writer. His constant and unflagging support made the Congress-and the things it stood for-possible. He attended its twenty sessions consecutively. To

MOVING A STEAM DONKEY UPHILL was done very simply: Fire it up, run out the line and tie it down to a tree, stump, etc. - then drag the machine under its own power! *Stan Parker*

show his sturdy, consistant nature he came to the Longview Congress with his leg in a plaster cast as the result of a fractured limb. Nothing could keep him away. Mr. English's conspicuous figure will be missed at its sessions by the hundreds of men who knew him and by none more than the writer, who treasured his friendship.

Mr. English was a pioneer in the use of wire rope in logging on Puget Sound, at the time when the trusty ox team propelled the turns of logs over the greased skid road to the landing. He came to Washington territory a number of years before it was admitted to statehood. He saw the lumber industry of the Evergreen

AFTER TAKING A SPILL, crews are hard at work to reclaim their Ohio Crane. The drawhead of Shay No. 7 is supplying power to this maze of rigging along with one steam donkey. When the signal is given, Art Barringer will crack the throttle and the Ohio will right itself onto the temporary ramp built for that purpose. The accident occurred near Bald Mountain Mill, one and one-half miles east of Camp 7 when part of the bridge failed. *Bill Mason*

CLIMAX NUMBER TWELVE easing a train of logs down the Camp 11 hill. This descent from the slopes of Frailey Mountain was tricky and more than a few loads of logs were lost to the canyons. Note the log cribbings supporting the track under the fourth load. *D. Kinsey, Pete Brandt and Mrs. Denny Beeman*

state-which he loved-become the premier producing state of the union.

The sincere affection evinced at the funeral by the men who had worked with him, and the old friends and neighbors of his younger days from Mount Vernon, Washington, of which he was one of the founders, bore abundant testimony by their presence and the wealth of floral tributes which banked the chapel, of their appreciation for the sturdy pioneer logger. The funeral was held in Seattle. The active pallbearers were chosen from his own men. The afternoon was radiant with sunshine. A crispy March tang was in the air. The reflected glistening glory of the snow-clad Olympics made an ideal setting-nature's benediction, as it were, to the going home of "Uncle Ed." We left him in sweet sleep canopied by his flowers.

Following his death, adjustments in the English Lumber Company management were announced in **The Timberman** of April 1930:

James O'Hearne, for many years manager of the English Lumber Company's operations in the vicinity of Mount Vernon, who was named one of the executors of the will of the late E. G. English, has been designated to have active charge of the various English properties in the northwest. Norman English and T. W. Doan were named as executors to act with Mr. O'Hearne. The will of Mr. English recently filed for probate revealed an

PILEDRIVER AT WORK NEAR CAMP 11. Notice short piling set on top of stump. *D. Kinsey, Roger Fox*

FAT-BOILERED SHAY No. 13 at the Lima Locomotive Works plant in 1923 before shipment to Skagit County. She earned a reputation for being a good riding and reliable engine. Her place on the line was primarily the "swing run" from the woods to the log dump and she held this position often until the railroad closed down in 1952. The 13 was then cut up for scrap at the log dump. *Allen County (Ohio) Historical Society*

estate valued at approximately $1,000,000, of which $500,000 is bequested to the widow, $250,000 to a daughter, Mrs. Alice E. Doan, and $250,000 to a son, Hugh L. English.

The same month, Norman A. English, of Wood & English, Vancouver, and a nephew of the late E. G. English, was elected chairman of the British Loggers' Association.

During the Great Depression, English Lumber Company shut down for one full year.

About 1930, Camp 12 was established in the Deer Creek region. This was to be English Lumber Company's last camp.

Through the 1930s there was no more major expansion, but rather a systematic harvesting of the timber available to them. So many temporary spurs were laid

SHAY NUMBER 15 at Camp 10. Fuel trestle in upper left background where oil tank cars were spotted to provide fuel for locomotives below. L to R: Walt Cranston, Fred White, Tom Clevenger and Alvin Tate. *D. Kinsey courtesy Whatcom Museum of History and Art*

down and quickly removed following cutting that it is difficult today to imagine the spiderweb of steel that covered the country from Day Lake south into Snohomish County. English Lumber provided jobs for hundreds of men and they tell many interesting stories of life on the railroad and in the woods and camps.

Lud Sande still praises the cookhouse and dining facilities at the camps: *That cookhouse table was about as good as anyplace you ever seen. Clean! It was really good; and good food. All kinds of good beef, potatoes, vegetables and desserts. And you could have coffee or milk. The camp really fed good.*

Art Barringer remembers night-time snacks, after working long hours on the locomotives: *Sometimes we'd be two in the morning getting out of there. Lots of nights that you was pretty lucky to get two hours sleep. It seemed like every night we'd come in we'd give the whistle for the night cook and he'd come down and fry us up a bunch of ham. We'd have some ham and eggs before we went to bed. I'd start getting undressed before I got in the house...leave a trail of clothes all the way to the bed. My wife would put a burlap sack over the pillow 'cause my hair was covered with oil and grease. They had a big one lung diesel engine that ran the light plant and you could hear that bark all through the canyon. But at nine o'clock that quit and everything went dead. Everything went black. We'd lay in bed and listen to the hootie owls. Then we'd whistle out at 6:10 in the morning with the locomotive.*

We had different things happen to us with the train. One day we run right through a swarm of bees going up the grade but we got out of it with no trouble.

We had a shotgun in the cab with us all the time, a single barrel Champion 16 gauge. We run into them grouse. We'd see up the grade ahead a black area, they were grouse, running ahead of us. And we rolled right up into the flock and stopped. There was something

ENGLISH LUMBER COMPANY Caboose No. 1 built by Pacific Car and Foundry, Renton, Washington in November 1921. *PC&F, John Taubeneck*

SHAY NUMBER FIFTEEN came to English from Day Lumber Company who purchased her new in 1913. This photo taken in a rainstorm in April 1937 near Camp 9 shows the cross-compound air pump installed during the years since the scene to the left. *D. Kinsey courtesy Whatcom Museum of History and Art*

THE LAST LOCOMOTIVES operated by English Lumber Company are seen here. In a few months they and the railroad will be gone. This final scene at Headquarters was taken April 16, 1952. *Albert Farrow*

about that locomotive and the air pump running all the time that attracted their attention. They'd just sit around there and look at ya. The fireman would say, "your ol' lady want a grouse?" "Yeah, take that one right there, that's a young'un, I want him." BOOM! "Well," I said, "I guess I could take a couple, makes no difference, any two." BOOM! BOOM! The other brakeman said, "I don't want any of your grouse with buckshot in 'em, I'll get my own." And he'd climb down and start throwing rocks at them! He hit one in the side with a rock, knocked the grouse off the log; the grouse shook his head and climbed right back on the log. The brakeman hit him again and got him. We used to fill up the fireman's seat box, 25 or 30 grouse. Then later we'd start to *Headquarters. We whistle at the crossing and ladies knew that whistle. Here they come, lined up past the cab. They took every grouse we had, 'course they enjoyed them.*

Millard Anderson, an engineer who spent a lot of time on the Camp 11 hill, speaks of his experiences: *Going up Frailey Mountain from Camp 9 to Camp 11 was pretty steep, we used to think it was about 7%. And what hurt you so much was the tremendous curves and in order to get traction for the locomotives you had to sand the rails heavily and the combination of the two is a bad thing. Sand on the rail going around a curve is terrible. I've seen where it would cut a fine shaving, like a lathe, where the flanges on the locomotive are hugging so they just peel it right off going around. Well they changed that later, they put water pipes to each wheel and run a little water on them. Oh, that was the biggest help; they wouldn't squeal or anything then.*

Coming down we had to be careful. We could only take 15 cars because with that weight, once we got started, you couldn't do anything with them.

I've seen the time when the air gauge would drop, you wouldn't feel much, but I would look back around some of those canyons, and they're pretty deep, and you see these cars going over the bank, end over end. Cars, logs, bunks, the whole works right down into the gully. It's really something to see.

I was running the 12, relates Millard. There wasn't another locomotive engineer in camp. They'd been shut down for six months. They got Pete Brandt and I to steam this locomotive up and get her ready and haul this crew up so they could start rigging the tree for logging. This was at Camp 11. So in the morning we hauled the rigging crew up pretty well on top of the mountain towards Oso. And after we had everything put away up there, we left the Mulligan car, we had Bob and Charlie and Denny Beeman, the foreman. They were all sitting outside the cab on the running board. We were drifting down, running backwards. We came down a grade that curved onto a bridge and derailed right on the bridge. Well, when a locomotive derails, there's nothing you can do. She will not run on the ties. She goes down and takes everything with her, right onto the stringers. That's as far as she goes. So the only thing I could do was set the brakes and reverse her, turn on the sand and get out of there-all done in a moment. It was a crib bridge so it was a little stronger. I got to the gangway and there was no place to go unless I went over the bridge. The engine stopped and nothing fell through.

ENGLISH LUMBER COMPANY

Logging Camps

CAMP 1	1903 to 1924	Adjacent to Headquarters. Ora Williams, foreman. Permanent railroad shops in later years were at the wye where the Camp 5 line connected.
CAMP 2	1905 to 1912	Two miles east of Headquarters.
CAMP 3	1909 to 1913	High on McMurray Hill.
CAMP 4	1912 to 1914	Northeast of Lake 16. Oscar Rose, foreman. Camp moved directly to Camp 5.
CAMP 5	1914 to 1920	Little Mountain. Oscar Rose, foreman
CAMP 6	1917 to 1928	About two miles west of Bryant. After closure was moved to Camp 10.
CAMP 7	1921 to 1930	About three miles east of Finn Settlement on Pilchuck Creek. Chris Nederlee, foreman.
CAMP 8	1922 to 1924	At Finn Settlement. Followed purchase of Parker-Bell Lumber Company. Denny Beeman, foreman.
CAMP 9	1923 to 1940	West end of Lake Cavanaugh. Denny Beeman, foreman.
CAMP 10	1924 to 1930	East end of Lake Cavanaugh.
CAMP 11	1925 to 1936	Frailey Mountain and Stimson Hill on Crane Creek.
CAMP 12	1930 to 1952	Deer Creek
TYEE CAMP 1	1904 to 1908	Oscar Rose farm. Two miles southeast of Headquarters.
TYEE CAMP 2	1908 to 1910	Less than one mile southwest of Lake McMurray.
TYEE CAMP 3	1910 to 1913	Originally known as Victoria Mill. Five miles east of Stanwood. Area now known as Victoria Heights.

Ed English operated Tyee Logging Company and logged those lands with other normal business of the English Lumber Company. Dates reflect the best information available.

SHAY No. NINE at Headquarters. This is February of 1938. *Albert Farrow*

And there we were, sitting right on the bridge. She had spread the rails, bunched up the ties and all three trucks were on the bridge stringers.

Well, we whistled for the speeder. George Campbell came up with it to see what we wanted. All we could do
46
was to take our tools and get off. The next step was to go to Camp 9 and get another locomotive, and that was the 14. She was cold, been sitting there all winter. We had to load wood on the 14, put the boiler plugs back in....all that takes time. We got her steamed up and went back. By this time we had the whole section crew with us. We had to jack that whole Climax up to get under her and put the track back to the right gauge under the wheels.

During the hard winters at English Lumber Company, the high camps were forced to close. However, a skeleton crew usually stayed to watch the property. Millard has fond memories of beautiful snows and winter operations: *In the wintertime when the snow would get so terrific the camps would shut down. Well, a few men would stay to watch the camps and they had to have food and supplies. So we had a car that was a combination flatcar/boxcar. We would take that when we delivered supplies.*

We'd leave Headquarters, where there would be no snow, get to Finn Settlement and the ground would be white. A little farther, following Pilchuck Creek, the snow would be heavier and hang on the trees. The trees would bend over and you'd swear there was never a railroad in there.

We would pick up a tank car and use it for weight ahead of the locomotive. We'd pile some ties on the front end of the tank car and when the snow got really deep those ties would be dropped on the rail ahead of the tank car and wedge the top tie under the coupler. With that ahead of us we'd push snow. Away we'd go. In the high country that snow would pack into a huge pile then fall away. Beautiful to see. You don't have much trouble because with snow on the rail that's the best traction there is.

For about the last two decades of English's operation, the firm had adopted the practice of placing a caboose at the end of their trains used on the mainline. Two cabooses were obtained from the Great Northern Railway. When each second-hand caboose was purchased, the first thing English would do would be to remove the toilet to make more room. Then the inside would be cleaned out

ONLY THE SCRAPPER'S TORCH now awaits Shay No. 6 as she sits forlornly at Headquarters. In this scene taken February 22, 1938, her useful days are over. *Albert Farrow*

and a sliding side door added. The railroad now had a combination caboose and supply car.

Following the death of Ed English, the company retained much of its old flavor and feeling for operation. Certainly the results of the management of Jim O'Hearne. Closely allied with Jim were two other fine men, John O'Leary of Mount Vernon, a graduate of the University of Washington civil engineering department, and Bill Mason, also of Mount Vernon, who was trainmaster and bookkeeper.

THE END - LOAD OF SCRAP RAIL, seen from the locomotive, is headed to the dump in 1952. *Monte Holm*

In the early 1940s, Jim O'Hearne passed away. A sense of eminent change prevailed over the company until December 6, 1944, when the following article appeared in the **Mount Vernon Daily Herald**:

ENGLISH SALE IS MILESTONE

Sale of the 50 year old pioneer English Logging Company, famous throughout the state for half a century, to the Puget Sound Pulp and Timber Company, of Bellingham, is an open secret, according to persistent rumor in northwest Washington.

In talking with a representative of the Puget Sound Pulp and Timber Company by telephone today, the sale was said to be still pending and the Bellingham office would not verify the matter.

Since the death of its founder, Ed English, and the subsequent death of his manager and long time associate, Jim O'Hearne, sale of the logging firm located at Lake Cavanaugh has been pending. No official announcement has yet been made from the Bellingham office of the Puget Sound Pulp and Timber Company regarding the sale although they have been issuing checks, for operation of the English concern, it is said.

Change in ownership of the logging property marks a milestone in timber operations which have contributed greatly to the growth of Skagit county.

Details of the sale were completed fully by the summer

THE LAST TRAIN to operate is seen here as it arrived at the log dump. Shay No. 13 is dead behind the two-spot. Engineer is Dudley Hansen and the date is September 27, 1952. *Monte Holm*

of 1945, and Puget Sound Pulp and Timber began evaluating their purchase.

The Canadian interests of Ed English were also sold in 1944. Wood and English Logging Company in British Columbia became the Englewood Logging Division of Canadian Forest Products, Ltd.

Puget Sound Pulp and Timber received considerable physical plant with their acquisition of English Lumber Company. It included 28.5 miles of mainline railroad from Camp 12 to the log dump laid with 56, 60 and 70 pound steel. Sidings and passing tracks amounted to an additional 10 miles, for a total of 38.5 miles of railroad. Four locomotives were inherited, numbers 12, 13, 14 and 15. Two hundred log cars were included, fifty of those in need of repair. There were also six 40-foot flat cars, two 48-foot crew cars, four oil tank cars, three water tank cars with pumps, one 100-ton moving car, two cabooses, one model 4-40 Skagit speeder, three Kalamazoo No. 35 speeders, two Kalamazoo No. 25 speeders, one Washington car mounted skidder, one Lidgerwood car mounted skidder, one Skagit diesel yarder, one Willamette cold deck donkey, one 30-ton Ohio locomotive crane, one Washington Tyler yarding and loading unit on a steel car, five Washington duplex loaders, one Marion model 21 steam shovel, ten Roger ballast cars, three Western side dump ballast cars, two pile drivers, one 4,000 barrel oil tank at the log dump,
 two power boats, camp buildings, fully equipped machine and blacksmith shops, wire rope, bucking saws, tools, light plant, 627 boom sticks, 675 boom chains, pike poles, peavies, office equipment and surveyor's compass.

The biggest concern for the new owners was the condition of the railroad, especially the bridges. There were 34 bridges in use whose combined lengths totaled 7,703 feet. Safety inspectors touring the line labeled them, "in very poor condition." Over the next three years Puget Sound Pulp and Timber crews were constantly working on bridges. The toughest job was building a complete new trestle at bridge No. 5, adjacent to Headquarters camp on Conway Hill. The new bridge was built alongside the old 368 foot structure without disturbing traffic.

By the summer of 1947, numerous construction projects had eliminated several bridges entirely through relocations or fills. Some 200 feet of the 1,454 foot trestle crossing the Northern Pacific had been filled in. The railroad was now in good condition.

While reconditioning the mainline was being conducted, an extension of the railroad was built north of Camp 12 to Day Lake. Along the east side of the lake, at about its mid-point, the Washington tree-rigged skidder performed its last show. Even while it was still operating, motor trucks were appearing on the west side of the lake, building truck roads and making steady advances on railroad territory. Gravel trucks were loaded on flatcars and taken to the Day Lake area. There, they were unloaded and put to use building roads which later would be connected to the outside world over abandoned railroad grades.

In the mid 1940s, Shays 14 and 15 were scrapped along with the big 12-spot Climax. Two locomotives were surplus at the recently acquired Puget Sound Pulp and Timber holdings in Clear Lake, namely road numbers 2 and 3. They were transfered to the English operation at Headquarters. Along with the fat-boilered 13, they were the last motive power in use on this once vast system.

By 1948, the railroad had been removed back to the vicinity of Camp 12. A reload was in operation near the Deer Creek shops. Another reload was working near old Camp 7. As more and more truck roads were built the railroad was "pushed" westward toward the log dump. In 1952, the mainline was in the hands of the Alaska Junk Company. Puget Sound Pulp and Timber Company made locomotives and rolling stock available for the use of the salvage firm. The last logs came out by rail the early summer of 1952, scrap trains thereafter. On September 27, 1952, Shay No. 2 was fired up for the last time. She coupled up to the 13-spot and pulled out of Headquarters on the final journey. When the 2-spot arrived at the

REMINDER OF THE PAST is seen here in the early 1970s at Headquarters. The railroad is gone, however, the old water tank was still in use by the local fire department. Even this has now disappeared. *Dennis Thompson*

log dump with her lifeless charge, the engineer climbed down and asked, "What do you want to do with them?" The answer was, "leave 'em, we'll cut 'em up in the morning."

The event did not even rate space in the local newspaper. It was the end of over a half a century of railroading.

49

Lyman Timber Co. Ry. trestle
Hamilton, Wash., 136 feet high.
Highest pile trestle in the world. Aug 31 1918
105H
Darius Kinsey
Seattle

CHAPTER 2

SCOTT PAPER COMPANY AND EARLY HAMILTON LOGGERS

The Puget Sound and Baker River Railway

The Seattle and Northern completed their railroad into Hamilton in 1891. Close on their heels was Ed English, looking for transportation opportunities in the lumber business.

English was busy supervising a lumber camp near Lyman by 1898. In May 1899, he incorporated the Lyman Lumber Company. After only eight months' operation, he re-incorporated the firm under the name Lyman Lumber and Shingle Company with a capital stock of $10,000, in January of 1900. However, English continued to hold Lyman Lumber Company as a separate operating entity. That month he had enough of his own railroad completed to the landing that he purchased a used rod engine and put her to work on the little spur.

In 1902, the camp burned but was rebuilt. The financial backer of the firm was W. C. Butler, officially listed as president of the Company. Butler was an Everett banker. Lyman Lumber and Shingle Company had mills in two locations. The larger sawmill and shingle mill was at Minkler's Spur and the smaller shingle mill was about one mile east of Lyman. The smaller mill was sold to Bixby and Triplett, of Lyman, in March of 1903.

A further, though unwelcome, divesting of property came six months later when, in September 1903, the entire remaining plant burned to the ground. The loss was estimated at $50,000, to be rebuilt at once.

During 1904, car shipments of logs and lumber over many area railroads was undergoing scrutiny due to alleged excessive shipping charges. The climate of those times is reflected in the **Hamilton Herald** of March 1905:

> *E. G. English, manager of the Lyman Lumber Company, came up Tuesday afternoon to visit the company's camp north of town, which has closed down for several weeks.*
>
> *Mr. English stated that the company is seeking a lower rate than has here existed, from the Great Northern Railway company, who are hauling their logs to the Sound and until a satisfactory contract can be made, the camp will not resume operations. How soon an agreement can be reached is a matter of conjecture.*

LYMAN TIMBER COMPANY, August 31, 1918, two years after this second crossing of Red Cabin Creek was made. This is Shay No. 4 with Matt Snider as engineer. *D. Kinsey, courtesy Whatcom Museum of History and Art*

When asked to what course would be taken, should he fail in securing the rate asked for, Mr. English said: "In that event we will extend our logging road to the river, put in a pocket boom with a capacity of several million feet of logs, and at any time when the water is at a favorable height, drive them down the river. After reaching a point a short distance below Mount Vernon we can handle the logs easily, no matter what the stage of the water, and while the preliminary expense of putting in booms will be large, we are determined to do so if we cannot make a satisfactory agreement with the transportation company."

PASSING THROUGH BURLINGTON on her way to work at Hamilton, Shay No. 1 reveals, by her lettering, the controlling interest of the up-river operation by Ed English. English Lumber Company equipment traveled frequently between his various enterprises. Train is bound for the newly completed Puget Sound & Baker River Railway connection at Hamilton. *Courtesy Skagit County Historical Museum.*

Mr. English stated that the cost of extending the logging road to the river and the building of booms would amount to about $8,000. He figures, that after the preliminary work is accomplished, the cost of transporting the logs to salt water will be about 50 cents per 1000 feet. This will be a big saving over the cost of transportation by rail at the existing rates, and the initial expense of making the water route possible would soon be made up.

The lumber tycoons of Skagit County must have had many long meetings that Spring in 1905, for a major undertaking was taking shape. July of that year found big news in the **Sedro Woolley Morning Courier**:

A NEW RAILROAD FOR UPPER SKAGIT VALLEY. The long-delayed, long expected moment has arrived. Failing absolutely to gain the desired concessions from the Great Northern company in the way of freight rates the three biggest lumber companies now operating in the Skagit Valley have decided to build a road of their own. The proposed road will commence at Sterling, a short distance east of Burlington, and will extend to Hamilton, running north of the G.N. road the entire distance, and tapping the richest timber region in Skagit Valley. The road, altho primarily for the transportation of logs, will also be a common carrier.

DOUBLE-HEADER IN CAMP ONE. Lead Shay in this Hamilton Logging Company consist is first No. 3, c/n 1881, with engineer Eddie Adams; second Shay is second No. 3, c/n 2618, engineer Matt Snider. *Mrs. Fred Bacus*

Nick Dowen, of the Dempsey Lumber Company, was in town this week. He stated positively that the road would be built, and moreover, that the work would begin at once. The Dempsey people own 4,000 acres of fine timber land in this valley, the greater part of which will be reached by the new road. One-half the stock will be taken by this company, the balance by the Lyman Lumber

HEADING DOWN THE SWITCHBACKS, Hamilton Logging Company Shay No. 3 is seen here in the hills north of Hamilton. Dexter Hooper standing on foot board. *Dennis Thompson collection*

CROWNED by her classic Baldwin capped stack, 4-6-0 No. 1 sits at Dempsey Headquarters about 1912. She was new in 1907. Her price tag: $9,975. The little ten-wheeler handled all mainline runs taking Hamilton Logging Co. and Dempsey timber to the Riverside dump. *Courtesy Mrs. Al Stewart*

54

CHOKER SETTING IN THE WOODS at a Hamilton Logging Company show about 1908. *C. Kinsey, University of Washington*

> *Company and the Tozier Company.*
>
> *Surveyors are now at work and actual road building operations will be begun as soon as possible.*
>
> *A prominent local lumberman is authority for the statement that the Lyman Lumber company's camp north of town, which has been closed down for a period of 6 months, will be in operation within the next few weeks.*
>
> *The Dempsey people will in the near future install a new logging camp in the vicinity of Hamilton. The proposed works will be very large, plans now maturing calling for the employment of about 200 men.*

The balance of ownership was actually tipped in favor of Dempsey, as they held 51 percent of the interests. This arrangement remained throughout Dempsey's activities in Skagit County.

The name of the new railroad was Puget Sound and Baker River Railway. Work began promptly with M. F. McNeil of Hamilton, leading a survey party along the route in the fall of 1905.

Articles of Incorporation for the Puget Sound and Baker River Railway were filed August 30, 1906, following the preliminary survey work and right-of-way acquisition. Signing the papers were William C. Butler, the Everett banker-promoter-financier, and Lawrence T. Dempsey. Capital stock was $100,000; with one thousand shares of stock.

That same month active construction began laying out and grading the right-of-way. Track-laying began at Hamilton in January 1907, and continued westward. The new line reached Sedro Woolley in April 1907, and crossed under the Northern Pacific mainline. Construction was completed to the Riverside log dump by the end of the year.

During the summer of 1907, a new Baldwin 4-6-0 locomotive had arrived for use on the PS&BR. She was purchased under the authorization of L. T. Dempsey at a cost of $9,975.

In December 1907, capital stock for the Railway was increased to 150,000. As of January 1908, the PS&BR was ready to roll.

While construction of the new railroad was carried out, the lumbermen behind the new venture were getting ready for business. Dempsey built a headquarters camp at the eastern terminus of the new railroad. This was

HIGH HERCULES LOG TRUCKS line up along light rail waiting to be loaded. This scene recorded by Clark Kinsey, brother of Darius Kinsey, at Hamilton Logging Company landing about 1908. *C. Kinsey, University of Washington.*

two miles west of Birdsview located on the bench of land above today's Highway 20, at the north end of the Pinelli Road. Dempsey had also acquired a new Heisler locomotive for woods duty.

Lyman Lumber and Shingle Company now embraced some changes that puzzle the historian. Somewhere between 1905 and 1908, Lyman Lumber seems to have been reorganized under the name Hamilton Logging Company. It is known that simultaneous to the operation of Lyman Lumber and Shingle Company at Minkler Lake, Ed English also operated a small logging camp at Hamilton using a locomotive. During these years the Hamilton camp seemed to have rapidly grown and the Minkler activities decreased.

When the PS&BR began hauling logs in January 1908, no shipments originated at Minkler or from Lyman Lumber and Shingle. Yet references continued to be made to the Minkler firm as late as 1914. Another interesting note is that in the first few years of the PS&BR operations, a log flume existed at Minkler Lake passing over the new railroad and emptying into the lake.

Birdsey D. Minkler, from whom the town of Birdsview and the above lake gained their names, was a principal in the Lyman Lumber and Shingle Company.

Regardless of what business entanglements really occurred, the outcome was that E. G. English's major "up-river" business emerged as Hamilton Logging Company.

LOADING DISCONNECTS AT LANDING. Hamilton Logging Co. about 1908. *C. Kinsey, Univ. of Washington* 55

56

VERY EARLY VIEW AT HAMILTON LOGGING COMPANY. Even the flat car and log trucks look weary in this scene. *Burmaster collection, Ed Marlow*

The first major building achievement of Hamilton Logging Company was the construction of a large pile trestle over Red Cabin Creek in 1908. The bridge stood 136 feet above the water and became a local landmark. Camp 3 was built near the south end of the new trestle. Camps 1 and 2 had been lower on the hill.

Hamilton Logging Company began shipping over the PS&BR in March 1908; Dempsey began six months later. At the log dump the locomotive was turned on a turntable that had originally belonged to the Great Northern when that line had ended in Hamilton. After the Great Northern built on to Rockport, the old turntable was sold to the PS&BR and installed near the log dump at a point just before the line passed under the Great Northern Skagit River bridge approach.

The year 1911 found English's enterprise operating three Shay locomotives and an 0-4-2 Davenport. Twelve portable bunkhouses were built to accommodate ninety-six men.

A bad forest fire occurred the following year, which is recalled by Matt Snider:

I began running a logging locomotive for the English Logging Company at Conway in 1903 and I have since then run engines for some of the largest logging companies in the state where we have had to use our engines and their equipment for fire fighting with no let up until the fire was subdued or the equipment was put out of commission.

One of the worst forest fires that I can remember was in 1912 when the terrible fire that was started at Birdsview by the carelessness of some rancher on a dry and hot morning of May 12, 1912 took to the tall timber when a strong East wind with great force carried it out of control. Like a roaring furnace it crossed Grandy Creek and took a north course until it got into the Dempsey logging works where the slashings had never been burned and the family homes and the Dempsey camp had no protection from such a rushing fire that would soon consume or destroy homes, houses and camp. The people made a wild rush for safety. Some made it in one way or another while five men lost their lives in the woods near the camp. Others come to safety in a railroad cut near the camp where there was a small spring of water that ran from the bank that some said "was a life saver." One little short camp laborer climbed up and got into the water tank where the locomotives

FROM THE ORIGINAL BALDWIN negative, this print shows the One-Spot as she appeared at the factory in 1907 before being shipped to Washington. *Both photos Railroad Museum of Pennsylvania (P.H.M.C.)*

57

took on water. The water in the tank was deep, too deep for him to stand on the bottom and he could not swim. He had to hold on to the top of the tank with his hands and let his body float. The tank was full to the brim and he kicked over enough water that the tank did not burn down, but the fire was so intense that his hands and fingers were so badly burned to cause his fingers to be amputated. I knew him well but can't remember his name now.

That day I was on an engine for the Hamilton Logging Company of Hamilton and we were logging about 6 miles west of the Dempsey Lumber Co. camp when we saw the black smoke rolling up over the tall fir timber that was between the two camps. At first no one thought we were in danger. We could see that the fire was spreading north, south and west. The miles of green fir timber between the two camps gave us a lot of encouragement. They logged on and we switched the loaded logs from yarding donkeys to side tracks and spurs until the call came from Lyle McNeill to close down all logging operations and for the three locomotives to pick up all their fire fighting equipment and stand on the east side of the camp.

Lyle McNeill was camp foreman and we, the three train crews, made haste to fill his orders. The fire at that time had broken through the green timber to the east of us and had entered the Hamilton logging works. All the families that were living near the camp had gotten orders to leave camp by walking a distance of two miles on the trail that would lead them down to the siding near Hamilton. One locomotive was coupled to a flat car and parked in front of the office so all the office supplies

58

ORIGINAL RED CABIN CREEK BRIDGE just before completion about 1908. Locomotive appears to be Hamilton Logging Company first No. 3. *D. Kinsey, courtesy Whatcom Museum of History and Art*

(left) - **FIRST RED CABIN CREEK BRIDGE** under construction by American Piledriver Company about 1908. This bridge became a landmark in the area. *Stan Dexter*

could be loaded and gotten out of danger before the fire cut them off on the south. They made it by the skin of their teeth.

Looking toward the East we could see that the fire was almost two miles wide, north and south and with the hot wind that sometimes would form itself into whirlwinds that would carry the fire straight up from the ground and land it several hundred yards ahead where it would immediately flare up into a roaring blaze with no possibility of heading it off in time to save the camp. The water pumps we had with the two locomotives were of no avail against such odds as we were facing. The fire was fierce and the smoke terrible until we could not take chances any longer. For soon our exit would be cut off with out any possible escape. We pulled in our water hose and wet our handkerchiefs for our face protection, put our engines in reverse position and backed out while the smoke behind us was so bad we could not see anything. As we passed by the office and blacksmith

HAMILTON LOGGING COMPANY second No. 3. *C. Kinsey, Univ. of Washington*

SHAY No. 3 in a nice broadside view taken about 1914 near Camp 1 at Hamilton Logging Company. Engineer is Matt Snider 59
in cab window; Fireman, George Wilson in gangway. Head brakeman Arlo McCracken on running board. Second brakeman June Moore on ground with brake stick. Note the unusual lens distortion of the spark arrestor shape. *D. Kinsey, Mrs. Fred Bacus/Harley McCalib*

WOODS SPUR, Shay locomotive and Hercules log trucks - standard operations for Hamilton Logging Company for many years. This engine is road number three. Dick Woodring standing on running board in front of cab. *C. Kinsey, University of Washington*

shop they were both on fire with the flames lapping across the railroad with such force we had to lie on the floor of the cab and let the engine roll. After we passed the blacksmith shop we had gone through the worst of the fire and smoke.

Then we could see that the line was clear and we would try to reach Camp No. 3, two miles below Camp No. 1 where we thought the locomotives would be safe. The railroad grade from Camp No. 3 to Camp No. 1, on an average, ran from 4 to 7 per cent. We got about half way down to Camp No. 3 when we found a trestle was on fire and we had to find a level piece of track where we could "spot" the locomotives and leave them there. We found such a place in a small cut and while the line of fire was some distance from that place we blocked

HAMILTON LOGGING COMPANY Shay No. 3, c/n 2618, later re-numbered as No. 4 of Lyman Timber Company. This 1913 view shows, l to r: Matt Snider, engineer; Walter Sherrill, fireman; June Moore and Harry McInterfer, brakemen. *Matt Snider, Lawrence Perrigo*

"THE TURTLE" was the nickname of this little 0-4-2 locomotive. She was considered the company switcher and is seen here after the 1912 fire claimed her cab as well as other burnable trimmings. She continued in use after the fire. Although her eventual disposition is unknown, her lineage can be traced back to J. A. Veness Lumber, as seen on her tank. From left to right, third man is Jim Hooper, then John Dahl. *John Pinelli*

them well and filled the boilers with water and pulled the fire. In the words of a railroad man "we killed them," and beat it on foot until we reached Camp No. 3, our headquarters. From there we could look back on the mountain near Camp No. 1 and imagine what a great loss was taking place up there.

Later on we began to count noses and found that Lyle McNeill, the foreman, was missing. Also Mr. Kearney, an old man who looked after the hogs and other animals at the Camp, was not present. But in a space of time both men showed up. Kearney had brought out a horse and Lyle had followed Muddy Creek all the way out to safety. So no one lost their lives at Hamilton Logging Camps but the fire roared on and to this day I don't know where it stopped.

After the smoke around Camp No. 1 had cleared away E. G. English came up from Mt. Vernon. He was the general manager of the Hamilton Logging Co. and part

AFTER THE FIRE at Hamilton Logging Company, Shay No. 3 shows evidence of her loss. She was actually operated like this for a short time before her new cab was fabricated in the company shops. *John Pinelli*

62 **HAMILTON LOGGING COMPANY** Camp 2. Mount Josephine is seen in the background. Two Shays work the camp. *John Pinelli*

WHEN NEARLY NEW in 1913, this scene was captured on film at the Riverside log dump along the Skagit River, near where the Burlington Northern now crosses the river. L to r: Rube Morgan, engineer; Walter Welch, fireman; Therman Fisher, brakeman; Grover Welch, conductor; Howard Wilson. *Wilfred Richmeyer*

THE ONE-SPOT AT RIVERSIDE DUMP, circa 1917. This is the old turntable from the Great Northern at Hamilton. L to r: unknown, Al W. Stewart, Louis LaMar, Jim Ward. *Courtesy Mrs. Al Stewart*

63

(above) **MORE WORK FOR THE REPAIR SHOP.** In the early days of the Riverside dump an obstinate High Hercules model log car does battle with the caboose. There is no winner. The little side-door "crummy" develops a major leak in the roof, while the log truck on the right seems to have its toes stepped on. In the background, the Pacific Northwest Traction Company Skagit River bridge carried interurban cars as they traveled from Mount Vernon to Bellingham. The track in the foreground was extended westward in 1913 with the intention of reaching the town of Avon. It is not known if the mile-and-a-half addition was ever completed. *Vern Harris, Ed Marlow*

(right) **A CLOSER LOOK AT THE CABOOSE**'s intruder reveals the log end protruding from the car's roof. *Peter Replinger Collection*

WASHINGTON DUPLEX LOADER at Hamilton Logging Company. Machine is manufacturer's serial number 2533. *C. Kinsey, University of Washington*

HAMILTON LOGGING COMPANY yarder on left. Small loading donkey on right. *John Pinelli*

owner of several camps in Skagit County. I got with him up at Camp No. 1 where I went with him on a general survey of the actual damage that had been done. The camp itself was practically new buildings with a large cook house and dining room close to all the bunk houses that were in a straight line away from the cook house. The office was located just across the railroad track from the bunk houses and just east of the blacksmith shop. All were a total loss with nothing left but twisted iron and steel. The residential district that housed many of the working men and their families was completely

THE SECOND RED CABIN CREEK BRIDGE. In 1916, Hamilton Logging Company undertook a line relocation. This was done for several reasons. First, it was a move about one-half mile downstream on Red Cabin Creek; this replaced the old pile-driven bridge near Camp 3. It allowed a mainline railroad with no adverse grade. The maximum grade on the new line was 3.75 percent in favor of the load. Locally the new relocated line was called the Lyman Pass Railroad, as it was laid out through Lyman Pass and on toward the Nooksack River. Fresh timber was also accessed through this route.

The new Red Cabin Creek bridge was 600 feet long and 132 feet high from water level to the top of the rail. Douglas fir poles were used in various lengths from 70 to 130 feet. Construction was interesting, mud sills were placed on the ground on 20-foot centers. Twenty-one bents were framed, squared and braced on the ground. A sky-line was used to assemble the parts, and later to raise them into position. These two photographs illustrate the construction. *C. Kinsey, University of Washington*

(below) - VIEW FROM GROUND LEVEL beside stacked bents ready to be raised into position by the yarder.

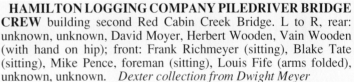

HAMILTON LOGGING COMPANY PILEDRIVER BRIDGE CREW building second Red Cabin Creek Bridge. L to R, rear: unknown, unknown, David Moyer, Herbert Wooden, Vain Wooden (with hand on hip); front: Frank Richmeyer (sitting), Blake Tate (sitting), Mike Pence, foreman (sitting), Louis Fife (arms folded), unknown, unknown. *Dexter collection from Dwight Meyer*

LYMAN TIMBER COMPANY Marion Steam Shovel digging railroad cut 51 feet deep. James R. McIlraith (in shovel doorway) is operator. *D. Kinsey, courtesy Whatcom Museum of History and Art*

destroyed. They did not have a thing left but the clothes they had on their backs. All the many big fat hogs the Company had in the hog lot behind the cook house were cooked into a roast well done. After we surveyed the ruins of the camp we looked over a part of the burnt logs and donkeys with their lines and rigging, then we went over the railroad equipment such as flat cars, logging trucks and locomotives, all of which could not possibly escape part or total destruction from this raging and moving furnace of fire.

In the beginning of this article I pointed out how the train crews were ordered by McNeil to abandon everything else by switching loaded cars and empty trucks onto side tracks and spurs for the purpose of leaving the main line clear. On one side track we had nearly all the empty trucks with most of the loaded cars on spurs. On one spur which included a 45 degree incline where a donkey engine was used to pull the loaded cars to the top at which place a locomotive could couple on and take them away and replace them with empties. But at this time the train crew backed in a lot of loads to the top of the "incline" where they set the brakes and left them there. All the brake beams on those trucks were made of wood and when the fire came to this incline it set those loads on fire and burnt all the brake beams up and turned all the cars loose where they went over the incline into one of the greatest wrecks of log cars I ever witnessed in all the years of my railroad experience.

But I don't remember how much damage was done to

MACHINERY- QUAINT, PRIMITIVE and GIGANTIC provided the muscle as well as danger in the woods as men labored to harvest the forests.

(at right) **MARION STEAM SHOVEL** building railroad grade at Lyman Timber Company. A classic scene in the woods. It truly depicts steam powers' self-sufficiency: it runs on water and firewood. *Take along some lubricating grease and oil, and this rig could disappear into the brush and never be seen again, operating indefinitely.* L to r: unknown, Fred Pence, Dennis Medford (operator), and unknown. *D. Kinsey, courtesy Whatcom Museum of History and Art*

LYMAN
CLYDE
TIMBER
CO
NO
352

THE "WHITE ELEPHANT" of Lyman Timber Company. Heavy logging machinery arrived in late 1922 with the addition of a large cableway skidder built by Clyde Iron Works of Duluth, Minnesota. Put right to work in the hills north of Hamilton, the big machine was oil fired and boasted three sets of steam engines on its single frame. The main engine was next to the boiler and operated the skidding, haulback and slack-pulling drums. Each of these drums was capable of two-speed operations.

The center engine also contained three drums, namely, the transfer, heelblock and grassline.

The front engine was the duplex loader equipped with a car-spotting drum.

All of the above could be in operation at the same time. The railroad car upon which this machinery was mounted was of all steel construction and equipped with swiveling trucks such that the skidder could be turned around on a switch. The Clyde was designed to use a tree as a spar pole.

A normal crew (photo below from John Pinelli) consisted of 18 men as follows: foreman, skidder operator, loader leverman, three loaders, one fireman, unhooker, hooktender, four chokerman, and a rigging crew consisting of a head rigger and four helpers and one or two additional as the particular days work required.

Lyman Timber experienced some difficulty in obtaining good operators for the Clyde as it was a tricky monster to handle. The duplex loader was so sensitive and fast to operate that the company shop eventually discarded the Clyde duplex and substituted a Washington duplex in its place. These things are likely to have precipitated the nickname *White Elephant* which was soon tagged onto the skidder. Even in these modern times, mention of *The White Elephant* around old-timers in Hamilton will bring a raised eyebrow.

The machine saw extensive service, however, and when working on Hightower Hill, was reaching out over 4,000 feet with its spiderweb of cable, plucking the green gold from the land. After 18 years in the woods the Clyde skidder was retired in 1941. Following many months of resting in the weeds by the company shops it was cut up for scrap during World War II. *D. Kinsey, Whatcom Museum of History and Art.*

THE CREW DURING JUNE 1936: L to R: Fred Gimmer, woods foreman; Dusty Rhodes, skidder fireman; Dan Isham, rigging; Kim Ensley, skidder engineer; Carley Larson, head loader; Al Nordstrom, chaser; George Snelson; Seated: Burlin Daves, whistle punk; unk; Gilbert Wylie & Brian (Baldie) Allen, chokermen; Bernard Davis; Keif Beckman; Ira Moffat; Theodore Metcalf; Bernie McCalib; Glen (Sparky) Sparks; Phil Grabinski, head rigger; Eddie Poore; Hank Snyder; Joe McCracken. *D. Kinsey, John Pinelli*

This view of the other side of the Clyde skidder was taken on the same day as the facing page view on the north lateral above the Camp 14 incline about a quarter mile north of Deer Creek. *D. Kinsey, Dennis Thompson Collection.*

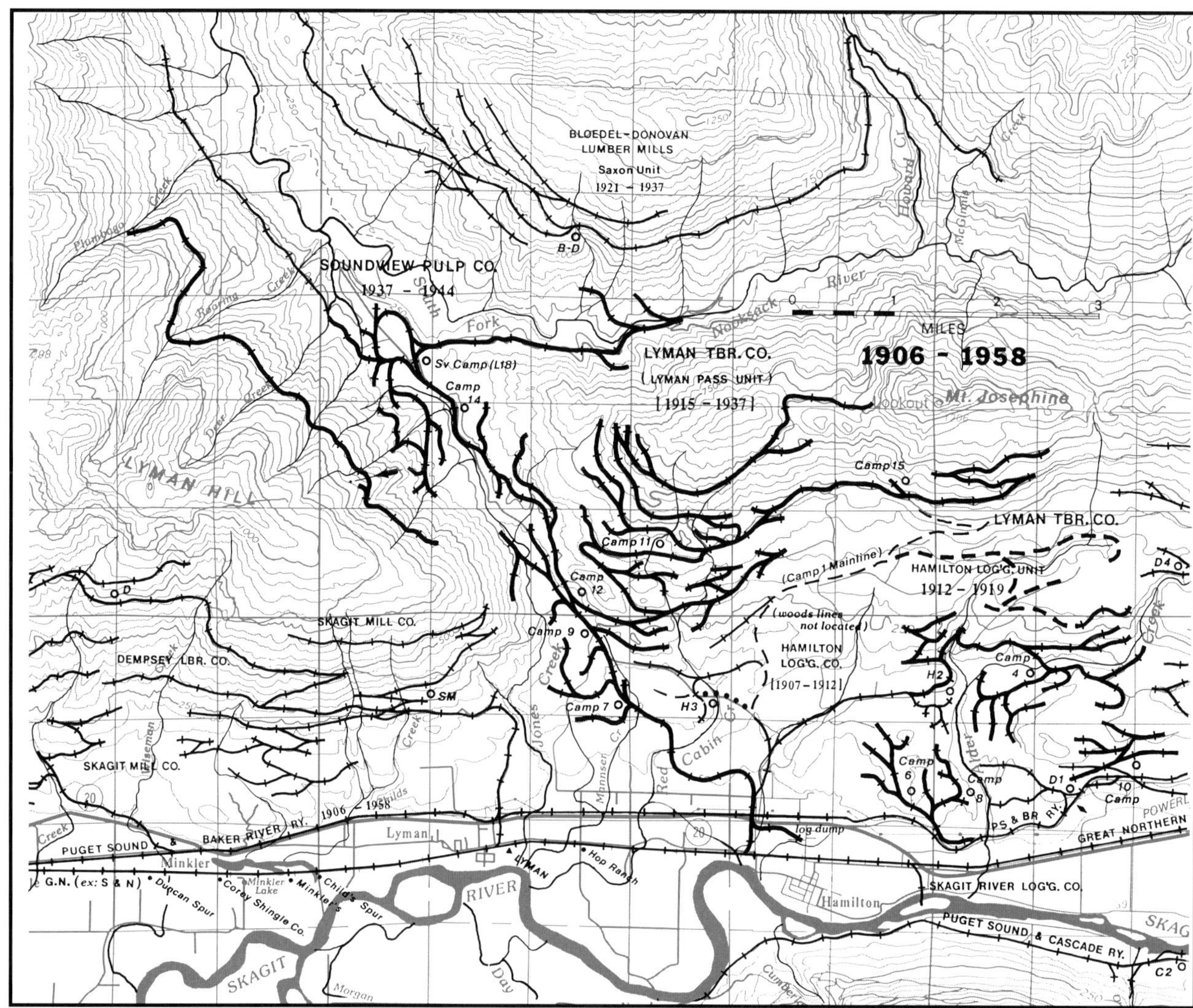

Map No. 5: **The Puget Sound & Baker River Railway** was constructed in 1906 by English & Dempsey. The terminus at Birdsview (just off above map at right) marked the beginning of Dempsey's logging railroad and timberlands.

Hamilton Logging Co. began operations adjacent to and concurrently with Dempsey. Hamilton's earliest operations were not documented. Astonishingly detailed timber cutting records after 1910 have allowed for the "approximated" grades shown. The company came under the name Lyman Timber Co. in 1917. Early camp numbers and origins are difficult to establish. Hamilton Logging Co. appears to have fostered "even numbered" camps to Camp 10. Lyman Timber Co. (under the veil of no documentation) seems to have set up odd numbered camps and its identity also merged into Lyman Timber Co. in 1917.

Soundview Pulp acquired Lyman Timber in 1937. Soundview logged extensively with motor trucks and built numerous truck roads into the area north of the Nooksack River along routes originally surveyed for railroad by Lyman Timber Co. Soundview did, however, construct one 3 mile spur northwest from Lyman Pass.

All of the woods lines were gone when Scott Paper Co. acquired Soundview Pulp Co. in 1951. The railroad yard and shops at Hamilton Junction along with a small amount of track at Similk Bay remained into the early 1960s with "re-loaded" log trains operating over the Great Northern in the last years. At its demise, the last physical evidence of railroad logging in Skagit County passed into history. *Map by RD Jost 1989*

Dotted line at Hamilton Logging Co. Camp 3 (H3) indicates original crossing of Red Cabin Creek (photo. pg. 58).

72

the "incline donkey" nor the yarder at the bottom of the incline. I am sure they were both badly damaged along with lines and rigging. Many of the long string of empty trucks that we left on the siding were badly damaged and all the wood parts were burnt off. Fortunately they were on a level track where they burnt up and stayed there.

The two locomotives (both Shays) that we hurriedly abandoned about half way down to Camp No. 3 on the main line did not escape the fire either. The cabs that were made of wood were completely burned up as well as all other parts of wood about them. They both looked to me, when I saw them, a good deal like a muley cow. The throttles were there, the reverse levers were there with nothing over head and but little space to put my feet. But, after road repair was finished we got them down to Camp No. 3 for repairs which was hastily made and I ran the "Old 3 Spot" for some time with a temporary homemade cab built by Mike Pence out of fir lumber that had never seen a dry kiln. Needless to say that it drawed up some in a hurry from the dry heat from the fire box over which it was built.*

Camp No. 3 was made headquarters for carpenters and mechanics with Lyle McNeill, one of the best camp foremans, placing his men here and there until soon a new camp was finished and all the loggers were back on the job and it was my turn to do the switching for all the yarders with the "Old 3 Spot" with a "Mike Pence" built homemade cab with a whistle that was worth a million dollars to my ears. But I can never forget the words that Ed English spoke to me as we conversed regarding the loss, that him and I could only make a feeble guess at the time, and these are his words, "Matt if you had all the money that I have lost in forest fires you could make a trip around the world."

The motive power stable on the Puget Sound and Baker River Railway doubled in 1913, with the arrival of 4-6-0 No. 2 - a near twin sister to the 1-spot. The new locomotive was factory fresh from Baldwin and added greatly to the flexibility of the railroad's operations.

The Riverside booming grounds on the Skagit River were busy preparing log rafts. These were towed to market by the little river steamer *Black Prince,* also company owned.

Hamilton Logging Company purchased two 8-1/2 x 10 Willamette steam loaders early in 1914, and about the same year the Red Cabin Creek trestle was replaced by a new bent-construction trestle lo-

PUGET SOUND & BAKER RIVER caboose No. 100 at Hamilton in 1937. *(below)* - **PS&BR CABOOSE No. 10** also at Hamilton in 1937. *John Taubeneck*

PS&BR CABOOSE No. 101 seen at Hamilton August 12, 1948. Scott Paper renumbered it 94 in 1956 and in 1959 donated it to the Puget Sound Railroad Museum at Snoqualmie, WA. *Ernie Plant, Callie Sparks*

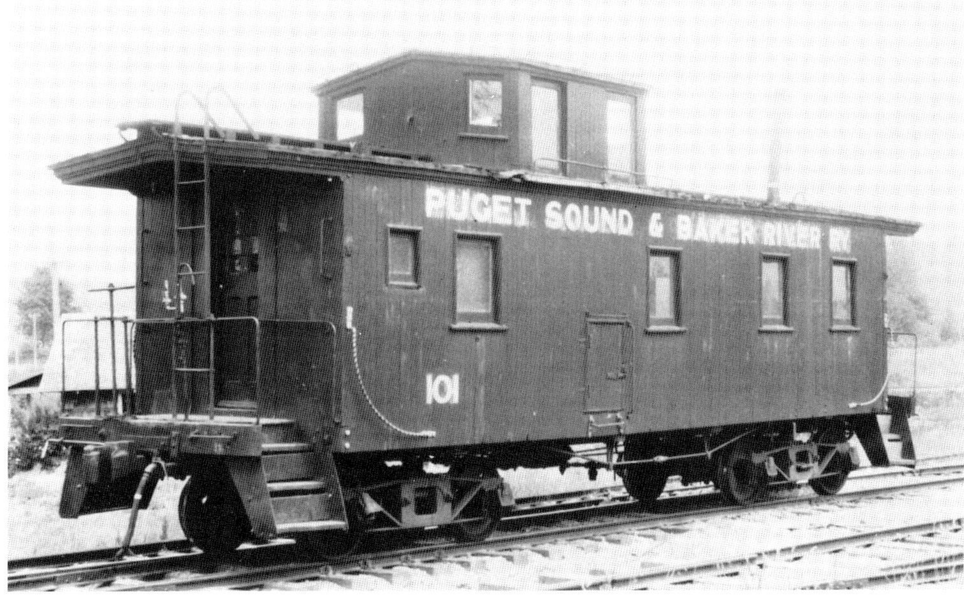

94 TONS OF SHAY LOCOMOTIVE rest on this trestle while the crew watches Darius Kinsey snap the shutter in this scene from the early 1920s. Classed as an 80-ton engine, the extra weight was added putting her in working order; on the road each of the 12 drive wheels support over 15,600 pounds. Photo taken near Camp 5. L to r: June Moore and "Happy" Pulsipher, brakemen; J. Oscar Robinson, fireman; George Wilson, engineer. *June Moore, Lawrence Perrigo*

LIMA BUILDERS' CARD for Lyman Timber's new Shay no. 5 delivered in 1920. *Allen County (Ohio) Historical Society (below)* - **SPECIFICATION DATA** on back of builders' card

LIMA LOCOMOTIVE WORKS, INCORPORATED

LIMA, OHIO

Class: 80-3 Truck Shay Geared — Road No. 5

Built for LYMAN TIMBER CO.

GAUGE OF TRACK	DRIVING WHEEL DIAMETER	FUEL KIND	CYLINDERS NO.	CYLINDERS DIAMETER	CYLINDERS STROKE	BOILER DIAMETER	BOILER PRESSURE	FIREBOX LENGTH	FIREBOX WIDTH
4'-8½"	36"	OIL	3	13½"	15"	50"	200 LBS.	72¼"	54¼"

WHEEL BASE TRUCK	WHEEL BASE ENGINE	WHEEL BASE ENGINE AND TENDER	MAXIMUM TRACTIVE POWER	FACTOR OF ADHESION	TUBES NUMBER	TUBES DIAMETER	TUBES LENGTH
4'-8"	32'-2"	44'-6"	35100 LBS.	5.35	194	2"	12'-5"

AVERAGE WEIGHT IN WORKING ORDER, POUNDS ON DRIVERS	AVERAGE WEIGHT IN WORKING ORDER, POUNDS TOTAL ENGINE	GRATE AREA SQ. FT.	HEATING SURFACES, SQUARE FEET TUBES	HEATING SURFACES FIREBOX	HEATING SURFACES TOTAL
188000	188000	27.2	1254	108	1362

Capacity, Water 3000 Gallons — Fuel 1200 Gallons

Negative Order No. 316

LYMAN TIMBER COMPANY Shay No. 6 in April of 1948. She was purchased from Sultan Railway and Timber, their No. 4, about 1930. After twenty years at Hamilton, she was cut up for scrap in 1950. *R. M. Hanft, D. S. Richter Coll.*

cated about one-half mile downstream from the original structure.

The Puget Sound and Baker River, as well as other English controlled railroads in the county, converted their locomotives from coal to oil burners in 1915.

A change in names occurred in 1917, when Hamilton Logging Company became the Lyman Timber Company. Filing for new incorporation on January 4 of that year, were William C. Butler, Eleanor E. Butler, L. L. Crosby, E. G. English, Alice K. English and N. A. English. Capital stock was $1,000,000. Other than the name change, the logging operations continued about the same.

The beginning of 1918 marked the tenth anniversary of the Puget Sound and Baker River Railway. The railroad handled the output of Dempsey Lumber Company and old Hamilton Logging Company as well as two smaller producers.

For the ten year period Skagit Mill Company shipped a total of 3,110,272 feet of timber over the PS&BR. In the same period, David Tozier Company, which appears to have been a holding company as Hamilton Logging Company did their only known active harvesting, shipped 90,606,168 feet.

The Dempsey and Hamilton companies were surprisingly close in their ten year output. Dempsey shipped 250,816,687 feet, being edged out slightly by Hamilton

75

LYMAN TIMBER COMPANY CREW, October 1939 at the Hamilton car shop. Man sitting on locomotive is unknown. L to r, rear: Sam Beck, car whacker; Henry Harps, Ohio Steam Crane operator; Bill Pulver, fireman, brakeman, car shop worker; Charlie Elliott, car whacker; Phil Hancock, machinist; Axel Jensen, welder, mechanic; Front row: Walt Hopgood, dozer operator; Hal Johnson, blacksmith's helper; Al Stewart, locomotive engineer; Dick Phillips, mechanic; Johnny Elving, blacksmith; Frank Houston, car whacker. *Dennis Thompson collection*

AT THE TOP OF THE CAMP 16 INCLINE this Washington snubbing engine waits for the next car to use the track running down toward Grandy Lake, and the mainline of the railroad. This machine was moved later to another incline near Camp 14. When that operation ended, the snubber was left in place and abandoned. It was still there in 1988. *D. Kinsey, Bill Pulver*

Logging Company with their 261,627,195 total for ten years.

The grand total of timber carried by the Puget Sound and Baker River Railway for their first ten years was over 606 million feet dumped into the Skagit River.

In 1922, statistics for the "new" Lyman Timber Company were as follows: three sides operating, ten donkey engines, five high leads, commissary, machine shop, electric light plant, fifteen miles of railroad using 56-pound rail, three geared locomotives, one hundred skeleton cars, ten flat cars, one hundred and seventy five men employed with a daily output of 200,000 feet.

Changes in operation occurred on the Puget Sound and Baker River in 1923. Annual freshets had been taking their toll of the river rafts and the decision was made to open a new log dump and booming grounds at Similk Bay, between Anacortes and Burlington.

Accordingly, in May of that year, trains

LYMAN TIMBER COMPANY Camp 14 incline. This was the car the crew rode daily to work. Two wires strung along the track were to signal the snubbing engine at the top. Jumping off the car and touching the wires together would signal the snubber to stop travel of the car. Date is June 1936. *D. Kinsey, Howard White/Ed Marlow*

LYMAN TIMBER COMPANY "Unit" l to r on sled: Lornie Campbell, "Tar" Rhodes, Grover Welch, unknown, "Happy" Pulsipher, Ransom Herl. Leaning: Ed Woods, engineer. Man with oil can is "Dusty" Rhodes. Two men on bottom: Harry Kell on left, Gus Hill. *D. Kinsey, Callie Sparks*

began traveling as far as Butler Station, west of Sedro Woolley, on PS&BR trackage; thence over the Great Northern Railway through Burlington and on 10.3 miles west of Burlington to Whitmarsh Junction where the last mile was again on PS&BR rails. Trackage rights over the Great Northern always included PS&BR equipment and crews. The Riverside dump was abandoned and the turntable moved to Similk Bay.

Lyman Timber continued to log at full capacity under the management of H. A. Moore with N. A. Dameron as superintendent. Three sides were running using

LYMAN TIMBER COMPANY 12 x 14 Washington Yarder crew. L to r: John Pinelli, Walter Allen, George Snelson, Clarence Lundberg, Hokie Lund, Herbert Fisher, Scoop McCully, Shirley Allen, Mr. Green, Ovel Thomas. *John Pinelli*

LYMAN TIMBER COMPANY CAMP 15. This camp was located well up the slopes of Mount Josephine, in Section 25, of Township 36 North, Range 6 East. Several logging camps were arranged in this fashion, built on tiers laid against the mountainside.

78 *(above)*- These were not good bunkhouses for sleepwalkers who walked through doors. *D. Kinsey, Harley McCalib*

(to the right) - Upper track terrace of the camp. Lower track is to the left of the water tank. The two ladies are Mollie Dowdle on the left and Francis Freeman. *D. Kinsey, courtesy Whatcom Museum of History and Art*

five donkey engines, four high leads and a new Clyde skidder. The woods railroad was fifteen miles in length and the hillsides echoed to the whistles of four Shay locomotives as they busily shuttled over one hundred logging cars back and forth. On the payroll were 175 men toiling in the forests.

By 1927, Dempsey finished logging its holdings. It was unable to negotiate the purchase of one section of timber adjacent to its old Camp 5. The block of timber was owned by Stimson interests and referred to locally as the *Stimson Claim.* Failing to strike a deal, Dempsey pulled up their railroad back to the end of the Puget Sound and Baker River, and moved to fresh logging north of the town of Lyman. Removal of the old track was done in February and March of 1927.

The next year Lyman Timber Company did purchase the Stimson Claim and relaid steel eastward on a slightly different route. Lyman Timber purchased Dempsey's incline snubber and built an incline into the Stimson Claim. The base of the incline became Lyman's Camp 16.

Logging the Stimson Claim required about one year, after which they extended the railroad on to Grandy Lake where they built Camp 17 on the shore of the lake. They logged here until the Great Depression shut them down in June of 1930. While these expansions were being made toward Grandy Lake, other camps were still running in the Lyman Pass area.

Pre-depression times were indeed busy. Lyman Timber maintained locomotive shops and car shops. The car shop not only repaired company equipment, but built new railroad cars as well. The woods force usually produced twenty-five to thirty cars per train leaving the landing and there were normally two trains per day. Log trains to Similk Bay from Lyman Timber were usually handled by 4-6-0 No. 1. The mainline haul for Dempsey was made with 4-6-0 No. 2.

Life on the mainline haul was not always dull. Al Stewart, engineer of 4-6-0 No. 2 related some incidents to Ray Jordan some time ago:

Motz Hamilton was easing the Two-Spot down the hill from the Dempsey Camp with a drag of logs crowding hard behind. Albert Nielson was hauling milk in ten-gallon cans from the John Cook place to the Dempsey cookhouse with the gas speeder and highballing to make it up the hill to camp before the Two-Spot came by.

Whizzing around a curve Al suddenly saw a big shiny brass Number Two staring him in the face. He became tired of riding right away and promptly dived off into the

(at left) **LYMAN TIMBER COMPANY Camp 11** in 1920.
D. Kinsey courtesy Whatcom Museum of History and Art

LYMAN TIMBER COMPANY Shay No. 4 at the Hamilton enginehouse April 18, 1941. This was the junction for the Puget Sound & Baker River Railway. *Al Farrow*

salmonberry brush, understandably forgetting to slow down first.

The speeder smacked our old girl friend; the can lids flew off and dunked Motz Hamilton with a barrage of milk. Motz was a busy man for awhile, what with clawing milk out of his eyes, applying the air and doing all the 83
things that an engineer has to do in a crisis like this, with nothing to see with.

ALAS, IN LATER YEARS, Lyman Timber No. 5 shows her age as this photograph depicts taken at Hamilton shops. *Al Farrow*

LYMAN TIMBER COMPANY M.A.C. 4-40 Rail Car. Carl Schaffer on left; Carl Johnson on right; both men employees of the car's manufacturer, Skagit Steel and Iron Works. Location is Hamilton. This unit was soon rebuilt to fully enclose the deck, providing protection from the weather to the men riding to and from work. John Pinelli recalls coming home from a day's work in the remodeled car in 1936: "There was the gas mechanic named 'Andy' who drove the speeder. We were all standing in there like sardines coming home from working on the incline by Camp 14. We'd stopped in Camp 9 to let off some guys, and started up again. 'This car don't ride right' said Andy, and he stopped to look around. 'I'm gonna ease her on home,' he said, starting up again. We went across the high bridge and around the corner into 'Punkin Center.' Some more guys got off and we started up again. I was watching out the window. Pretty quick I saw one of our wheels roll out in front and go down the bank. We were lucky. Four years later going along the Nooksack River the same speeder lost a wheel again." *(Author's note: these cars usually had a good reputation for reliability and usefulness). Skagit Steel and Iron Works*

LYMAN TIMBER COMPANY Camp 18 Truck re-load. This photograph was taken when Camp 18 was still under construction and this scene is about one-quarter mile northwest of the camp site. Davis and White (Claude Davis) was the contract truck logger and this was his fleet of Kenworth trucks. *D. Kinsey, Whatcom Museum of History and Art*

LYMAN TIMBER COMPANY Camp 18. This was the last railroad camp for the company, and also a truck reload. *D. Kinsey, courtesy Whatcom Museum of History and Art.* 85

DAVIS AND WHITE, CONTRACT LOGGERS. When Soundview took over Lyman Timber, internal combustion gained a foothold. In this scene, taken in the fall of 1939, a Kenworth truck is high above the Nooksack River, ready to start down to the railroad reload. Top to bottom are: Vivian Bates, "Speed" Bowman, Hank Snyder and Ira Moffat. Driver is unknown. *D. Kinsey, Bert Kellogg*

HERE IN APRIL 1952, following her last days of general use, Puget Sound and Baker River No. 1 looked like this. She is mated to the tender from 4-6-0 No. 2. *Doug Hubert, D.S. Richter Collection*

(below) - **IN THE DRINK,** 2 views of the one-spot Baldwin. Tender and back of cab seen sitting in the salt water of Similk Bay. Original photo stamped "June 10, 1946." She was pulled out and placed back in service for a short time. *Callie Sparks*

No one was hurt much, but the engine had to visit the shop doctors for the removal of some serious wrinkles in the front parts.

And one evening when the Two-Spot was standing on the trestle at the log dump on Similk Bay, Walter Welch fumbled and dropped his lantern overboard. The lantern stayed lighted, and Walter, never one to pass up an opportunity, called to Clarence Love, the fireman, and asked if he had ever seen an electric fish. Clarence hadn't, so he came over and displayed quite an interest in the "fish."

It is well now to note certain events of the 1930s that impacted Lyman Timber Company.

First, Ed English passed away February 23, 1930, at the age of 79. Even with competent management in place this must have left its mark.

Second, with clouds on the national economic horizon, Dempsey Lumber Company, having finished logging in this region, chose to leave the county within six months after English's death. As Dempsey left they sold their 51 percent interest in the Puget Sound and Baker River Railway to Lyman Timber Company.

Finally, the Great Depression closed the doors of Lyman Timber in June of 1930; a shutdown that lasted almost four years. The

THE TWO-SPOT is seen here on April 12, 1952 sitting behind the Scott Paper Company shop near the Great Northern interchange. She had received a general overhaul in 1937, right after Soundview Pulp took over the line. From early 1948, until 1957, she sat here, waiting her fate. *Doug Hubert, D. S. Richter Collection*

(below) - **THE LEFT SIDE** of No. 2, near the end of her career. Photo taken at Hamilton September 2, 1948. *Al Farrow, D.S. Richter Collection*

87

mainline remained silent except for one trip made with 4-6-0 No. 1 to Similk Bay to get fuel oil to have on hand in case of fire.

A fire did occur in the early 1930s - this time in the Lyman Timber enginehouse. Shay No. 2 was caught in the fire and her girder frame sagged clear to the railhead from the heat.

However, times again improved, and Lyman Timber resumed logging again in October of 1933. It appeared the darkness had passed.

It was business as usual for almost four years. E. T. Clark was manager and the firm was logging 250,000 feet daily, running two sides. The Clyde skidder was back in service. Ed Seabloom was logging superintendent.

In 1937, came an event that not only changed the company's identity once again, but reshaped the organization's philosophy, policies and operations for all time. Soundview Pulp Company purchased Lyman Timber Company, "lock, stock and barrel," in the spring of

"MIKE" No. 3 was built new for Monroe Logging Company in July of 1923 and appears here 25 years later - September 2, 1948. Her days at Hamilton ended when she was scrapped in the spring of 1958. *Al Farrow, D. S. Richter Collection*

88

(right) - **AT HAMILTON JUNCTION**, Mikado No. 3 waits for the run to Similk Bay. L to r: Ed Woods, engineer; Adrian Strong; J. O. Robinson, fireman. *Callie Sparks.*

(below) - **THE THREE-SPOT HELD DOWN ROAD ASSIGNMENTS** during the last years of the Puget Sound and Baker River. She is seen here at Hamilton, August 12, 1948. The big Porter product has ten years of her life remaining. *Ernie Plant, Callie Sparks*

STORMING OUT OF HAMILTON JUNCTION, Porter Mikado No. 3 heads for the Great Northern switch, and Similk Bay 27 miles to the west. Small building left of the locomotive is telephone shack where clearance was obtained to move onto Great Northern track. *Al Farrow*

that year. Soundview operated the largest bleached sulphite pulp mill in the world in Everett, Washington. About this time, Soundview also acquired the holdings of Canyon Lumber Company, in Snohomish County. The intention was to provide a long-term supply of raw materials for their Everett plant.

Because of the new focus on pulp production, hemlock logging, not fir and cedar, became the goal. Revitalization of the Skagit operations not only included plant already in place, but included plans for truck logging in the future. The internal combustion age was just around the corner.

Camp 14, located about twelve miles northwest of the Hamilton headquarters, was running two sides.

The "high side," was well up on Hightower Hill, a high ridge extending from Hamilton to Wickersham. An incline was in use down which logs were lowered, one car at a time, over grades as heavy as 52 percent in places. The incline length was 4,600 feet. Ordinary skeleton cars were used. A cable was placed around the load, the top and side logs being slightly notched to keep the cable from slipping. A system of notches and hooks on the bunks kept the line from fouling. Each round trip took about eighteen minutes. By operating the incline day and night, it hand-

RUNNING GEAR of the Porter road engine provides setting for this portrait of Louis LaMar, brakeman (left) and Ed Woods, engineer. This is the summer of 1948. *Ernie Plant, Callie Sparks.*

90

PUGET SOUND AND BAKER RIVER RAILWAY DUMP AT SIMILK BAY. In the last days of the railroad, this was the unloading operation on the salt water. These four photographs taken August 27, 1952 depict the sequence of operations in the dumping - the locomotive leaves the loaded cars on the dump trestle, the unloader moves down the parallel track, car cheese blocks were dropped, the unloader then pushes the logs off the car. *All photos Steve Russell, Callie Sparks*

52
52

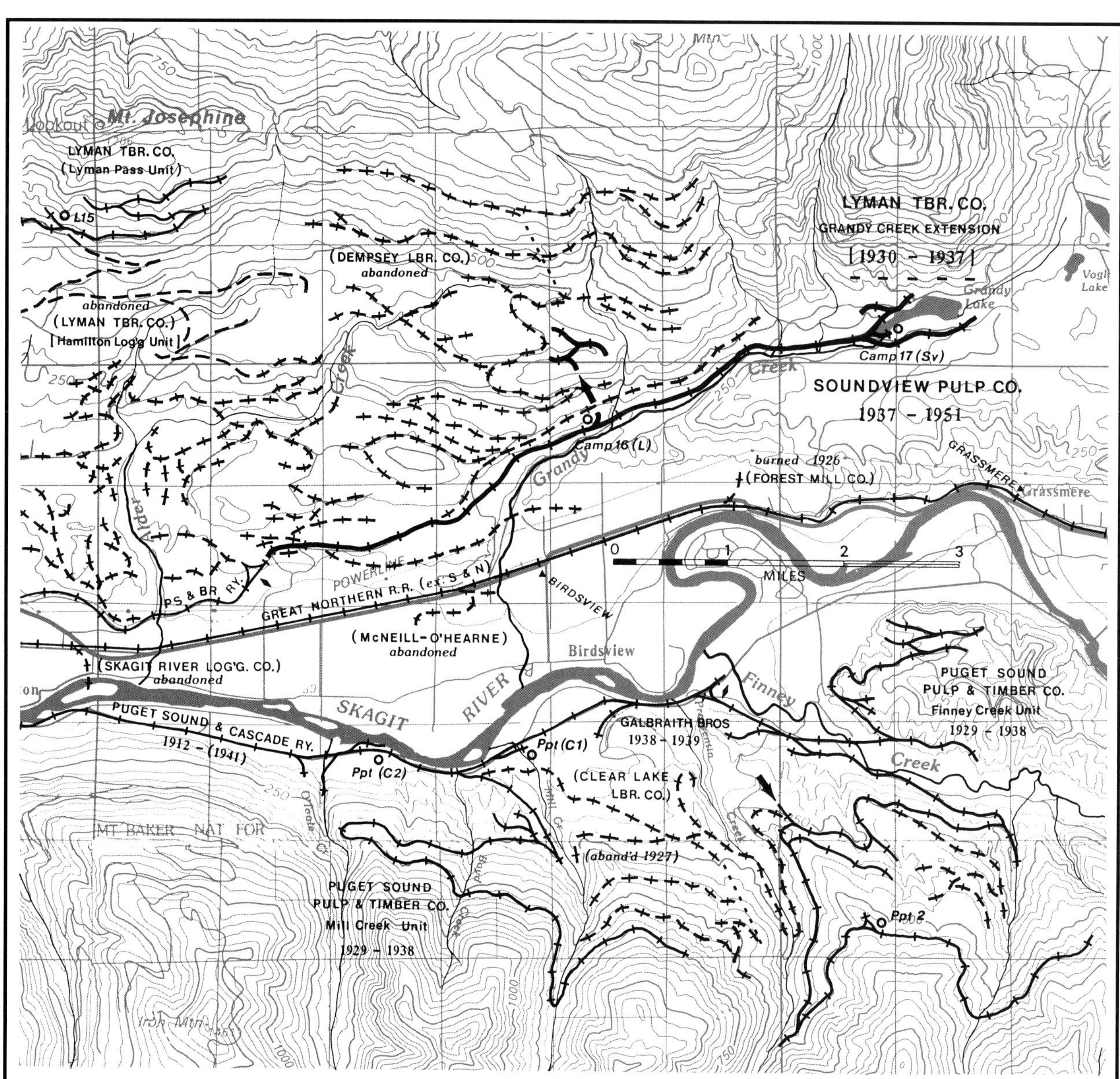

Map No. 6 In 1928, the Camp 16 spur and incline shown here was constructed to log a half-section of timber known as the *Stimson claim.* The subsequent extension of this spur to Grandy Lake in 1930 (Grandy Lake Extension) marked the last railroad construction at Birdsview, and its projected goal of Baker Lake was never reached. The Extension remained for several years, becoming a reload point for Soundview Pulp Co.

To the south, Puget Sound Pulp & Timber Co. had taken over the Clear Lake Lumber Co. *(see page 151)*. The Finney Creek unit was repaired, the Pressentin Creek unit was torn up and a new line built to Mill Creek. PSP&T discontinued railroad logging in favor of motor trucks in 1938. Some thought had been given to retaining the mainline Puget Sound & Cascade Ry. but such plan was dropped in 1941. Removal of the track occurred about 1942. *Map by RD Jost 1989*

led all logs brought to it. Feeding the incline was the huge Clyde skidder. The incline snubber was the same Washington machine purchased from Dempsey. This was to be its last setting - when logging moved on it was abandoned to the forest. It remains there to this very day.

A new tractor camp was now begun on the "high side." Operated by Halterman and Knudsen, they had a contract to remove eight million feet of timber near the top of the hill. Using an RD8 and an RD6 "Caterpillar," and a Skagit gas donkey, they brought logs as far as the tracks where they were loaded.

The "low side" of the operation was east across Lyman Pass. In use was a Washington skidder. Cold decking was done with a Skagit Waukesha powered, 225-horsepower donkey.

For additional activity in late 1937, a new steam side was planned up the Nooksack River where some 600 million feet of timber was waiting. This timber would come out through Camp 14.

A new incline had been planned for the future, however, with new management the emphasis began to shift toward truck logging.

Another immediate decision of Soundview manage-

PUGET SOUND AND BAKER RIVER'S ONLY DIESEL. She held two distinctions: one as the only diesel to operate private logging trains in Skagit County. Second is that she ran the last private logging train in the county in 1960. Photo taken at Burlington July 1, 1959. She is an ALCO product built in 1938. *Lloyd Graham*

ment was the shutdown of the Puget Sound and Baker River mainline. Evidently expanded trackage rights over the Great Northern appeared cheaper than maintaining their own railroad. The track from Hamilton to Butler Station was abandoned with the exception of a small portion used for a short time by Skagit Mill Company west of Minkler Lake. Now all Soundview trains traveled via Great Northern from Hamilton directly to Similk Bay. During 1939 and 1940 the steel was taken up on the old mainline using the 2-spot Shay from Soundview. Ed English's inspiration to avoid Great Northern's high freight of 1905, had lasted almost thirty years.

A new plan was now under way for the Grandy Lake area. The old Camp 17 was modernized. A new cookhouse and dining room was erected. And a large, new truck operation was taking shape with a contract logger.

The new outfit was named Grandy Lake Logging Company and was owned by Ed Ward and Pat Archibald. Part of the plan now was to use Grandy Lake as log storage in case of disruption in logging. It was estimated that fifteen million feet of logs could be stored in the lake.

On the east side of the lake a forty-car passing track was built on the railroad. A steam loader was installed to facilitate loading a steady stream of log cars that could be routed directly to Similk Bay.

Another contract logger joined the company by 1938,
hauling in the Lyman Pass area. The logs were loaded 93
on railroad cars at a truck shop and reload in Lyman Pass. The new firm was Davis and White of Marysville,

ALCO No. 95 sits at the rear of the Scott Paper Company shops at Hamilton. She came from the Chicago & Eastern Illinois. Date is June 1956. *George Hartwell, Fred Spurrell*

ONE OF THE LAST REMAINS of Hamilton railroad logging was the old Lyman Timber car shop seen here February 17, 1982. It had been built about 1937 after the old shop burned. The building, pictured here, was torn down in December 1986. *Dennis Thompson*

who owned a fleet of Kenworth trucks. The trucks boasted 428-cubic-inch Buda motors, Brown-Lipe transmission sets and dual worm drive rear axles. Top speed was thirty-nine miles per hour on the highway, which they never achieved on these back roads. Brakes were Roadmaster vacuum. There were fourteen trucks in the fleet and the average haul was five miles on Soundview's private roads.

Other equipment on the job consisted of seven Caterpillar tractors with blades; one Hyster arch; one Carco arch; one 11 x 14 oil-burning steam skidder; one Pacific Iron and Steel Works diesel skidder with 250-horsepower Cummins motor; one 12 x 14 Washington two-speed oil-burning steam donkey used for yarding; one 300-horsepower Skagit gas yarder; two Skagit 170-horsepower gas donkeys; two Clyde 200-horsepower gas donkeys used for cold decking and one 12 x 14 Washington oil-burning steam donkey used for reloading.

An 85-ton Shay locomotive had been obtained from Sultan Railway and Timber Company at Oso. This and the 5-spot Shay, already there, were the woods engines.

A Porter 2-8-2 mainline locomotive was on the way from Monroe Logging Company at Monroe, Washington. When she arrived at Hamilton she spent some time in the shop "getting the bugs worked out of her." Over the next few years she gradually replaced the Baldwins on the haul to the dump. The 10-wheelers had often double-headed fifty to sixty car trains, which the Porter now handled alone.

As the war years passed, trucks handled an ever greater share of the work. In 1946, the Grandy Lake branch of the railroad was pulled up.

Camp 14 made its last move about 1939, to a flat area just south of the Davis and White reload. This became Camp 18 - the final railroad camp for the Hamilton operation. From this camp back to Hamilton became the only woods railroad left.

Camp 18 was used as a reload only in later years. About 1948, the camp buildings were moved to Hamilton, and a reload was set up north of the Hamilton railroad yard. Soon after, the old track to the woods was removed. The Hamilton reload operated until the end of the railroad.

Baldwin No. 1 made its last run in 1949. The 2-spot finished a year earlier. The two 10-wheelers sat in the Hamilton yard until 1956. At that time the 1-spot and the tender from the 2-spot were cut up for scrap. The remaining locomotive and tender were held for a few months, then given to the city of Sedro Woolley for display on September 23, 1957.

Soundview Pulp Company merged with Scott Paper Company on November 9, 1951. The donation of the

2-spot to Sedro Woolley was a gift from Scott Paper.

About 1956, Scott brought to Hamilton a 1939 vintage diesel locomotive to replace the Porter. In the spring of 1958, the 2-8-2 was scrapped at Hamilton.

After a few months' service with the diesel locomotive, Scott experimented with truck hauling from Hamilton to the log dump in the winter of 1959-1960. The Puget Sound and Baker River Railway never turned a wheel again. Trucks took over and the last logging railroad in Skagit county disappeared into history.

95

CHAPTER 3

HEISLERS AT BIRDSVIEW

The Dempsey Lumber Company

The Dempsey Lumber Company came to Skagit County from Manistee, Michigan, where they had exhausted their timber holdings. James Dempsey, who first engaged in the lumber business in Manistee in 1854, was looking for fresh timber in the Pacific Northwest and planned to build a new sawmill in a central location. Tacoma was chosen as a mill site and standing timber was found available in Skagit County. The summer of 1905 found James' sons, John J. and L. T. Dempsey, making a tour of the Portland, Oregon mills to determine the best methods of modern mill construction. By Christmas of the same year property had been purchased in Tacoma and construction of the new facility was expected to begin promptly.

The scope of the company's new venture can best be understood from the following items taken from **The Timberman** magazine, February 1906:

L. T. Dempsey, of the Dempsey Lumber Company, of Manistee, Michigan, has placed an order with the Allis-Chalmers Company, through the Seattle office, for one of the largest and most complete sawmill outfits ever sent to the Pacific Coast. The mill will be erected at Tacoma, where they have secured about 50 acres for the mill site, located on tidewater. The machinery in this mill will be of the heaviest type that ever has been built. It will include an 11-foot band mill carrying band saws 18 inches wide, and a 9-foot band mill carrying double-cut saws 18 inches wide, with a complete equipment of log deck machinery, Pacific Coast carriages, etc., for handling logs up to 19 feet in diameter and 120 feet long. The edger is capable of handling 10-inch timber, and is 84 inches wide. The slashers and trimmers will take lumber up to 50 feet in length. The mill building will be 66 feet wide and about 500 feet long. The power plant will consist of eight 72-inch by 18-foot high pressure boilers with Dutch oven settings, connected to a concrete stack 100 inches in diameter and 120 feet high. A twin Reliance engine will be furnished, having cylinders 26 inches in diameter by 36 inch stroke. The wheel on this engine will be 16 feet in diameter and 90 inches face, carrying a belt 88 inches wide. The electric plant will be driven by separate engines which will generate electric current for lighting purposes as well as running the planing mill, where each machine will be driven by a separate motor. The dry kilns will be constructed of concrete blocks, making them fire-proof. The lumber from the mills will be handled by the improved method

DEMPSEY LUMBER COMPANY. Steam pot and crew. *D.Kinsey courtesy Whatcom Museum of History and Art*

DEMPSEY HEISLER No. 1 is shown here with what is said to be the first train of logs from their Skagit operation. The location is on the mainline above Headquarters. Matt Snider is the engineer with Bert White, fireman, Perry Francisco, brakeman and "Bruiser" Richardson, brakeman. Dempsey signed a purchase contract for this first geared engine in November 1906. The price was $9,400. *Lawrence Perrigo*

HEISLER No. 1 pauses in the woods above Birdsview. No longer a new locomotive, footboards have replaced her factory pilot and her headlight had disappeared. Five years of logging have left their mark. In the gangway stands Wilfred Richmeyer, fireman. Resting in the cab window is Al Stewart, engineer. Brakeman Jim Raby reposes on the footboard. *D. Kinsey photo, Jesse and Elsie Ingersoll*

and when completed will be one of the finest plants ever constructed on the Pacific Coast. The erection of this plant has already commenced and it is expected to be in operation by September. The Dempsey Lumber Company has a large amount of standing timber in the State of Washington; in fact, enough to run their mill for many years. For over 30 years they have operated at Manistee, Michigan, completing their cut there in the past season.

The new mill began operation in the spring of 1907. Then, after less than two months operation, the industry trade journals for June carried the news that the new plant burned to the ground.

Testifying to the steadfast determination of the Dempseys,

(left)
DEMPSEY HEISLER No. 1 sans headlight. Dexter Hooper on left, Jim Raby in center. *Ed Marlow*

(below)
IN THE EARLY DAYS OF DEMPSEY'S LOGGING, Heisler No. 1 shows some coal smoke as she puffs across West Grandy Creek. *Vern Harris, Ed Marlow*

40 ft. Bridge over Grande Creek at Dempsey's

99

within thirty days of the fire they had built a small mill on the site to enable them to begin cutting lumber to rebuild the large plant.

The Dempsey Lumber Company began logging in Skagit County shortly before 1907. This first operation was located two miles west of Birdsview and just north of the present Burlington Northern Railroad.

Dempsey skidded logs with horses over an old skid road that had been built and used by the John Hightower Mill Company some three or four years earlier. The first forty acres were cut primarily for boom sticks and piling and the logs were put in the Skagit River at the old C. Green homestead near the south end of today's Pinelli Road.

The main office for the Dempsey Lumber Company was also located in Tacoma and remained there throughout the life of the firm. In 1906 Dempsey entered the railroad business when on October 2 of that year the Stearns Manufacturing Company of Erie, Pennsylvania, made a proposal to construct a 52-ton Heisler locomotive for Dempsey's Skagit operations. The transaction and delivery of this machine was handled by Dempsey's Tacoma office and Stearn's western agent, Whitney Engineering Company, also located in Tacoma. The

THE ONE-SPOT HEISLER halts her work to allow the photographer to catch Wilfred Richmeyer and Al Stewart in their work clothes. The steam brake actuating cylinder is clearly seen next to fireman Richmeyer as he stands with hands on hips. Light rail, rough ties with tops hewn flat and few spikes show the typical signs of a woods line. Date: 1912. *Wilfred Richmeyer*

sales contract for the Heisler was dated November 27, 1906.

Dempsey's railroad operation quickly became two-fold as they entered into an agreement with the Hamilton Logging Company (English interests) whereby the two firms would build a railroad from the vicinity of their logging camps to a Skagit River log dump just north of Mount Vernon. Incorporated September 7, 1906, with a capital stock of $100,000, the name of the new railroad was The Puget Sound & Baker River Railway Company. The first trustees were L. T. Dempsey, J. J. Dempsey, W. C. Butler, E. G. English and Fred Pape and this firm was destined to continue in operation after all other logging railroads in Skagit County had ceased to exist. Dempsey Lumber Company owned 51 percent of the Puget Sound & Baker River Railway.

Four months after the purchase of the Heisler, Dempsey concluded purchase of a new 52-ton Baldwin 4-6-0, to be lettered for the new PS&BR Ry. The Baldwin appears to have been Dempsey's first locomotive on its Skagit property. **The Timberman Directory** of 1907 records Dempsey Lumber Company as having five miles of railroad under construction using one rod locomotive.

Dempsey's Headquarters Camp, enginehouse and shop were located north of the Pinelli Road, and about three miles west of Birdsview Siding. At that point the PS&BR "officially" ended and the track beyond was the Dempsey Lumber Company's woods lines which were built north and east of Headquarters. It was in this area the Heisler was used. Number "One" (as was the PS&BR Baldwin), the Heisler came to Dempsey with a price tag of $9,400. She had 16-$^{3}/_{4}$ x 14 inch cylinders, carried 1,700 gallons of water and burned wood.

Disconnected trucks were used by Dempsey and loads were brought to Headquarters by the Heisler to be interchanged to the PS&BR for the trip to the Riverside log dump which was located between the interurban and highway bridges on the Skagit River in north Mount Vernon.

The first record of logs to be shipped from Dempsey over the PS&BR occurs in 1908,

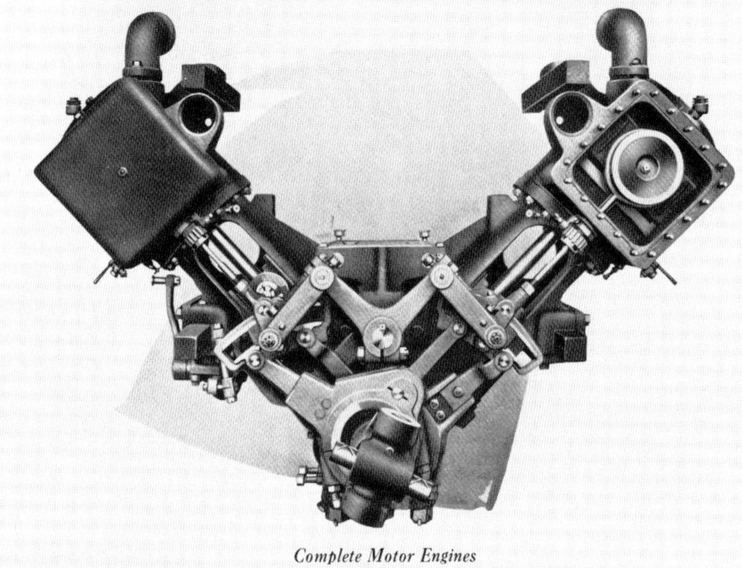

Complete Motor Engines

HEISLER RUNNING GEAR is shown here, the "V-2" engine above and the power truck with gearing below as illustrated in a Heisler catalog. *Jim Gertz Collection*

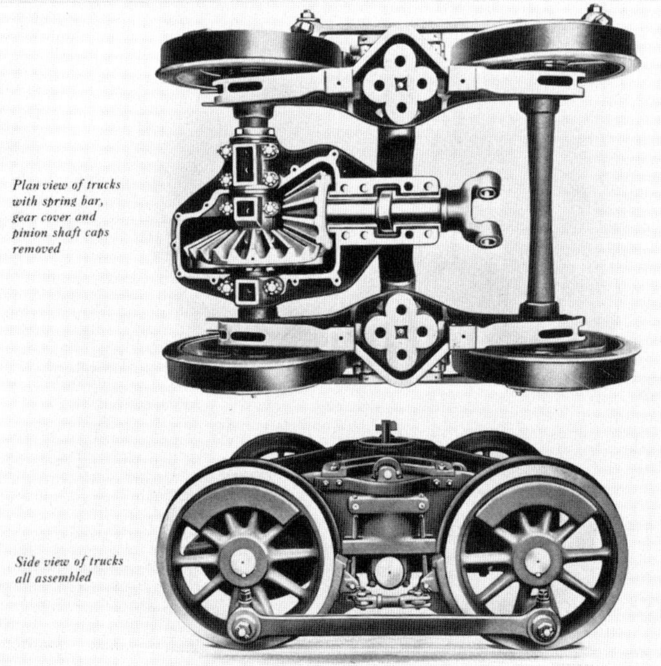

Plan view of trucks with spring bar, gear cover and pinion shaft caps removed

Side view of trucks all assembled

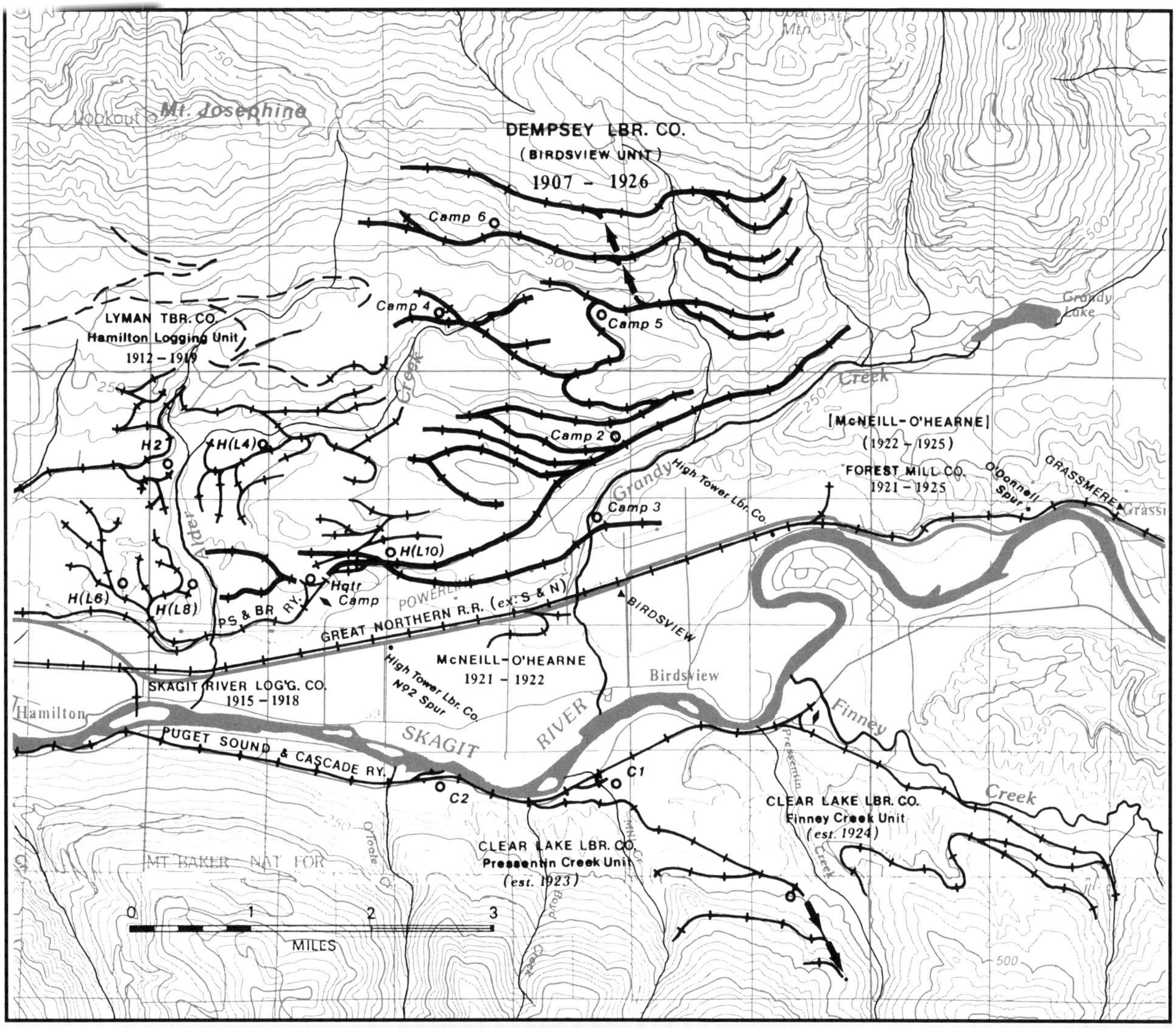

DEMPSEY LBR. CO.
(BIRDSVIEW UNIT)
1907 - 1926

Mt. Josephine
Lookout
Camp 6
Camp 4
Camp 5
Camp 2
Camp 3
Grandy Lake
Grandy Creek
LYMAN TBR. CO.
Hamilton Logging Unit
1912 – 1919
[McNEILL-O'HEARNE]
(1922 – 1925)
FOREST MILL CO.
1921 – 1925
O'Donnell Spur
GRASSMERE
High Tower Lbr. Co.
H2
H(L4)
H(L10)
H(L6)
H(L8)
Hqtr Camp
Alder
POWERLINE
PS & BR RY.
GREAT NORTHERN R.R. (ex: S & N)
BIRDSVIEW
Birdsview
McNEILL-O'HEARNE
1921 - 1922
High Tower Lbr. Co. No2 Spur
SKAGIT RIVER LOG'G. CO.
1915 – 1918
Hamilton
SKAGIT RIVER
PUGET SOUND & CASCADE RY.
C1
C2
Finney Creek
Pressentin Creek
CLEAR LAKE LBR. CO.
Finney Creek Unit
(est. 1924)
CLEAR LAKE LBR. CO.
Pressentin Creek Unit
(est. 1923)
MT BAKER NAT FOR
0 1 2 3
MILES

101

Map No. 7 The complete logging railroad of the Dempsey Lumber Co. at Birdsview is shown here. Note that Dempsey logged the upper laterals of their Camp 5 incline first, then moved down to build the mid-laterals later. There is reason to believe that much of the railroad as shown remained in place until the conclusion of operations in 1926. The bridge which crossed Alder Creek just east of Camp 4 is remembered for its "Y" configuration as the spur to the northeast split off from the middle of the span!

Hamilton operations shown are those occurring after Hamilton Logging Co. became Lyman Timber Co.

As logging railroad activity neared conclusion on the north side of the Skagit River, Clear Lake Lumber Co. arrived on the south side, linking their Pressentin Creek and Finney Creek units with the Finney Creek Extension. Financial difficulties stopped Clear Lake's operation in 1925 *(see Chapter 6 and page 153 for further details).* *Map by RD Jost 1989*

when 159,580 board feet were shipped in the month of September. The passage of only two months brought a sharp increase in production and over one million feet of timber left for market in November. The Tacoma mill cut 23,605,400 board feet of lumber in 1909, the first year of the new operation.

DEMPSEY CAMP 2 as it was rebuilt after the fire of 1912. The portion of the camp shown here includes some family houses and a new donkey sled under construction to the left of the water tank. *Dennis Thompson*

102 **ON THE THIRD SWITCHBACK** above Birdsview, Heisler No. 2 is caught in a classic pose by the lens of Clark Kinsey. She trails a string of High Hercules logging trucks built by Seattle Car and Foundry. Each set of two trucks (often called "disconnects") weighed in at 18,000 pounds. The train length appears to contain about 11 sets. That equates to a 198,000 pound train weight this 62-ton Heisler is taking uphill to Camp 4. Later, returning downhill loaded with logs, the only air brakes are those on the locomotive, the cars have only hand brakes. Standing in the gangway is Louis LaMar, Al Stewart, engineer, is in the window. Man on front is unidentified. The year is 1917. *Clark Kinsey, Univ. of Washington*

DEMPSEY HEISLER No. 2 steams quietly in front of the camera about 1918. On the cab steps is Louis LaMar, Al Stewart leans out of the cab window and Dexter Hooper rests his hand on the air pump. *Clark Kinsey photo, University of Washington*

DEMPSEY HEISLER No. 3. This scene was photographed at Camp 5. Men in picture are (l to r): unknown, Harry Winters, Louis Huff and Ashe Huff. *Mary McCloud*

The hot breath of flame again brought destruction to the Company when on May 12, 1912, a forest fire began in the area east of Grandy Creek. It burned rapidly north and west crossing Grandy Creek and moved into the Dempsey Lumber Company operations. Dempsey was operating two camps at the time and both were lost in the fire. Five men died in the burn near Dempsey's camps: Joe Rucich and J. C. Nelson, both cooks; James Rawson, donkey engineer and Fred Clebank, donkey fireman. The fifth man was found at a later date. Matt Snider recalls finding "safety in a railroad cut near the camp where there was a small spring of water...."

One camp laborer took refuge in a railroad water tank. He could not swim and the tank was too deep to stand on the bottom. He splashed water over the sides of the tank to keep it from burning and hung onto the tank top to stay above the water. Although his hands were badly burned his life was spared.

The fire continued to burn north and west and heavily damaged Hamilton Logging Company's operations there.

Following the fire Dempsey quickly rebuilt both camps. Camp 2 was rebuilt approximately a quarter of a mile from its original location. Limited camp activity and log production was restored within thirty days.

Nick Dowen was company manager at the time and Hugh Sutherland was office manager.

In 1913, PS&BR purchased a second Baldwin rod locomotive; she was a near twin to the 1-spot and was given road number 2 on the PS&BR roster.

OFF HER FEET, Dempsey No. 2 rests on her side somewhat north of Birdsview. This could be the accident described in the text when the company attempted to pull and straighten snubber cable for the incline. *Stan Dexter*

JOINT OPERATION at Dempsey's Lyman Enginehouse. In view is Puget Sound and Baker River Railway's 4-6-0 No. 2 under steam; Dempsey's Heisler No. 2 in foreground and their three-truck Heisler in background. Fred Nielson was Dempsey's car shop foreman and the photo was snapped from Fred and Nellie's back porch. *Myron Nielson*

Dempsey Lumber Company then ordered their second Heisler from a proposal dated April 25, 1914. At a cost of $11,055, Heisler No. 2 was shipped to Dempsey in May of 1914. She was 62-tons, had 40-inch drivers, 200 pounds boiler pressure and carried 2,150 gallons of water.

The 2-spot Heisler arrived in Skagit and was found to have a defect in the side sheet of her firebox. Hartford Steam Boiler Inspection and Insurance Company sent a letter to Whitney referring to welding done on the Heisler and enclosed a letter from Olson-Klopf Welding and Cutting Company, Seattle. The Olson-Klopf letter, dated June 27, 1914, guaranteed the weld for one year, and indicated the work was done at Sumner Iron Works, Everett. From Everett the locomotive was brought to Birdsview and operated without any further reported difficulty.

The working day for the Heisler crew began at 5 a.m. At that time a train of empty cars would leave for the woods returning again with loads about 10 a.m. The loads would then be set out on a siding at Headquarters and the locomotive would take on water. The engineer would "oil around" the Heisler and after the short fifteen minute layover they would be off to the woods again with more empties. The second trip down the hill would arrive about 2 p.m. and after setting out the fresh loads and retiring the Heisler for the day, the crew went home about 3 p.m.

One of PS&BR Railway's 10-wheelers would pick up Dempsey's waiting train and take it to the Riverside dump, returning empty to Birdsview in the late evening. The mainline trains to the dump were then running 14 to 17 cars per train. Most of the early timber came out of the woods cut in 64 foot or 84 foot lengths to be used for boom sticks.

The family camps at Dempsey Lumber were small independent communities. Families that moved into camp had to build their own house - the Company provided the lumber. Every family in camp had a cow and other livestock were common, especially hogs. The men all walked to the work sites as there were no gas speeders at that time and it was not Company policy to use a locomotive to transport men to work. (In later years some companies did provide rail transportation to the work location.)

A well-worn path led from Camp 2 into Birdsview. The two mile route was heavily traveled including regular deliveries by the mailman who trudged faithfully back and forth to camp.

Camp 2 sported their own school and the single class usually numbered something under a dozen students.

Shortly after the 1912 fire Camp 3 was built on what is now the Cruse farm on Grandy Creek one half mile north of Birdsview siding. This was the smallest of the Dempsey camps employing only about thirty men. Another fire destroyed Camp 3 about 1917 and it was not rebuilt.

Camp 2 finished about 1915 and moved to the site of Camp 4 about 1½ miles farther north and a bit west. The only family remaining at the location of Camp 2 were the Prestons. John Preston was section foreman and for approximately four years his gang worked out of old Camp 2.

Camp 4 was short lived and by early 1918 Camp 5 was in use on a site about one mile east of Camp 4. A contingent from the Spruce Division was located at Camp 5 working for the war effort.

This was an active time for Dempsey; Camp 5 was their largest camp, the Company was growing and to log the highlands above Camp 5 an incline was constructed on the northeast edge of camp in 1922.

The Timberman magazine reported in its September 1919 issue that Dempsey was building 1½ miles of new railroad under the engineering direction of Blaine H. McGillicuddy. Jim Shields was logging superintendent in the same year.

During the spring of 1919 Dempsey experienced their third forest fire. Lyman Timber Company had a slash fire go out of control and it burned several miles east threatening Dempsey's camp and equipment. Without help from the Lyman manager, Dempsey crews fought the fire for three days until the wind changed and reversed the fire to "burn the Lyman sides out."

A third and final Heisler locomotive was ordered by Dempsey in December of 1919. The factory called for delivery of the new machine in March of 1920. She weighed in at 75 tons and was a 3-truck locomotive. Price: $24,844. She was lettered with road No. 1, which appears to be evidence that Dempsey management desired to dispose of their first Heisler No. 1. The big 3-trucker was shipped, towed on her own wheels in regular trains, via the New York Central, Northern Pacific and Great Northern railroads. A Heisler factory "messenger" rode in the cab the entire trip to watch the engine. The Heisler's drivelines were removed to allow her to roll free without turning her

WORLD WAR I, August 29, 1918. U.S. Army uniforms appear in Dempsey's Camp 5 as representatives of the U.S. government's Spruce Production Division - an intensive effort to provide aircraft-quality spruce for the Nation's war efforts. *D. Kinsey, Mary McCloud*

A NEW CAMP FOR DEMPSEY LUMBER COMPANY. The following commentary from that period describes this scene at Camp 5 in 1918: "All the buildings in this new Dempsey camp are new and all the bunk houses have been painted dark red. They have been painted with real paint. Three dining rooms have been provided. They are the cars in the left background of the picture. On the walls of the dining rooms are a number of fine pictures. The Stars and Stripes also are hung in the dining rooms. Window boxes and potted plants add to their attractiveness.

"The kitchen is adjacent to all three dining room, forming the fourth side of the cross. A separate car has been provided and equipped for the women employees of the camp. Next comes the quarters of the officers and next the general camp office. The camp also has a social hall and a car containing shower baths and drying rooms, etc.

"The bunk houses in the foreground of the large illustration are divided into two sets, one in which the bedding is furnished by the company, and the other set for the use of loggers who wish to furnish their own blankets, but in this case, the bedding furnished by the men is subjected to the most rigid supervision.

"In front of the camp a lawn has been prepared from which rises a tall flagpole.

"The camp is supplied with a splendid water system and very great pains have been taken to insure perfect sanitary conditions." *D. Kinsey photo, Mary McCloud; commentary from the West Coast Lumberman, October 1918*

"HEADWORKS" for Dempsey's Incline. This scene shows foul-weather protection for snubbing engine and the Sessoms incline "block" or "lowering" car hooked to loads waiting for the descent down the incline. When the system is in operation, the lowering line extends from the steam snubbing engine, which is placed to the right of the incline, through a block on the lowering car, then back to a stump or deadman near the engine, but on the opposite side of the track. This gives the snubber double the pulling and holding power. *D. Kinsey , Whatcom Museum of History and Art*

engines over. The messenger set up the new locomotive and attended to its proper operation when they arrived at Birdsview. The factory man's expenses were $325, which was included in the price of the locomotive.

A photograph appeared in **The Timberman** October 1920, showing all three Dempsey Heislers in front of the Camp 5 enginehouse. Shortly thereafter their eldest Heisler was sold to the Hetch Hetchy Railroad at Groveland, California.

The Heislers seemed to perform well for Dempsey.

(facing, right) **THE DEMPSEY INCLINE.** Almost a mile in length, with grades to 45%, this incline operated immediately northeast of Camp 5 in the early 1920s. Three loaded log cars were dropped down the incline each operation. Heisler No. 2 switched cars at the top. In this view, the cars are just arriving (note cable beside track). *D. Kinsey , Al Hodgin*

(below) **SESSOMS BLOCK CAR.** Designed by Hugh W. Sessoms and built by Pacific Car and Foundry. This "traveling block" provided power advantage for lowering heavy loads down the incline. Block car is hidden by logs (right) but cable and car side guides can be identified. See drawing - Appendix D-4. *D. Kinsey, Whatcom Museum of History and Art*

DEMPSEY'S CAMP 5 showing dining rooms, lawn and flagpole. Standing timber directly in back of the camp was Stimson owned and Dempsey was never able to successfully deal with the owners to log the tract. Years later Lyman Timber Company purchased the 160 acres of timber and rebuilt a railroad to log it. *D. Kinsey, Mary McCloud*

Many men on the train crews had fond memories of them as they were part of their daily lives. Even those not working with the trains gained impressions of the big black machines. Blaine McGillicuddy, a forest engineer for Dempsey, recalls the 3-truck Heisler simply as, "...a big greasy bucket of bolts but it did its work." And work they did, but heavy grades and a few accidents took their toll. Maintenance was an important job at Headquarters. All but major repairs were handled in the Company shop.

An interesting accident occurred in the days of Camp 5 and is recalled and told by Myron Preston who grew up in Camp 2 and later worked for Dempsey as did his father. It seems that the big Washington Iron Works incline snubber carried some 9,000 feet of cable on its drum to move log cars up and down the forty percent grade incline above Camp 5. After months of almost daily use, it was necessary to replace the cable. At any time when there was slack in the cable there were problems of "kinks" or loops in the line and with the cable being over one-inch in diameter, it was no easy task to untangle the mess. This situation was especially troublesome when the cable was being replaced.

On one occasion when cable replacement was due Myron remembers that an inspired employee had a new idea to prevent kinks in the new cable. Quick to implement innovation the management agreed to using the new idea of "dragging" the snarls out of the new cable. Not far out of Headquarters the end of the new line was attached to the drawbar of the 2-spot Heisler and she in turn was coupled to the rear of her sister engine, the No. 1. The two locomotives, totaling over 137 tons, started out toward Camp 5 trailing the cable "to straighten it out real good." Near the top of the hill the strange procession entered a long curve and the cable moved to the inside and began to run against an old snag. Following some hard pulling by the two locomotives the snag broke suddenly and the quick movement of slack in the cable flipped the 2-spot over on her side! The bigger Heisler escaped injury but was no longer able to pull the 9,000 feet of cable.

The 2-spot could be removed from the ditch; however, the railroad now possessed a third shiny ribbon of steel for almost two miles: the cable was in the way of everything! Drawing from the deep well-spring of loggers' ingenuity the Company shut down operations, crews were called off their jobs and what was to be a week-long task was begun.

The old cable on the snubber was unreeled and taken down the incline and through the brush toward the scene of the accident. Failing to reach far enough an additional 2,000 feet of line was removed from a nearby skidder and sweating hands were finally able to link up the entire mess to the upper end of the new incline cable at the wreck site.

A fire was built in the huge snubber and the sturdy machine worked its drum into the weight of almost four miles of steel line! Anchored firmly into the hilltop the Washington bit into the load and slowly began to wind the cable back onto its drum. As the snubber bellowed and snorted the cable pulled high into the air over the Camp 5 flat - a giant kite string stretching from mountaintop to the outer edge of the shelf of land below. The aerial movement reduced the load on the snubber as

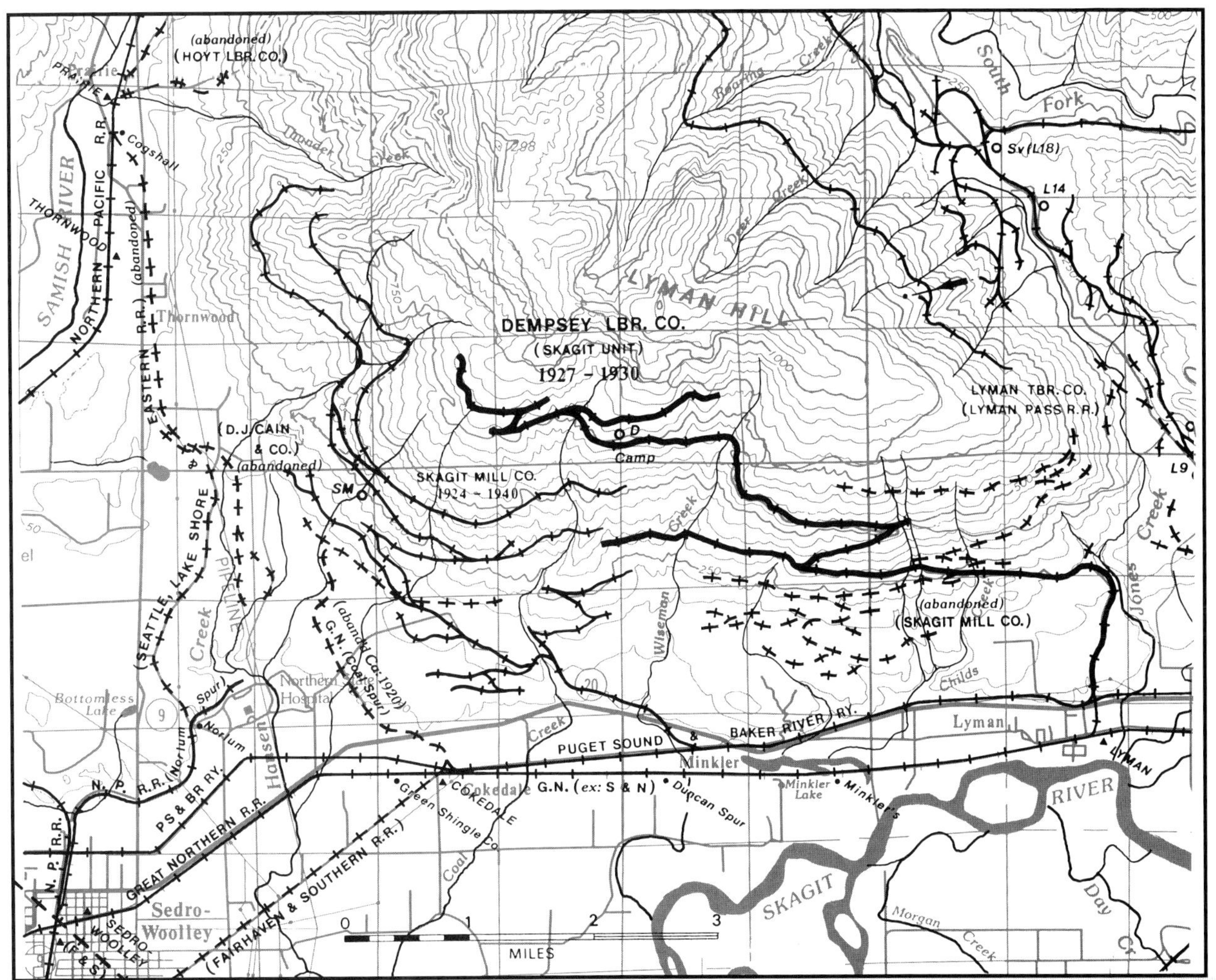

Map No. 8 Dempsey concluded Skagit County operations by utilizing the abandoned mainline of Skagit Mill Company's first unit. Skagit Mill Co. in turn, established a second unit on the western slope of Lyman Hill, where they continued operations until 1938. *Map by RD Jost MD1989.*

109

the cable did not hang up in brush and logs for that distance.

But even as the week's troubles seemed near an end, as if in angry protest, one last incident happened. The cable broke one time while high over Camp 5 and like Paul Bunyon's great whip the line sliced through the air to cut a bunk house in half and shear the end off the cookhouse as it crashed to earth. Thereafter, no further difficulties interfered with rewinding the cable. And Myron feels there were truly no kinks in the new snubber cable.

Not all the accidents that plagued the woods were as glamorous or as interesting. At one time a load of logs struck the 2-spot in the front end which "laid her up for a spell." One of the Heislers was out-of-service in 1923 and a used Heisler was rented from Whitney to fill the vacancy.

A letter from Dempsey to Whitney dated May 14, 1923, mentions "enclosed invoices from Skagit Steel & Iron Works" covering work done by Skagit on a Heisler. Again in the same Whitney file folder is a parts bill dated March 1924, totaling $1,347.42 including "express to Hamilton" and Heisler mechanics' wages of $160 (sixteen days at $10 per day).

The year 1924 found J. J. Dempsey as manager of the company and M. B. Kurth, superintendent and purchasing agent. They were running two sides using one Lidgerwood skidder, eight donkey engines, one high lead, sixteen miles of railroad using 56 to 60 pound rail, fifty-five sets of disconnected trucks, five flat cars and the two Heislers burning oil. Maximum grade for the railroad was six percent.

It was about this time that Dempsey converted from disconnected trucks to skeleton cars. Reasons behind the change were several: disconnects did not offer air brakes as did skeletons, the new cars would be safer. The incline above Camp 5 was not suited to operate with the older cars and the PS&BR was soon to be operating in part over Great Northern track. GN insisted on connected trucks equipped with automatic air brakes.

When the incline was built about 1921, the first logging was done at the very top. After that area was finished the incline was shortened a bit and a slightly lower lateral was built west about three miles long-see map 7.

About one and a half miles out this lateral a dinner camp was built to provide hot meals for the crews. At the end of this spur was located the last setting of Dempsey Lumber for their Birdsview operations.

The Stimson Timber Company had a quarter section of timber standing within an eighth of a mile of Camp 5 with Dempsey's railroad on all four sides. Late in 1926 an attempt to purchase the timber was made; however, Mr. Ives who was manager for Stimson, never saw eye-to-eye with Dempsey and the proposition failed. The available timber gone, Dempsey closed their Camp 5 in early 1927. In February and March of that year they pulled up all the steel in the Birdsview operation and moved to fresh timber at Lyman.

In Lyman the Dempsey Lumber Company built an enginehouse on the old Skagit Mill Company property on the northwest edge of Lyman. Their railroad left the PS&BR mainline at that point and was "relaid" over Skagit Mill's old right-of-way, north about one mile then curved west and worked its way west and north up the mountain. Dempsey opened up the area above Skagit Mill's early logging.

A new M.A.C. 4-20 speeder was purchased in May of 1926. It was followed by a larger M.A.C. 6-60 in February of 1928, both products of Skagit Steel & Iron Works. They were used to transport tools, supplies and small crews from place to place on the line. Cost of the 6-60 was $6,778.25.

About 1927, Lyman Timber Company succeeded in negotiating for the Stimson timber where Dempsey had failed. Lyman Timber purchased Dempsey's Washington snubber and built an incline to reach the Stimson claim from the lower side of the mountain at their Camp 16.

In 1927, E. F. Cardin was Dempsey's superintendent and purchasing agent and J. C. McCormick was master mechanic. They employed one hundred and forty men and were still using the Lidgerwood skidder and eight donkey engines. Skeleton cars numbered fifty-six along with five flat cars, one moving car, three tank cars, two speeders, one steam shovel and one diesel shovel. Grades ran as steep as seven percent.

Dempsey had at least two camps during their years at Lyman and there is no evidence they were ever identified by number. Both known camps were located high on the mountain commanding a beautiful view of the Skagit River Valley. Electric light plants were now provided and life was quite improved over earlier logging camps.

Dempsey's 75-ton Heisler was out-of-service for repairs in 1928 and the Company obtained use of Clear Lake Lumber Company's 3-truck Shay No. 2. The Clear Lake firm had closed and gone into receivership at that time. There seemed to be considerable delay in getting parts for the Heisler and the Shay ran on the Dempsey line for most of a year.

After fewer than four years in Lyman, Dempsey exhausted the last of their timber holdings in Skagit County

A sampling of classified advertisements for the logger who needs everything. Back issues of **The TIMBERMAN** provide fascinating reading to the railroad logging fan. *Dennis Thompson Collection*

May, 1941 THE TIMBERMAN 103

Classified Advertisements

1000-GALLON
Centrifugal Pump
8 x 8 Allis-Chalmers with 100-H. P. motor, fire fittings and control panel.
DEMPSEY LUMBER CO
TACOMA, WASHINGTON

Logging Equipment
1 75-ton Heisler locomotive
1 63-ton Heisler locomotive
Relay Rail
3 Skagit speeders
12x14 Wash. 2-speed yarder
12x12 Wash. Comp. steam yarder
10x12 Wash. duplex loader
12x12 Lidgerwood skidder
Wire rope, blocks, etc.
Liquidation Prices
WRITE
DEMPSEY LUMBER CO.
Phone Broadway 3737 Tacoma, Wash.

12 x 17 Washington SLACK LINE FLYER
This machine is completely equipped with sled, lines, blocks, etc., and has transfer drum as well as strawline drum.
•
Also have 16-wheel moving car 56 ft. long, with special heavy construction
DEMPSEY LUMBER CO.
Phone BRoadway 3737 Tacoma, Wash.

SAWMILL FOR SALE
Located in British Columbia
35M capacity, steam operating, ample timber, A-1 opportunity.
Address: Box E-152
THE TIMBERMAN
623 S. W. Oak St., Portland, Oregon

"DON'T WAIT FOR LOWER PRICES! Buy Now!"
2-8-2 American Saddle Tank Locomotive, 85 ton.
75 ton Willamette Locomotive
200 ton All Steel 8-wheel Moving Car
300 ton 16-wheel Moving Car
3 Oven Lang Range, with Canopy
15 ton Brown Hoist Locomotive Crane
Tank Cars
Rail—practically all sizes
4-40 Skagit Speeder
6-60 Skagit Speeder
35 man NORTHWESTERN SPEEDER
Harmer Steel Products & Supply Company
Supplies and Equipment for Logging Operations and Railroads, etc.
138 S.W. 1st Ave., Portland, Oregon

and ceased operation in the summer of 1930. At this time Dempsey sold their 51 percent interest in the PS&BR to the Lyman Timber Company. Track was pulled up and all equipment including the two Heislers, donkey engines and flat cars loaded with cable sat at the PS&BR siding at Lyman until fall, when they were moved to Ohop, Washington.

At their new location at Ohop, west of Mt. Rainier, Dempsey logged until about 1935. After that the company seemed to close out their activities in the woods and began to disperse their physical plant. By 1941, they were advertising equipment for sale. Failing to find a buyer for their locomotives, in January 1942, Dempsey offered the Heislers for sale to the War Department. Asking price was $3,500 for the 2-spot and $5,000 for the 3-truck engine. A reply from the War Department stated: "We find that these locomotives are not adapted to the work we have on hand at the present time." Shortly thereafter the locomotives were scrapped in Seattle and the company liquidated.

CHAPTER 4

SALT WATER AND INCLINES

The Blanchard Logging Railroad Company

The town of Blanchard was named in honor of George Blanchard who began a logging operation there in 1885. When the first post office opened in 1886, Blanchard was named postmaster. The post office closed in 1891, but was opened again in 1903, under the town name of Fravel, also in honor of local residents. In 1915, popular support for the original name succeeded in restoring Blanchard to the map permanently.

In the late 1880s, the only transportation link with the outside world was by the *Salt Chuck* at Samish Bay. To facilitate use of this water route a long wharf was constructed just north of where McElroy's Slough emptied into the bay. The slough was named after James H. McElroy who is credited with starting the first horse tram railroad at that site. By 1886, the tram road and logging operation was in the hands of George and Dudley Blanchard. They, in turn, had entered into association with two gentlemen from the East. The first was a retired military man, politician, lumberman and investor, General Russell A. Alger of Detroit, Michigan. The second man was Ravand K. Hawley of Cleveland, Ohio. During 1887, George Blanchard, with the help of Dudley Blanchard, negotiated extensive land, timber and right-of-way purchases in behalf of Hawley and Alger who put up the money. The contract language provided the Blanchards the option of purchasing one quarter of the holdings themselves when they could raise the money. John Labbe relates that Alger was a senator from Michigan and during the late 1890s also Secretary of War. He was a lumberman with extensive interests in the Lake States and the South and he owned many millions of feet of timber in Skagit and Whatcom Counties. It is not believed he ever operated in the Northwest, but he may have backed others, as he did Blanchard, on a small scale to test the market. Weyerhaeuser did the same. At that period they were dubious of meeting the prices of producers east of the Rocky Mountains, and were uncertain of the export market. When ventures proved successful, they moved out in force.

February 1887 found the Blanchard tram road about five miles in length and was laid with 40 pound steel rails. Five Russell log cars were used, each log car carried about 5,000 feet of timber and the motive power consisted of mule teams. Supplies were moving

THREE RAILROADS SERVED BLANCHARD in the 1920s: Great Northern, The Pacific Northwest Traction interurban and the logging railroad. This scene shows the bustling mill belonging to Samish Bay Logging Company and a string of box cars from the serving common carrier. *Ina Burkhart*

114 **SAFETY VALVE LIFTED**, steam pot and crew pause in their labor. *D. Kinsey, Dale Thompson*

CLIMAX No.2 at the Blanchard road overpass which is now Chuckanut Drive. This is the site of the present concrete highway overpass and just northwest of the Blanchard log dump. *Ina Burkhart*

THE TWO-SPOT pauses on her way home. This scene is on the east side of Chuckanut Mountain. *Bob Sherwood*

smoothly across the new wharf and into the woods. There was even talk of purchasing a steam skidder.

A new steam locomotive was ordered from the Baldwin Locomotive Works and she was shipped from the factory on the East Coast in August of 1888. The shiny new machine arrived in Blanchard on a barge and was unloaded on the long wharf. She was a small pot by railroad standards with 38-inch drivers in a 2-6-0 wheel arrangement and had 14 x 18 inch cylinders. However, she stood head and shoulders above the Blanchard Railroad's mules and the latter surely sighed with relief to retire from the railroad business.

The little railroad operated throughout the 1890s; however, it slowed to a halt by 1899-1900, evidently influenced by the age and health of its financial backers. Hawley died in 1900, and this precipitated the remaining principals to look for a buyer.

Charles Marquart, who grew up in Blanchard, remembers playing on the old railroad wharf at the age of twelve. The railroad had ceased to operate but the rail was still in place. The year was 1901.

Another pioneer logger, Charles Dinsmore, came through Blanchard a few months after Marquart's ex-

YARDER WITH EXTENDED FIREBOX and crew at Samish Bay Logging Company. *D. Kinsey, courtesy Mrs. L. C. Burkhart*

THE MILL AT BLANCHARD, looking north from the slough, reflects a more thriving era for the little town. It was later enlarged as pictured on pages 113 and 123 near the end of this chapter. *Ina Burkhart*

perience and noticed the little Baldwin sitting forlorn in the engine house and all the rail picked up and gone. Grass was already growing in the right-of-way.

Peter Larson, of Helena, Montana, was at this time operating near Lake Whatcom as the Lake Whatcom Logging Company, and became interested in the Blanchard area properties. By the summer of 1901, a sale was consummated giving over the vast Hawley-Alger tract, along with the little Blanchard Logging Railroad Company, to Lake Whatcom Logging Company. Senator Alger died during the winter of 1906-07, without ever making the final move west.

The remains of the idle Blanchard Railroad was removed as new management intended to harvest their timber from a base near Alger. The Baldwin 2-6-0 went to work for Peter Larson, near Lake Whatcom.

One of Skagit County's more obscure lines, The Blanchard Logging Railroad Company will always have the distinction of being the first local operation to purchase a brand new steam locomotive solely for use in the Skagit woods. What arrived by salt water that day in 1888, must have provided an exciting day for the people in the vicinity of the town of Blanchard.

The Samish Bay Logging Company

The year 1901 found Great Northern Railway construction crews busy relocating their mainline from the old route through the town of Alger, to a tide water route through Bow, Blanchard and north along Chuckanut Mountain on the shore of Samish Bay. The first train over the new line rolled through Blanchard in February of 1903. The "High Iron" had arrived and would remain.

The Hazel Mill Company was incorporated in early 1906 with a capital stock of $75,000. The principals were George A. Cooper, F. D. Alpine and D. A. McMartin. Their mill was built on the pleasant little inlet between Blanchard and the edge of Chuckanut Mountain to the north. McElroy's Slough became an industrial area once again.

Another new era arrived for Blanchard in 1912 when the Samish Bay Logging Company was formed. C. B. Howard and Company of Emporium, Pennsylvania was another eastern logger that had finished harvesting their timberlands and, in search of new holdings, moved west.

The men involved in setting up the Samish Bay Logging Company came directly from C. B. Howard and

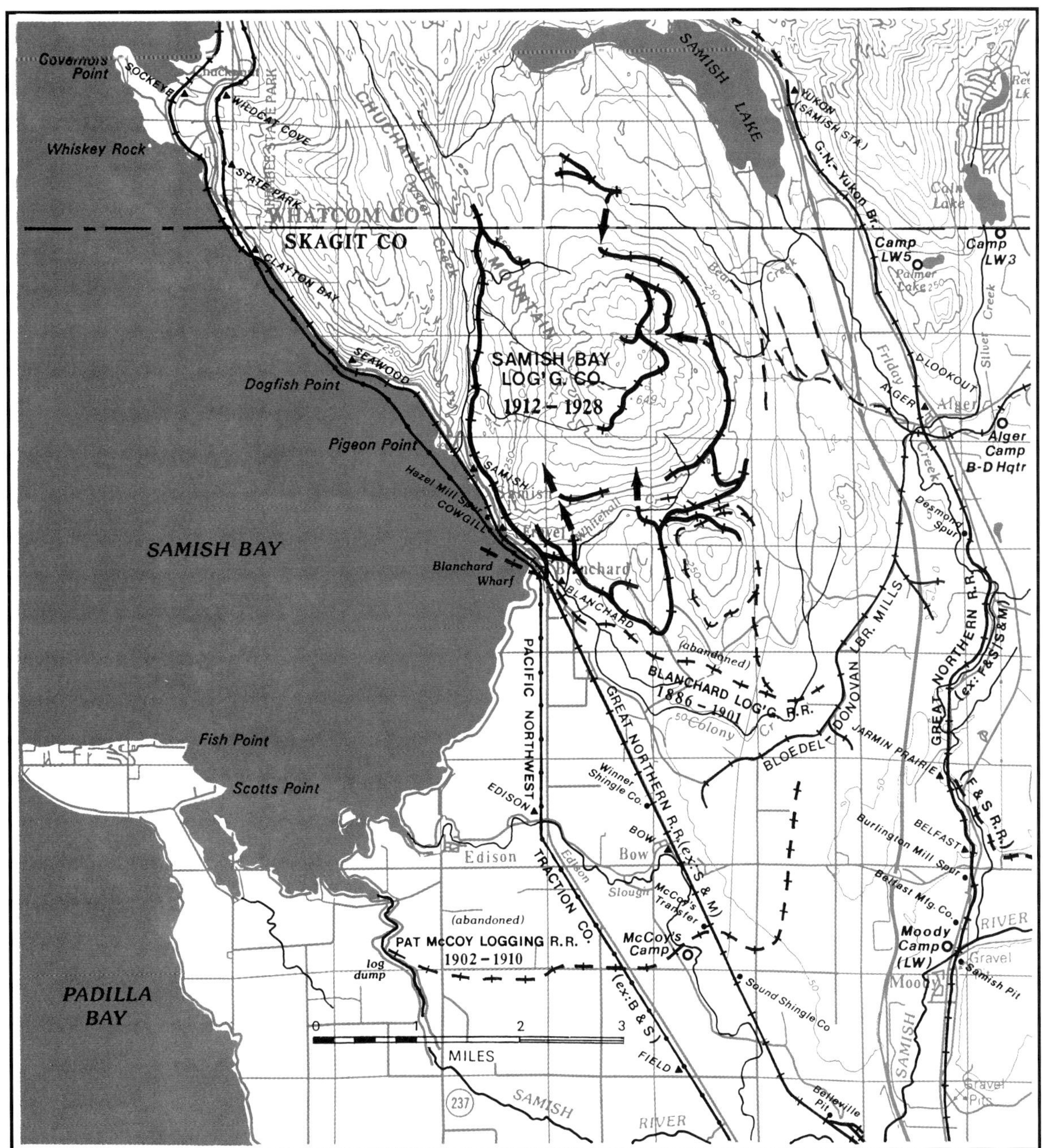

Map No. 9 First railroad activity at Blanchard took place at the wharf in 1888 when a Baldwin 2-6-0 arrived by water for the new Blanchard Logging Railroad, shown here as abandoned prior to 1912. Those holdings were later sold to the Lake Whatcom Logging Co. in one of the largest timberlands transactions of the period. Lake Whatcom camps 3 through 7 were located in Skagit County; Moody Camp became Camp 6. Lake Whatcom Logging Co. became Bloedel-Donovan Lumber Mills in 1913, whose railroads are shown here.

The high reaches of Chuckanut Mountain were the exclusive domain of the Samish Bay Logging Co. The terrain was such that, of necessity, the firm distinguished itself by constructing more railroad inclines than any other logging company in Skagit County.

Pat McCoy (see McCoy and Pullman Palace Car Logging Co., pg. 214), shown abandoned, had moved on to Hoogdal, near Sedro Woolley, where he began a partnership operation known as McCoy-Loggie. Theirs was a brief endeavor at Hoogdal, after which they moved permanently to Whatcom County. *(see endpapers for legend)* *Map by RD Jost 1989*

Company and were James Norie, a son-in-law of Joseph Kaye, one of the principals in the Howard Company, Josiah Howard and Henry Auchu, another principal. Joseph Kaye also became general manager of another Howard enterprise, the new Parker-Bell Lumber Company, of Pilchuck.

Samish Bay Logging Company obtained timber holdings over a large portion of the southern half of Chuckanut Mountain. In early 1912 the Company had set up a camp and began building Blanchard's second shortline railroad. The line was constructed some 2-1/2 miles north from town up what is now Chuckanut Drive

118 **AT THE TOP OF THE INCLINE** Climax No. 1 switches out cars. At the far left is seen the stack of the snubbing engine and denotes the actual top end of the incline. A fuel car is perched near the left side of the hilltop, just below which is a loaded logcar beginning its descent. This incline is still traceable by a hiking path. A ten-minute walk uphill from this site brings one to Lizard Lake. *Ina Burkhart*

to Oyster Creek, thence northeast up the creek into company-owned timber.

A new 75-ton Climax locomotive was purchased in 1912 and the new engine left the Climax plant at Corry, Pennsylvania on November 20, 1912. Asa M. Howard, a Climax employee, traveled with the locomotive and according to his diary Samish Bay was not quite ready for the machine when they arrived.

C. B. Howard and Company owned a 3-truck Shay which they had used on their Pennsylvania operation and that locomotive was shipped to Blanchard about the same time. The Shay was never successfully used at Blanchard and spent most of her time sitting in town. Facts about the Shay are few and obscure, however, she did earn a reputation for being troublesome and unpopular. It has been strongly rumored that she "just didn't have the guts for the tough grades on the railroad." She was eventually

COOKHOUSE CREW at camp above Lizard Lake incline. Notice water tank that uses large stump for main support. *Skagit County Historical Museum*

sold.

After less than four years operation on Oyster Creek, a right-of-way conflict developed when the State of Washington decided to build Chuckanut Drive. It seems the logging railroad was located exactly where the highway was planned between Blanchard and Oyster Creek. And so it happened that in late 1915 the steel was picked up and plans were made to reroute the railroad around Chuckanut Mountain in a southeasterly direction. The railroad grade up Oyster Creek was converted into a truck road and timber in that area was removed by Bulldog Mack trucks.

During this period the Hazel Mill Company was having their difficulties as can best be seen in this item from **The Timberman** of May 1914: *The Hazel Mill Company started operations on May 4 after a seven months' shutdown. George Cooper says that it is "just about as well to go busted running as to go busted closed," and there is some little amusement in seeing the lumber come out of the tail end of the mill in a musical fantasy created by the rythmic music of the saws. George says this is a poetical effusion but in reality there is more truth than poetry in the situation.*

A LOADED LOG CAR makes its way slowly down the incline below Lizard Lake. The cable controlling its descent measures over one inch in diameter and is connected to the drum of the steam snubbing engine far out of sight up the hill. *Ina Burkhart*

Construction gangs were busy in February of 1916 building seven miles of new railroad for Samish Bay Logging Company. A camp was established east of Blanchard. Known locally as *Firstcamp* it was in later years called *Oldcamp*.

The Hazel Mill was again idle for a period during early 1917, but extensive improvements were made and it

SAMISH BAY LOGGING COMPANY'S FIRST NEW LOCOMOTIVE is seen here in fresh factory paint. She worked out her life on Chuckanut Mountain and was the engine used on top of the Lizard Lake incline in the 1920s. *Walter C. Casler*

120

resumed operation again in March. The daily capacity was increased to 75,000 to 100,000 feet of lumber and 300,000 shingles daily. In 1919 the Samish Bay Logging Company purchased the Hazel Mill.

The year 1919 was a banner year for expansion at Samish Bay Logging Company. Acquisition of their own mill gave them a more self-sufficient position with the market. Their railroad had reached beyond the seven mile mark into fresh timber and now plans were finalized for the building of an incline on the east slope of Chuck-

NOT QUITE LIKE HOME but this was camp living in the woods. Most of the crew at Samish Bay went home for the weekends and returned each Monday. *Ina Burkhart.*

MACK BULLDOG TRUCKS were used to finish logging the Oyster Creek area after the railroad was hastily removed to allow construction of the *Chuckanut Drive* highway. Plank roads were used and an incline was part of the operation where the trucks were lowered down by a cable and snubbing engine. Man on far right of log is R. E. Gray. *D. Kinsey, R.E. Gray* 121

(right) **BULLDOG MACK TRUCK ON INCLINE** of the Samish Bay Logging Co. near Blanchard. *R.E. Gray, courtesy Skagit County Historical Museum*

anut Mountain facing the town of Alger.

Magnus Anderson recalls that many Italian laborers were employed on the track gang and they preferred to live in their own section of camp. They baked their own bread in brick or rock ovens and the finished loaf was 12 to 18 inches in diameter. The locomotive engineer would often deliver supplies to these folks and he was occasionally rewarded with a loaf of bread which was highly prized.

The new Lizard Lake incline was finished about 1920. It was three-quarters of a mile long and the maximum grade was 38 percent. Upon its completion Firstcamp was moved to the top of the incline.

Lewis Clifford (Cliff) Burkhart was superintendent and he and his wife Ina lived in the newly relocated camp. The Willamette incline snubber performed its daily chores and graced Burkhart's front yard at the same time. Lizard Lake reposed a short up-hill stroll away. Ina relates that on many occasions when the families

ACCIDENT AT HAZEL MILL COMPANY about 1917. This was before the mill sold to Samish Bay Logging Company. White house in background was still a private residence in 1988. *Dennis Thompson Collection*

Editors note: *This is a fun page - the three views on this and the facing page provide a virtual panoramic picture but they have by coincidence been taken about 120 degrees apart in a manner that each shows the vantage point of one other photograph providing an unusual feeling for the use and "lay of the land." How many common elements can you tie together?*

CLIMAX No. 2 has delivered a train of loaded skeleton cars to the Blanchard log dump. Barely visible is the cable (thin white line) from the skeleton car to the gin pole. The locomotive spots the car to be dumped, uncouples it, hooks the cable to the coupler and backs away, lifting the cable and dumping the logs. *Courtesy Mrs. L. C. Burkhart*

SAWMILL on McELROY'S SLOUGH, Blanchard. As well as showing the extensive plant of the Samish Bay Logging Company, the Great Northern Railway mainline can be seen at upper right. The chapter introduction photograph provides another view of this scene. *Photo taken April 1927 by Bob Sherwood*

were ready to return to town for the weekends, she was reluctant to leave the high mountain camp. She enjoyed the view of the valley and the tranquility of the woods.

From time to time the minister at Blanchard would go to the camp above the incline to lead singing sessions and evening fellowship. Sometimes he would spend the night and other times he would walk all the way back to town.

Early in 1921, a second new Climax was purchased. Another 3-truck, she tipped the scales at eighty tons. A sales contract dated April 25, 1921, established her cost at $27,400. The new locomotive carried road number 2 and operated the mainline trains from the incline to the Blanchard mill pond. The 1-spot was kept on top of the incline to work the woods spurs and light locomotive maintenance was also done there.

The year 1922 found Samish Bay operating two sides with a daily output of 110,000 board feet. They employed one hundred men operating two high leads, six donkey engines and one skidder. The Company ran a commissary, machine shop and electric light plant. The railroad was now 8½ miles in length laid with 56 to 60 pound rail. Rolling stock consisted of twenty-six skeleton cars and two flat cars running on a maximum grade of 8½ percent. W. B. Hopple was manager with John Myers as master mechanic.

Samish Bay was plagued with several fires but the most talked about blaze took place about 1925 and endangered the camp above the incline. The women and children were ordered evacuated and were lowered down the incline on an empty skeleton car to be picked up by the logging train. On their arrival at the bottom they found the train had left without them. This proved to be to their advantage even though they were forced to walk through the woods in order to reach safety. The escaping train and crew found themselves running

SAMISH BAY LOGGING COMPANY. The mill pond at Blanchard - with a log of more than 8 feet in diameter. *D. Kinsey courtesy Mrs. L.C. (Ina) Burkhart*

124

ELDERLY CLIMAX NUMBER ONE shows her with log train in the woods above Blanchard. *Galen Biery*

SAMISH BAY locomotive crew. L to R: Roscoe Murrow, fireman and brother to Edward R. Murrow, well known radio commentator; George Kalk, head brakeman; Magnus (Maggie) Anderson, second brakeman; John Myers, engineer. *Magnus Anderson*

through burning forest and over burning trestles in their flight. They all reached Blanchard intact; however, some of the train crew were badly burned and found a stay in the hospital was required.

The last year for the incline was about 1926. After it was discontinued the railroad was extended north from the base of the incline about 1½ miles. At that point a decline was built down into what was then known as the Saling Timber. From its inception, Samish Bay had not been a financial success; now the Saling Timber offered a turning point and the Company seemed to do well the rest of its days. The Saling claim was the richest timber Samish Bay cut and was located close to the southern point of Lake Samish and even quite near the Lake's elevation. It is difficult in modern times to imagine logs traveling from this easily accessible location all the way by railroad to the town of Blanchard.

The second incline operated by Samish Bay Logging Company was near Oldcamp and the date of its use is not known.

By 1927 Samish Bay was logging the last of its Skagit holdings. A fourth and final incline was built immediately above the town of Blanchard 4,000 feet in length on a 42 percent grade. There was very little railroad built at the top of the new incline and it is even uncertain if a locomotive was ever used at the top.

Officials for the Company during the final days were: Josiah Howard, Emporium, Pennsylvania, president; W. B. Hopple, Blanchard, vice-president; R. W. Howard, Emporium, Pennsylvania, secretary; Alex D. MacDonald, Bellingham, treasurer; L. C. Burkhart, purchasing agent; Gerhard Larson, master mechanic.

Samish Bay Logging Company closed down in 1928. The 1-spot was scrapped at Blanchard and the 2-spot sold. The principals in the Company had developed a big operation in Panama to which they now turned their attention.

Although not an extensive railroad in terms of mileage, Samish Bay operated more inclines than any other Skagit County logger, and to this day offers pleasant hiking to anyone in the area of Lizard Lake where the incline operation can still be traced.

CHAPTER 5

RAILS FROM THE NORTH

Bloedel-Donovan Lumber Mills

In the early days of the Pacific Northwest, settlers stood in awe of the timberlands. The forests seemed to extend "forever" into the mountains. Indeed, the fine virgin timber was an obstacle and a nuisance to many; how could livestock graze or crops grow? The dark floors of the forests were so far below the treetops there was no light for grass to grow.

However, for scores of other men, young and old, the timber was a chance for entrepreneurship. Such was the case for Peter Larson, no newcomer to risking in business. Born in Denmark, Larson's modest investment in Whatcom and Skagit county timberlands in 1898, yielded a fortune of millions over the next ten years.

Organized as the Lake Whatcom Logging Company in 1898, his two respected partners were J. H. Bloedel, a lumberman, and J. J. Donovan, a civil engineer. Six thousand dollars of Peter Larson's money backed the three men who each subscribed to twenty shares of stock in the new firm.

Logging began at South Bay on Lake Whatcom and in the year 1900, two camps were operating with 1½ miles of railroad. Camp 2 was located at the head of the lake.

Expansion continued southward into Skagit County with Camp 3 at Cain Lake in 1902. Timberland purchases over the next ten years totaled almost 15,000 acres. The largest of these was the Hawley-Alger claim which allowed the company to log the area around Alger and southwest toward Bow. Another purchased property was that of E. L. Gaudette, who owned timber, a shingle mill and general store at Alger Station on the Great Northern.

Still another Skagit acquisition was the Belfast Manufacturing Company at Belfast, located also on the Great Northern, between Burlington and Alger. This new purchase included 1,280 acres of timber, four steam donkey engines, a shingle mill on twenty acres, boarding house, camp and houses and another general store. The Lake Whatcom Logging Company's new timberlands covered an extensive area and the loggers settled in for a long stay.

In 1907 several notable events took place. Peter Larson died on July 12, the same year the firm's large new *Larson* sawmill cut its first logs in Bellingham. On

RAILROAD LOGGING NEAR ALGER Most of the operation can be viewed in this scene showing log being brought to the landing by a high lead. Spar tree is 125 feet tall. Shay No. 4 waits with her little train. Taken west of Alger. *D. Kinsey, courtesy Whatcom Museum of History and Art*

WORKING IN THE WOODS, Bloedel-Donovan Saxon camp. *Courtesy Bernie Penley, Ed Marlow*

the railroad, another locomotive was put to work in the woods, this time a 30-ton Heisler. A telephone system was also installed this year, the lines running all along the fourteen mile railroad. A portable telephone was carried on each train. This enabled a connection to be made at any point and calls completed to the firm's camps and even on through to Bellingham numbers.

The Great Northern had relocated its mainline through Alger, moving it over to salt water and easier grades along Chuckanut Mountain. When this relocation was finished the Lake Whatcom Logging Company leased the Great Northern track from Alger south to Belleville, just north of Burlington. Part of this leased line had once been the old Fairhaven and Southern, the first common carrier railroad in Skagit County operating between Fairhaven (Bellingham) and Sedro Woolley. The only stipulation in the lease was that the Lake Whatcom Logging Company provide continued freight service to local industries along the line. For this work the Company's little 2-6-0 Baldwin, obtained from Blanchard, did most of the chores. Use of the old line lasted almost ten years under this agreement. The line was known as the Yukon branch.

"GENERAL ALGER'S FIRST LOCOMOTIVE" was the phrase used to describe this little 2-6-0 Mogul. She did indeed arrive new in Blanchard in 1888, to work the woods there for a company backed by General Russell A. Alger, of Detroit. Here she is seen continuing her career after the Hawley-Alger sale to Lake Whatcom Logging Company. For several years she ran on the leased Yukon branch of the Great Northern, from Burlington to Alger. *Courtesy Charles Dinsmore.*

By 1910 the area bustled. Camp 6 at Belfast was running as well as Alger itself. Camp 7 was begun about 1911 on the hill west of Cain Lake.

Motive power of the period included Alco 2-6-2 No. 1 on the run to the dump. Heisler No. 2 and Shay No. 4 handled the woods, and little Baldwin 2-6-0 No. 3 took care of the Yukon branch and odd jobs.

In 1911 the firm created a retail lumber corporation under the name of Columbia Valley Lumber Company. They established several retail lumber yards to market company products in eastern Washington.

The Company's largest reorganization occurred on March 1, 1913, when Lake

Whatcom Logging Company, Larson Lumber Company and the recently acquired Cargo Mill merged under the new name Bloedel-Donovan Lumber Mills. Assets were listed at $3,889,875. Articles of Incorporation were filed on May 6, 1913.

At this time seven temporary logging camps had been used by the Company to maintain its logging operations. Now Bloedel-Donovan consolidated its property in Alger and the existing buildings there. Using the old store, office and dismantled mill as a nucleus, a semi-permanent camp was built in what was to be Alger proper. Bunkhouse accommodations for 150 men were established. The old

A STRING OF DISCONNECTS trail behind Shay No. 4 in another view of the Camp 7 operation in 1909.

LAKE WHATCOM LOGGING COMPANY Shay No. 4 at Camp 7 in 1909. She is Lima c/n 820, built new in September of 1903. 129

L.W.L.Co. Shay No. 4 with *Eve Stevens* stack, seen at Camp 6 about 1910.

All three views courtesy Peter Replinger

mill building was transtormed into a dining room for 150 hungry loggers with suitable kitchen and storage upstairs.

A machine shop was erected 80 x 100 feet in size. Also a water tank, sand house and many other supporting structures.

Steam heat was provided to the buildings as well as electricity.

The machine shop maintained the Company's four locomotives, sixty logging cars and fifteen donkey engines as well as furnishing the hot water for the living quarters some 300 feet distant. Machinery was operated by a 7 x 12 Atlas stationary steam engine, and electric lights

BLOEDEL-DONOVAN Shay No. 4. Photo taken near Alger about 1916. Man on left is Bud Campbell, brakeman. Fourth from left is Melvin Adcox. *D. Kinsey, courtesy Keith Campbell*

kept bright by the 20,000 watt General Electric dynamo. The shop boasted two forges, power hammer, 12-foot New Haven lathe with a 26-inch swing, a shaper, 26-inch drill, 75-ton hydraulic press and power grinders, saws and cutters.

The recreation room for the men contained books, papers, card tables, two pool tables, barber's chair, bathroom and lavatory.

The bunkhouse provided eight steel bunkbeds per room with hard plaster walls in the rooms. The Company saw to it that the rooms were "swept daily." These furnishings "reduced to a minimum the danger from vermin, which often infect otherwise good sleeping quarters."

This new Alger camp was the center to some one billion feet of Bloedel-Donovan timber, all of which stood within a six mile radius of Alger. It was the intention of the Company to work all its operations out of Alger for several years. Logging locations beyond a "15 mile trip by railroad" could be handled by an occasional temporary camp.

Not far away Bloedel-Donovan soon purchased

THE CONVERTIBLE ALCO Two views of the One-Spot; *(below)* at Lake Whatcom Logging Company as a coal burner and *(above)* under the Bloedel-Donovan Lumber Mills name as an oil burner. American Locomotive Company offered this stock engine with optional wheel arrangements: one as an 0-6-0; the others with or without lead and trail trucks. *Dennis Thompson Collection and Peter Replinger*

3,000 acres from the Puget Mill Company at Delvan, about three miles northwest of Sedro Woolley. About 200 million feet of timber was located there and the Company set about building a camp as a separate operation in 1916. A new Shay locomotive was ordered for this camp, and some eight miles of railroad were on the drawing boards. A connection with the Northern Pacific was established as well as a small flag-stop depot. This new venture sparked considerable interest in the town of Sedro Woolley, certainly some of which was employment possibilities. Local road building was even affected as plans were quickly formed to build an automobile road over the abandoned Fairhaven and Southern Railroad grade from Sedro Woolley to Delvan.

THE PARK LOG DUMP. Tug boat is seen in background. *Dennis Thompson Coll.*

While the Delvan camp was under construction, more track was being laid southwest from Alger some 4½ miles towards Bow. This would allow Bloedel-Donovan to extend their operations right up to that of Samish Bay Logging Company, based in Blanchard. Approximately 35 miles of railroad were now in use by the Company, with one crew from Samish Bay Logging Company even cutting timber for Bloedel-Donovan.

Another venture worth mention in the Alger vicinity was the Alger Shingle Mill perched high atop Alger Hill. This mill and tiny isolated community was reached by a railroad incline which, according to some sources, was said to have been three miles long. In any event, the shingles were taken out by Bloedel-Donovan's railroad and supplies taken up the incline to those living there. A small school of some ten students even existed there for a few years. The mill existed from 1910 until 1918, and does not appear to have been part of Bloedel-Donovan's empire.

At Delvan 125 men were at work and a telephone was connected linking the camp to Sedro Woolley. Dining facilities were busy there and the office was built along with four bunkhouses. The new 70-ton Shay had arrived and was at work in the woods along with three donkey engines. Some employees rode bicycles from Sedro Woolley to the camp each day.

THE LOG DUMP AT PARK. This southern end of Lake Whatcom was host to many years of logging trains. Timber harvested in the Alger area was put in the water here. Locomotive is Lake Whatcom Logging Company ALCO No. 1. *Dennis Thompson Collection.*

131 132

THE ALGER LOG TRAIN led by Shay No. 2 and Climax No. 3. *D. Kinsey , courtesy Phil Swanson.*

Moves and expansions continued with Bloedel-Donovan. A camp near Sylvana, in Snohomish County, was operated in the 1920s, along with a camp at Marysville. Also a large operation at Skykomish including another company sawmill was in production. Closer to home available timberlands of any size were becoming difficult to obtain. An option with Pope and Talbot to purchase timber near Arlington was lost to the English Lumber Company and largely because of this, manage-

BLOEDEL-DONOVAN UNIT at a setting located about one mile north of the present Hickson Gun Club in 1927. This was in the Alger operation. *D. Kinsey, courtesy Al B. Johnson.*

(foldout, left) **CAVANAUGH CREEK BRIDGE** provided Bloedel's access route to Skagit timber in the Nooksack watershed. In this scene 2-6-6-2T No. 8 holds the point of the mainline log train headed to the log dump at Park on the shore of Lake Whatcom. The trestle over Cavanaugh Creek was an outstanding achievement when it was built in 1923. The main span stood 130 feet above the creek and the Howe truss was 100 feet in length. All piles were full length, the longest being 140 feet cut off to 125 feet, and sash and cross-braced in five panels. All materials were native timber. In this picture, Grover Welch is standing on the front of the locomotive. *D. Kinsey, Whatcom Museum of History and Art.*

THE CAVANAUGH CREEK TRESTLE passed over not only two streams but the ridge dividing them as well. *D. Kinsey, Whatcom Museum of History and Art.*

ment began to consider other areas, including Clallam County on Washington's Olympic Peninsula.

One last, large tract of timber was purchased in Skagit and Whatcom Counties. It was located east and south of Saxon, off the Northern Pacific and in 1920, Bloedel-Donovan added Saxon headquarters as yet another timber producing unit. The land was purchased from several firms, including the Michigan Timber Company, State of Washington, E. K. Wood Lumber Company, Sound Timber Company and later the Great Northern Railway. Bloedel-Donovan was to eventually build over fifty miles of railroad in this Saxon-Nooksack river valley region between 1920 and 1937. Also, in 1920 and 1921, Bloedel-Donovan took a major step when they concluded a purchase of over 12,000 acres of timber in Clallam County for future logging.

The Delvan camp closed in 1920, allowing equipment to be relocated to the new Saxon headquarters where the Company was hard at work building more railroad. A 4,000 foot railroad incline was completed in 1921, along with about five miles of railroad.

NEWLY COMPLETED CAVANAUGH CREEK BRIDGE An impressive structure measuring 1,000 feet in length and spanning the main creek and one tributary. The bridge was designed by J. Donovan, woods superintendent. Saxon Camp shipped 25 cars per day over this line. *D. Kinsey, courtesy Phil Swanson.*

In 1926 Bloedel-Donovan statistics appeared this way. The first six months of the year the Company cut 143 million feet of timber and processed 132 million feet of that in its own mills. The Cargo plant on the waterfront in Bellingham was located on 60 acres of ground and could load six deep-sea vessels simultaneously at its wharves. The Larson plant on Lake Whatcom occupied a 90 acre site and the two mills com-

CLIMAX NUMBER 10 eases out of the woods with a string of logs. This locomotive once found herself in the waters of Lake Whatcom in 1924. After considerable head-scratching, she was plucked out, dried off and put in steam again. *Courtesy Lew Hall*

bined employed 1,200 men. Sales offices were located as far away as New York, Boston, Chicago, Minneapolis, Denver, Los Angeles, San Francisco and other cities. The Company owned 78,000 acres of land in Whatcom, Skagit, King and Clallam Counties. Operating camps were Alger, Saxon, Skykomish, Beaver and Goodyear. These employed 800 men. Twelve locomotives were in use along with nine high-lead units, one Lidgerwood steel-tower skidder and more than twenty donkey engines. Ninety-five miles of railroad were in service with 325 log cars available to carry the logs.

Bloedel-Donovan had an operating agreement with

FIREWOOD NEATLY STACKED, the piledriver crawls slowly ahead, but will soon be followed by rumbling trains as new timberlands are opened to modern transportation. Standing on machine are Al Johnson and Tom Daves. *From original snapshot from Al Johnson.*

BUILDING DRY CREEK TRESTLE in 1926. Structure was located east of what is now the Parson Creek Road, and was 101 feet tall. In photo are: Tom Daves, Al Johnson (spiking braces), Wood Green and Mr. MacClellan. *Courtesy Al Johnson and Ed Marlow.*

BLOEDEL-DONOVAN Larson Plant, Mills "A" and "B". A tremendous amount of timber was processed here near Bellingham, on the shore of Lake Whatcom. *Jukes photo courtesy Phil Swanson.*

the Northern Pacific to run logging trains over their line from Saxon to the Company log dump at Park, on Lake Whatcom. For this run a 2-6-6-2 Baldwin tank locomotive was purchased new in 1924, and carried road number 8. She was the first logging mallet to see operation in this area, and was also used on the Alger to Park line. The 8-spot usually worked the dump run at night as the Northern Pacific had frequent traffic during daylight hours. The big mallet could take about 15 to 20 loads up the 3 percent compensated grade from Wickersham to Mirror Lake. "Doubling the hill" was a constant process. Bloedel-Donovan often shipped over 60 cars per day which kept the 8-spot literally working all night, every night, to push and pull logs to the dump. Wickersham was very active during the 1920s!

In 1928 the Alger camp closed for good and the last logs were hauled at the end of that year. Much of the equipment was moved to Saxon. Logs were coming out of Skagit County over the Saxon line and at times Bloedel-Donovan logged in cooperation with Lyman

THE BARKENTINE *COMMODORE* loads lumber at Bellingham. *Jukes photo courtesy Phil Swanson.*

M.A.C. RAILCAR on the Bloedel-Donovan Saxon Bridge. It was this span over the Nooksack River that the 8-Spot mallet fell through in 1924. The bridge was then replaced by a modern span which is still used today as the motor vehicle bridge. *Courtesy Ed Marlow,*

Timber Company as the two firms were working in adjacent properties along the Nooksack River.

138 Saxon operated consistantly until 1940, when the timber was exhausted. The last log was delivered from Saxon February 4, 1941, and only the dismantling crews were left. Bloedel-Donovan's last major logging was now entirely on the Olympic Peninsula, and had been producing since about 1923. Logging continued there until 1945, when the Company sold out to Rayonier, Incorporated.

THE SAXON BRIDGE COLLAPSED under the 8-Spot mallet and a tank car on June 19, 1934. The result is seen in these two photos. No one was killed and the locomotive was not only put back into service, but survives today. *George Nesset photos.*

A WELL KNOWN "LOKIE" in northwest woods was Bloedel-Donovan's 8-Spot mallet seen here near Alger in the late 1920s. She was one of the rare ICC approved engines on a logging line because she was used on through trains over the Northern Pacific between Saxon interchange and the Park log dump. Hence the flags and marker lights seen here. The stout little Mallet followed her owners to work on the Olympic Peninsula, later under the banner of Rayonier, Inc. She is preserved today in Shelton, Washington. *D. Kinsey courtesy Whatcom Museum of History and Art.*

A SECOND MALLET WAS ADDED to the Bloedel-Donovan roster in late 1924. She was a twin to the 8-Spot and was put through her paces at Alger, then shipped to the company's new operation on the Olympic Peninsula. *D. Kinsey, Dennis Thompson Collection.*

Presented on these two pages are the key elements in a logging show - - base camp (above); the source of logs (below) - a setting with spar tree and transportation to market; and the power (right) to gather the logs.

(above) **BLOEDEL-DONOVAN SAXON CAMP.** Although located in Whatcom County, considerable Skagit County timber moved through this camp on its way to market. This was the last large operation for Bloedel-Donovan on the mainland before the move to the Olympic Peninsula. *D. Kinsey, Phil Swanson.*

(right, facing page) **BLOEDEL-DONOVAN UNIT** near Saxon Camp. *Courtesy Bernie Penley, Bert Kellogg.*

(below) **SPAR TREE, HIGH RIGGER AND UNIT LOADER.** *Courtesy Bernie Penley, Ed Marlow.*

HAUFS

CLEAR LAKE LUMBER CO.
4
43462 FEET IN THE FOUR LOGS 107

CHAPTER 6

STEAM DUMMIES AND DISCONNECTS

The Clear Lake Holdings of Georgia-Pacific Corporation

The town of Clear Lake dates its industrial origin back to 1892, in which year Day Brothers built a shingle mill on the northwest edge of the lake. Day Brothers operated the mill three years and then it was acquired by the Bank of British Columbia who quickly leased it back to Hiatt and McMaster. They ran it for one additional year. Already established for some years locally, John McMaster bought out the mill himself about 1896, and continued alone until 1898. During that time he added a sawmill.

In April 1898, McMaster expanded his firm into a partnership with H. B. Waite, of Minneapolis, Minnesota and C. P. Bratnober of Waterloo, Iowa. The corporation formed was named McMaster and Waite Lumber Company and was capitalized with $60,000 stock. The stated purpose of the corporation was, "For lumbering, general mercantile business, logging railroads, etc."

Company property at Clear Lake consisted of 150 acres. In use were the sawmill, shingle mill, dry kilns, covered storage for four million shingles, automatic fire protection sprinklers with twelve hydrants, one boarding house, a dozen small homes, meat market, store and office building. The company store was operated by John McMaster's son, William. 143

A two mile logging railroad was in use to the logging camp.

The railroad was a quaint affair. Motive power arrived in town in the form of an old "steam dummy," discarded from an unidentified street railway. The wood-enclosed body of this locomotive must have been cozy quarters for the crew in the wet Washington woods.

The steam dummy was mated to four pairs of lightweight disconnected trucks to perform logging duties. The combination presented a bizarre sight in the forest. Clear Lake was certainly host to a notable railroad.

By the fall of the next year more investors were taken into the firm and the name was changed to Bratnober-Waite Lumber Company. To do their logging for them now was the contract firm of Kennedy and O'Brien. Their new affiliate brought in a Climax locomotive and built additional railroad out from the lake.

Everything was running well and at the end of 1899, the new company had cut 42 million shingles and over 6 million feet of lumber for the year.

A bad accident on the logging railroad occurred in the summer of 1900, when a train ran away and wrecked

TRAIN OF LOGS CUT FROM ONE TREE 12 feet in diameter. Log scales 43,462 board feet of lumber. *D. Kinsey courtesy Whatcom Museum of History and Art.*

the locomotive and cars. Damage was estimated between six and eight thousand dollars. This did not stall operations however, and at the end of 1901, the company had doubled the volume of lumber cut two years earlier.

Bratnober-Waite bought out Kennedy and O'Brien in 1902 and promptly ordered a new 40-ton Climax locomotive.

The lumber mill was lost in a fire early in November of 1902. Two men perished in the blaze. After a hard fight the shingle mill and store were saved.

In the process of rebuilding, an amendment to the Articles of Incorporation was made and filed by F. H. Jackson, now president, and J. E. Bratnober, secretary. It provided that the company would thereafter be named Clear Lake Lumber Company.

Several months work was required to finish the reconstructed mill. New equipment included a nine-foot bandsaw, live rolls, transfers, edger and new cutoff saws. Upon completion the mill was expected to employ 250 men.

The new mill opened for business and kept quite busy for the next few years. In 1908 a nine-mile railroad extension was begun toward Mount Vernon to connect with the Great Northern. The same year stock was increased to $300,000. The railroad continued using the two Climax locomotives along with eighteen sets of disconnected log trucks.

The following year the firm purchased 4,500 acres of timber located east and south of the lake. At the same time they sold 520 acres to Day Lumber Company of Big Lake. Stock now went to $450,000.

It is well now to take notice of other

SMALL DONKEY ENGINES in the woods around the turn-of-the-century produced this scene, taken near Clear Lake. *D. Kinsey, courtesy Mr. & Mrs. Jack Turner.*

McMASTER & WAITE LUMBER CO. steam dummy in woods service at a landing dated 1899. *D. Kinsey courtesy Peter Replinger.*

(facing page, right)

(top) **STEAM DUMMIES AND DISCONNECTS.** In these three photos, the travels of McMaster and Waite Lumber Company steam dummy No. 1 can be followed from woods to log dump. The first picture shows log rollway where cars were loaded.

(middle) **STARK CONTRAST** between "toy-like" locomotive and lengthy log portray Clear Lake's earliest railroad logging.

(lower) **THE DETERMINED LITTLE TRAIN** finally arrives at the log dump.

All three photos circa 1899. D. Kinsey, courtesy Bert Kellogg.

McMASTER & WAITE LUMBER CO.
No 1

McMASTER & WAITE LUMBER CO.
D.R. KINSEY
PHOTO.
1899

D.R. KINSEY
1899 PHOTO.

WOODSMEN HERE ARE SNIPING the ends of the logs so they may be better "trailed" down the track pulled by the little Climax locomotive waiting in the background. *D. Kinsey, courtesy Whatcom Museum of History & Art.*

events taking shape that were soon to affect Clear Lake Lumber Company. In 1906 Day Creek Lumber Company was incorporated by J. E. Potts, A. E. Freeman and C. E. Johannsen. The ambitious company barged a locomotive up the Skagit River to Day Creek, offloaded her, and proceeded to build a railroad. Within two years they boasted four miles of track and six sets of disconnected trucks. They dumped into the river and floated the logs to market. The firm sold out in March 1910, to become Miller Logging Company, under the direction of George Miller. A brand new Shay locomotive was purchased and taken to Day Creek. At that time arrangements were made to take the river tows to Utsalady, on Camano Island.

The new Miller operation at Day Creek was plagued with trouble from its beginning. Late in August, of the same year, the locomotive with two flatcars loaded with gravel started down out of the hills. On a steep grade approaching a curve followed by a bridge, the Shay became unmanageable. The engineer realizing the trouble, applied the air brake but to no satisfaction. Several men were riding the engine and cars and they began to jump, each more or less injured by his fall. Much to everyone's surprise the train remained on the track over the next two bridges before it "went into the ditch," rolling onto its side. A man riding on the Shay's running board, by the name of Jens Jensen, was pinned under the locomotive and fatally scalded by escaping steam.

SCENE AT LANDING of Bratnober-Waite Lumber Company near Clear Lake. Rollway is in foreground where logs are rolled onto waiting log cars. *D. Kinsey courtesy Whatcom Museum of History & Art.*

Within thirty days the same locomotive engineer involved with the first wreck, had another accident. He was caught between moving logcars and crushed to death; Walter Farmer became the second fatality at Day Creek.

By Christmas, 1910, Miller closed his Day Creek camp, having found it impossible to make a profit with the operation.

Another man entered into association with George Miller at this time. He was B. R. Lewis and his name is still well remembered in Clear Lake.

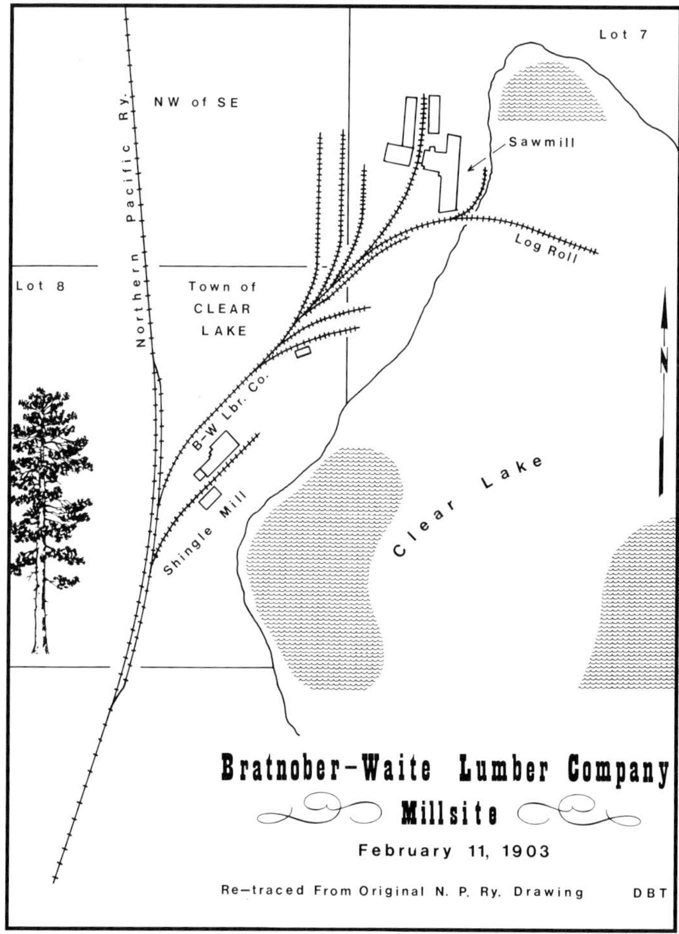

Byron R. Lewis was born in Ischua, New York, in 1864. His family owned and operated the Ischua Carriage and Wagon Company in that town. Mr. Lewis later became a timber cruiser in Minnesota where he also bought and sold timber. In the early 1900s he moved his wife and family to Spokane, Washington, and established the B. R. Lewis Lumber Company. His firm logged in the area north of Coeur D'Alene, Idaho, and Lewis built a common carrier railroad there named the Idaho and Northern Railway. He also organized the First National Bank of Coeur D'-Alene, an interest which he later sold in 1908. In 1909 he sold the remainder of his assets for about a half million dollars and the lumber firm became the Blackwell Lumber Company.

TRAILING A LARGE LOG, Climax No. 3 is seen here about 1904. Clear Lake made exclusive use of Climax motive power until B. R. Lewis came into the Company and began to purchase Shay locomotives. *Courtesy Stan Dexter and Joe Shelton.*

Mr. Lewis then purchased a large tract of virgin timber in Skagit County. It was located along the south side of the Skagit River and east of Clear Lake. He then founded the Skagit Logging Company and prepared to build a railroad from the Northern Pacific at the river, east. He named his new common carrier the Puget Sound and Cascade Railway.

George Miller and B. R. Lewis joined forces to log along the Skagit. It is said that Miller was to do contract logging and railroad building. At any rate, it was not long before Miller moved on to other interests in other places and Lewis remained in the local spotlight.

Construction of the Puget Sound and Cascade was underway in 1911, and that spring found fifteen flatcars

DUMPING LOGS IN CLEAR LAKE about 1901. Bratnober-Waite Lumber Company Climax No. 2 is seen here on the old log dump. *D. Kinsey courtesy Whatcom Museum of History & Art.*

of rail waiting in the Northern Pacific yards in Sedro Woolley for the new line.

Articles of Incorporation were filed that summer for the Puget Sound and Cascade Railway listing B. R. Lewis as president and treasurer. Other officers were Thomas Smith, T. J. Meagher, F. H. Jackson and J. C. Wixon.

Construction of the railroad required several months and in December 1912, the first load of logs was shipped from Day Creek directly to the new Northern Pacific interchange, now called Skagit Junction. The railroad boasted ten miles of track, three locomotives and forty cars.

ONE OF THE EARLY CLEAR LAKE LUMBER COMPANY MILLS on the north end of the lake taken before 1906. *Courtesy Walt Casler*

The impact of the reality of the Puget Sound and Cascade brought weight to bear on the other logging business around Clear Lake and in April 1913, a new Clear Lake Lumber Company was formed through the merger of the original Clear Lake Lumber with B. R. Lewis' Skagit Logging Company and Mt. Baker Timber Company. Puget Sound and Cascade, being a common carrier, retained its title, but was a subsidiary of the new Clear Lake Lumber Company. Immediately, another six mile eastward extension of the railroad was begun.

Expansion for Clear Lake Lumber was coming at an astounding pace: having built their own railroad from Skagit Junction into the town of Clear Lake, 1915 revealed renewed activities on the Mount Vernon extension which had begun in 1908. Washington Iron Works delivered three new donkey engines to the firm in 1915 and four more the next year. Another three miles of railroad was built southeast of Clear Lake to tap additional timber in 1916, and the Mount Vernon line was operating by June of the same year.

Several geared locomotives were busy on the railroad operations. As soon as Lewis took over the firm, no additional Climax locomotives were purchased. His preference for Shays was evident and only one Climax survived to see 1920. A new Baldwin 2-8-2 was ordered in 1916. On arrival in March of 1917, she was put to work on the mainline as road number 200.

During the height of World War One the mill was again heavily damaged by fire. This precipitated the construction of another new mill which was to become the largest and most modern inland mill in the state.

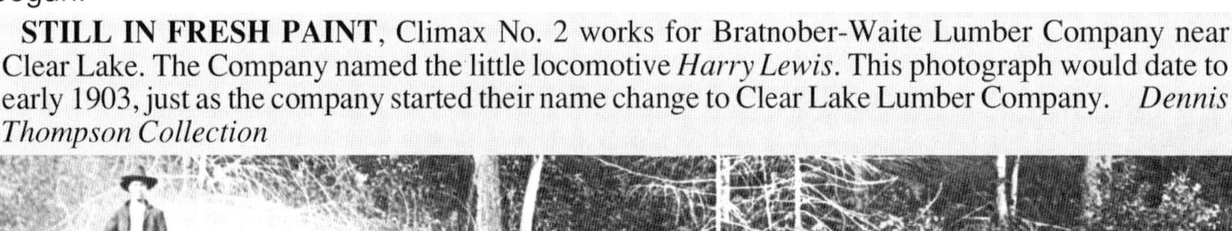

STILL IN FRESH PAINT, Climax No. 2 works for Bratnober-Waite Lumber Company near Clear Lake. The Company named the little locomotive *Harry Lewis*. This photograph would date to early 1903, just as the company started their name change to Clear Lake Lumber Company. *Dennis Thompson Collection*

149

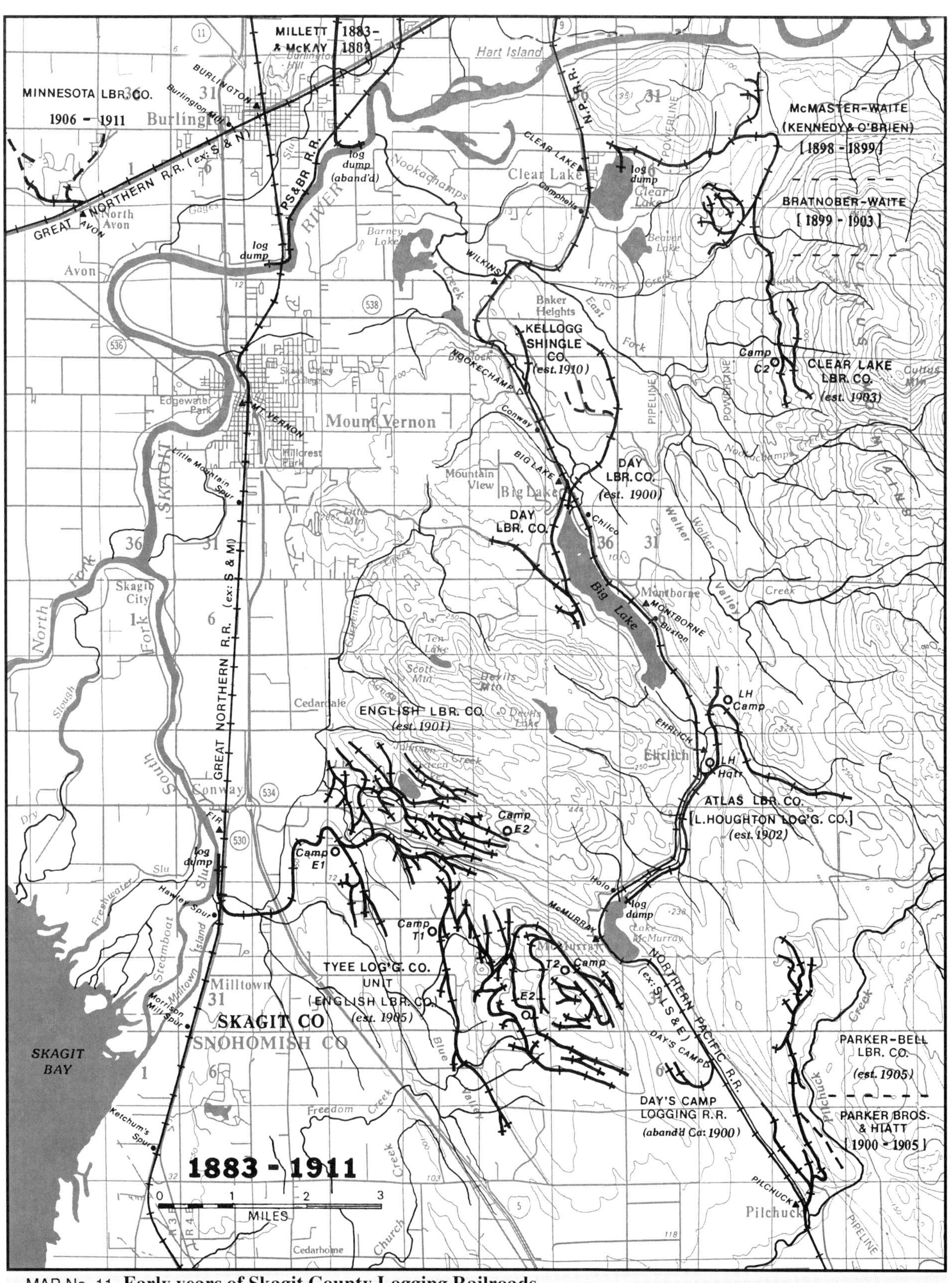

MAP No. 11 **Early years of Skagit County Logging Railroads.**
The first logging "railroad" in the county, Millett & McKay, is shown near Burlington. Note that "Day's Camp," near Pilchuck, was not related to Day Lumber Company, and leaves no documentation. Almost all of the logging grades shown in this map had disappeared by 1911.

DAY CREEK LUMBER COMPANY MILL in 1908. Before the Miller interests attempted their isolated logging railroad near Day Creek, mills such as this were the only "heavy" industry on the south side of the Skagit River. Miller absorbed Day Creek Lumber. *D. Kinsey, Dennis Thompson Collection.*

Woods locomotives brought loads out of Day Creek country to Potts Station. The eastern most harvest was collected at the Finney Creek "makeup," located on what is now the South Skagit Highway between Pressentin Creek and Finney Creek. The big Baldwin ran the mainline, picking up logs from both locations and hauling them to the Clear Lake mill or to the new river dump at railroad's end in Mount Vernon, depending on if the timber was to be cut or sold.

Frank Maddox, who ran donkey engines in the Day Creek country, remembers one log so large two chokers were broken getting it to the landing. After much difficulty it was loaded on cars. *They finally got it down to Clear Lake and had to dynamite the son-of-a-bitch before they could saw it. I bet they never made five cents on it.*

In 1923 stock was increased to three and one-half million dollars, with stockholders as follows: Frank Horton, Roscoe Horton, Jennie S. Horton, Laura H. Horton, Henry S. Horton, Belle H. Crangle, F. H. Jackson, C. H. Kinne, B. R. Lewis, S. B. Lewis, A. L. Lewis and E. P. Keefe.

During the next year Lewis purchased a new Baldwin 2-6-2 side tank locomotive and a new 80-ton Shay at a total price of $49,903. This was followed in January 1925, by an order to Pacific Car and Foundry for fifty skeleton logcars at $1,075 each.

Puget Sound and Cascade Railway operated 35 miles of mainline and over 60 miles of branchline which was growing daily. Seven locomotives were under steam using 225 logcars. Thirty-two donkey engines dotted the hillsides of the south side of the Skagit River. Employment ranged from 500 to 800 men. Camps and railroad were interconnected by Clear Lake's own telephone sys-

The new mill was finished and went into operation in March of 1919.

The arrival of the 1920s brought the Clear Lake Lumber Company to its height of glory, while at the same time storm clouds gathered on the horizon.

A railroad incline 2,680 feet in length was built near Day Creek in 1922, with another Sessoms incline of 5,375 feet in length following at Finney Creek in 1923.

MILLER LOGGING COMPANY Shay failed to negotiate a curve late in August 1910 with this result. A workman named Jens Jensen was riding the running board and could not jump free. He was trapped and scalded to death by escaping steam. This small railroad venture at Day Creek was discontinued shortly thereafter. *Courtesy Mrs. F. G. Brown, daughter of B. R. Lewis.*

tem.

Supplies of every description were consumed. The variety was as endless as it was varied. The company store sold a 25-pound sack of sugar for $2.55 per sack. Heavy material ranged up to an order, in the summer of 1924, for a single piece of cable 2 miles in length and 1⅜ inches in diameter for the Day Creek incline snubber.

The company also maintained company offices on 4th Avenue in Seattle, in room 1038 of the Henry Building. From there trips to Clear Lake were made in Lewis' new Packard automobile with chauffeur Billy Belford at the wheel.

CLIMAX NUMBER FOUR is almost new when this picture was taken about 1909. She was a pretty engine and very agile on woods rails. *D. Kinsey, courtesy Whatcom Museum of Hist. & Art.*

In the mill a new Sterling water tube boiler of 800-horsepower produced steam for a 3,200 KW turbine. The electric power generated not only had the capacity to handle the electrical requirements of the mill, but also all the business and residential power consumption of the entire town if necessary.

The theater in Clear Lake attracted first run movies before Sedro Woolley, which many considered a sign of eminence for the town.

Clear Lake Lumber Company reached its peak May 12, 1925 at the annual employee picnic. Employment at the firm was then 1,236 men. Visitors and picnic attendees were said to be triple that figure. It was ironic that before the end of the year the Clear Lake Lumber Company went into receivership. Men working on a new railroad trestle over Mill Creek received the news of the company's failure and the end of their jobs. They went home. For many years the half-completed trestle stood as silent and visible testimony to the end of a empire.

After months of litigation, the Clear Lake Lumber Company's assets were sold at public auction April 23, 1927. The properties inventoried at five million dollars and was the largest sale of its kind ever held in northwest Washington. The high bid received was refused by the court and the properties were resold August 20, 1927. The final buyer was the Bank of California and after a good deal of work, a new company was organized to take over in 1929.

PUGET SOUND PULP AND TIMBER COMPANY

In April 1929, a twelve million dollar corporation was organized at Everett, Washington. The new firm was named Puget Sound Pulp and Timber Company and was designed to merge pulp timber interests and to build

MANUFACTURER'S PHOTOGRAPH of Clear Lake Climax No. 6 when she was new. This was in December 1910. She weighed 57 tons. *Courtesy Walt Casler.*

WORKING ITS WAY UP DAY CREEK CANYON, Shay No. 3 is seen here one and one half miles upstream from Potts. This location is now a logging truck road. *Frank Maddox*

a large pulp mill in Everett. The company absorbed the properties of the San Juan Pulp and Manufacturing Company of Bellingham, Fidalgo Pulp and Manufacturing Company of Anacortes, the Rucker Brothers' properties in Everett and Snohomish counties, Clear Lake Lumber Company, the Hartford and Eastern Railroad, the Puget Sound and Cascade Railway and more than 70 million feet of timber in Snohomish and Skagit counties, as well as the Big-Four Inn on the Hartford and Eastern Railroad, and the shipyard site on the waterfront in Everett.

DAY CREEK INCLINE SNUBBER is in place, the new machine is now awaiting its hauling cable. *Frank Maddox*

Officers and directors of the new organization read like the who's who of northwest business. H. W. Bunker was chairman of the board of directors; Ossian Anderson was president, with P. F. Knight, first vice-president; William Morrison, vice-president; Neil Sexton, treasurer; H. R. Lawton, secretary.

152

The board of directors was composed of: U. M. Dickey, president of the Consolidated Dairy Products Company of Seattle; R. H. Miller, director of the National Bank of Commerce of Seattle; W. Neil Winter, president of the West Coast Telephone Company, Everett; H. M. Robbins, president of Clark-Nickerson Lumber Company, Everett; H. R. Lawton, vice-president of Pierce, Fair and Company, Seattle; O. M. Green, president of Olympia National Bank; Peter G.

Condensed Bankruptcy Inventory of Camp #4

(see appendix E for more complete listing)

1 Kitchen Car #1
2 Dining cars #3 - #1
1 Store and Office Car #2
1 Apartment car #1
1 Combination car #1
5 Sleepers - #1, 2, 4, 5, 6
1 Library car #2

Above cars are all on wheels, steam heated and electric lighted and modern in every respect

1 Sanitary Modern Toilet on skids
1 Girls Shack on skids
1 Foremans Shack on Skids 14' x 36'
1 Blanket House on skids 14' x 40'
1 Blacksmith Shop 14' x 40' on Skids
1 Filing Shack on Skids 14' x 36'

EVOLUTION OF RAILROAD OPERATIONS AT THE DAY CREEK INCLINE. When Clear Lake Lumber Company went into receivership in 1925, one of their operating inclines was near Day Creek. When Puget Sound Pulp and Timber emerged as the operator in 1929, an unusual engineering strategy caused the abandonment of both inclines in favor of building new switchbacks to gain access to fresh logging. This unexpected event can be followed in this series of 3 maps spanning the years 1921 to 1938 depicting proposed and actual railroad grades for this "logging unit," a term encompassing a defined area that was logged with one or more "shows." The term show referred to a logging operation consisting of a landing, skidder, etc.

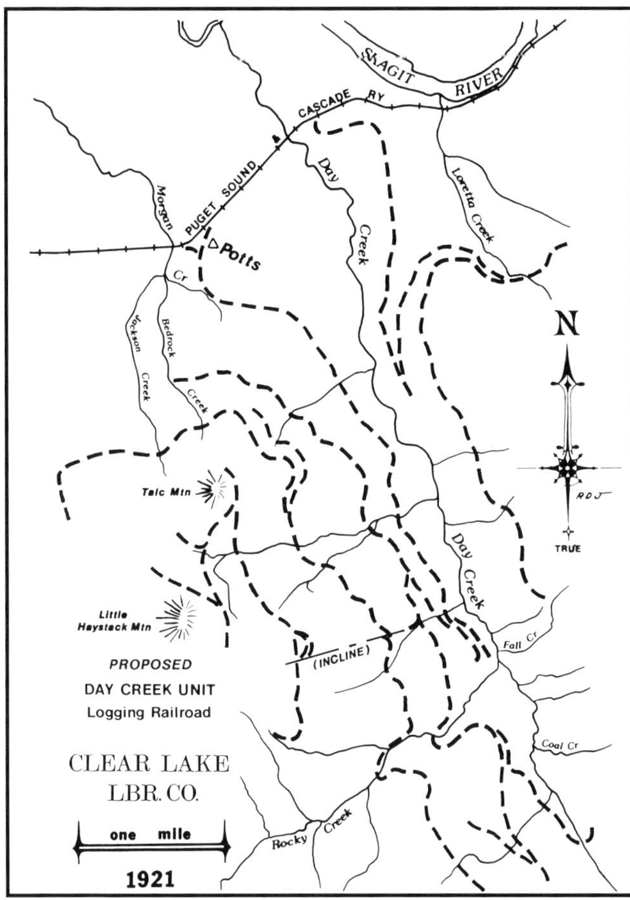

153

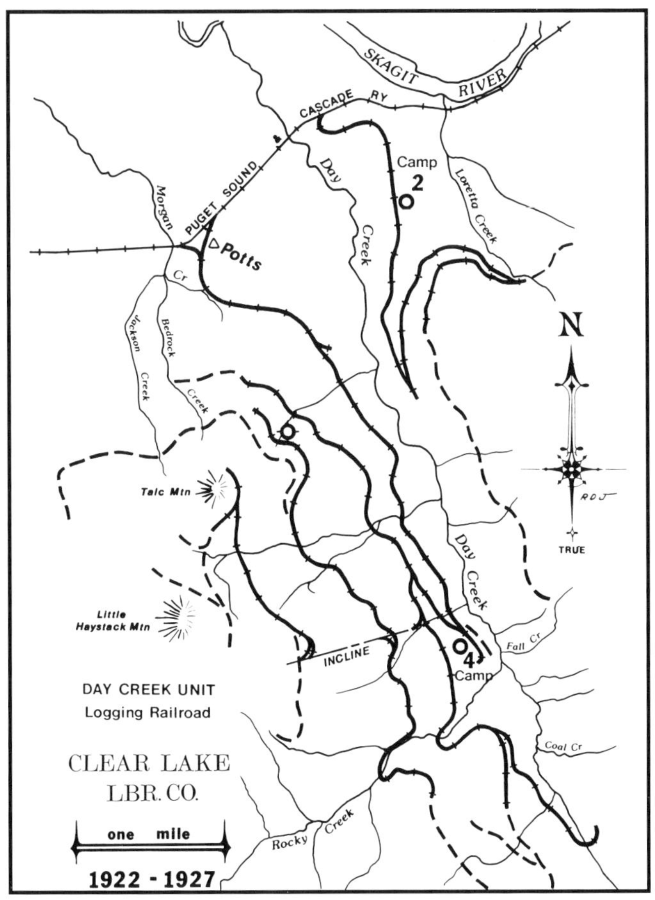

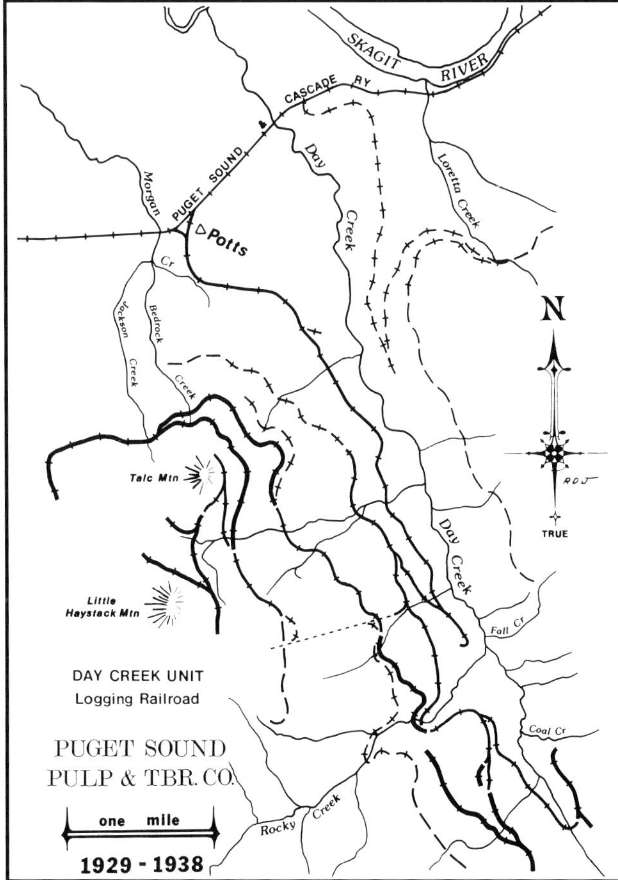

LIMA BUILDER'S PHOTO of Shay No. 2, taken at Lima, Ohio in 1916. She enjoyed a long life, eventually going to work on the old English Lumber Company line under the banner of Puget Sound Pulp and Timber. She worked there until that line was abandoned in 1952. *Allen County (Ohio) Historical Society.*

(right) **CLEAR LAKE LUMBER COMPANY SHAY** No. 3 on a temporary trestle. She is an 80-ton engine. *D. Kinsey, courtesy Whatcom Museum of History & Art.*

PERHAPS THE MOST WELL-USED Shay on Clear Lake line was No. 4, seen here during the last days of the railroad. She was the first engine put under steam when Puget Pulp took over in 1929. In 1940 she was offered for sale, but appraisal revealed she was "about worn out." *Dennis Thompson*

Schmidt, president of Schmidt Estate, Inc., Olympia, and secretary of the Washington Hotel Company; William Morrison, president of Morrison Mill Company, Bellingham; H. W. Bunker, president of the Coos Bay Lumber Company, San Francisco; P. F. Knight, vice-president and manager of the Mutual Lumber Company, Bucoda; and Ossian Anderson, president of the San Juan Pulp and Manufacturing Company, Bellingham and president of Fidalgo Pulp and Manufacturing Company, Anacortes.

Focus of this powerful conglomerate was directed toward the erection of a tremendous pulp mill in Everett and the rehabilitation of such logging operations as would be required to feed such a mill.

First activity along the old Puget Sound and Cascade Railway was observed in the

THE PRIDE OF THE PUGET SOUND AND CASCADE RAILWAY was this Baldwin Mikado built in 1916. Used on the mainline between Finney Creek, Clear Lake and Mount Vernon, she represented the glory days of Clear Lake's railroad. In the words of Frank Maddox, "She was a Dandy." Old No. 200 went on to serve on the Cowlitz, Chehalis and Cascade Railway as their No. 15. Thereafter she was on display at Chehalis, Washington. In 1988, the logging veteran was removed to the Mount Rainier Scenic Railway shops. She will be overhauled and returned to service in the Chehalis-Centralia area. *Railroad Museum Of Pennsylvania (P.H.M.C.)*

IRON WORKS
4589
JULY 1936
PUGET SOUND PULP
AND TIMBER Co CLEAR LAKE
TIMBERVIEWS © SEATTLE

(left) **PUGET SOUND PULP & TIMBER COMPANY Washington Two-Drum Yarder**. Bottom, l to r: Roy Wolfe, Elmer (Boone) Cabe, unknown; Middle row, unknown, Geronimo Ray, unknown, Mervin Bridge, unknown. Date is July 1936. *D. Kinsey, courtesy Whatcom Museum of History & Art.*

fall of 1929. Old Shay No. 4 was fired up and headed east up the mainline. One lone figure sat in the cab without benefit of the usual fireman, as life began again for the railroad. As it operated as a common carrier, the mainline continued under the name Puget Sound and Cascade Railway. Logging operations were now under the banner of Puget Sound Pulp and Timber, Clear Lake Division.

Additional work was also required now in Mount Vernon. The Pacific Northwest Traction Company had been abandoned in 1928, leaving Mount Vernon riverfront industries without rail freight service. The demise of the once pleasant and convenient interurban line to Bellingham, and its close proximity to the Puget Sound and Cascade Railway's log dump provided a natural course of events to take place. Puget Sound and Cascade took over the provision of freight service to the Mount Vernon waterfront. Thereafter, it was not uncommon to observe one of Clear Lake's Shay logging locomotives switching

COOKS IN THE WOODS. Clear Lake Lumber Company logging camp cooks pose by their kitchens. Two dining cars adjoined the cook car, each seating 100 hungry loggers. These mobile camps consisted of 13 cars as follows: 1. Combination car with boiler supplying steam and heat to run a 7KW generator for electric lights. This car contained four showers with hot water. 2. Cook car with York walk-in cooler, meat house and meat storage for 200 men. This car contained kitchen with ranges, sinks and all required supplies. 3-4. Two dining cars seating 200 men. 5. Office car with quarters for timekeeper and foreman and tools. 6. Library car with card room, reading room and writing desk, drafting room, 2 rooms for scalers living and accommodations for chief engineer and cruiser. 7. Compartment car with 7 rooms well ventilated, with wash bowl and hot and cold water. 8. Six sleeping cars, each with 4 compartments for 8 men each. The Tiger double-bunks were furnished with a felt mattress, 2 sheets, cotton blanket, pillow and pillow case, 2 wool blankets and bed cover of brown canvas. These camp cars were 14 feet wide and 64 feet long. Color was grey on the interior. Box car red distinguished the exteriors with white trim. In addition to this standard consist, accessory buildings were: home for superintendent, supply house, filing house, house for kitchen waitresses, blacksmith shop, oil house and sand house. These were built on skids to facilitate moving. *D. Kinsey, Dennis Thompson Collection*

CLEAR LAKE LUMBER COMPANY CAMP in the hills above the Skagit River. *D. Kinsey, Dennis Thompson Collection.*

cars into such industries as Carnation Milk Company. In addition, in 1932, Puget Sound and Cascade acquired 4.8 miles of old Pacific Northwest Traction line between North Mount Vernon and Burlington for a consideration of one dollar. The railway then began to serve the milk cannery in Burlington. Within a few

NEW AT BALDWIN FACTORY IN 1923, this photograph was taken by the Baldwin photographer. She is ready to leave on her journey west. Price tag for the little side-tank engine was $20,375. She was to work in Skagit County less than two years, however. Frank Maddox remembers her running up Day Creek canyon: "I used to like to listen to her going up the canyon - would sound like she was going to tear the whole country down - just a-barking. Then she'd come around the corner and she'd be just that little 'bitty engine. She could only pull seven empties up Day Creek canyon. But 'ol B.R. Lewis said 'I bought that to run on that hill and she's gonna run there!' She had blind center drivers, could get around the corners good. Only thing wrong with her was they had her where she didn't belong...she'd be O.K. on the flat. I wish I was back there again." *Railroad Museum Of Pennsylvania (P.H.M.C.)*

NOOKACHAMPS CROSSING by the Puget Sound and Cascade was made over this long trestle. (*above*) Seen through the underpass in the distance is what is now the Gunderson Road. Nookachamps Creek has always been known for flooding. One winter was so bad a loaded log train was left on this trestle to "hold it down." Water reached the journal boxes. (*below*) Side view of Nookachamps Trestle. Two bents still stand in 1988. *Courtesy Stacey's Camera Center*

THE CLEAR LAKE LUMBER COMPANY STORE. *Courtesy Bert Kellogg.*

months the Great Northern completed new industrial spurs in Burlington and the Burlington branch of the Puget Sound and Cascade was closed for good in the fall of 1936.

During Clear Lake's reorganization under Puget Sound Pulp and Timber, a considerable shuffle of equipment occurred. Forty-five skeleton cars, new in 1925, were repossessed by Pacific Car and Foundry, from the old Clear Lake organization and it appears the new 8-spot Shay followed. Locomotives changed hands to an extent that is still not clear. Baldwin 2-8-2 No. 200, pride of the railroad, had been sold in 1928. When Puget Sound Pulp and Timber had been organized, one of their acquisitions was the Rucker Brothers logging operation at Hartford along with the old Monte Cristo branch of the Northern Pacific. Some of the logging equipment there was brought to Clear Lake including Shay No. 7, which was in very poor condition. Mr. H. W. Bunker of the Coos Bay Lumber Company, in Oregon, now on the board for Puget Sound Pulp and Timber, seems to have initiated some motive power trades. Clear Lake's No. 7, the new 2-6-2T, turned up at Coos Bay, while an older Baldwin 2-8-2 left that Oregon firm and came to Clear Lake to replace the No. 200 on the mainline. After some two years of juggling equipment seven locomotives were on the property joining the menagerie of rolling stock already there. Non-railroad steam machinery in the woods was the same collection of Clear Lake Lumber Company equipment...thirty-two donkey engines, yarders and snubbers of various sizes and shapes. Condition of this mass of equipment ranged from pretty darn good to downright awful!

But while mechanics of the new Clear Lake operation settled down, Mother Nature did not, kindling a forest fire in the summer of 1930, which consumed thirteen railroad bridges. One locomotive was stranded in the woods by the blaze and for a time there was speculation that she might have to be left there. The timber in the area was almost logged out and it was not practical to rebuild the railroad. It appears, however, the locomotive was later removed by other means.

Over the next year Puget Sound Pulp and Timber completed a new 200-ton pulp mill

THE BOARDING HOUSE AT CLEAR LAKE during the days of Clear Lake Lumber Company. Date is prior to 1912. *Courtesy Mary Meins.*

ON THE NORTHERN PACIFIC AT CLEAR LAKE. At its peak, some eight passenger trains per day passed through Clear Lake, serving N.P.'s territory through the Skagit logging country. Here 4-4-0 No. 1147 takes her turn through town. She was a Rhode Island product of 1888. *Courtesy Roger Fox*

CAMP FOUR ON ROCKY CREEK. This camp was literally built on the tail track of the mainline's switchback. *Frank Maddox.*

162

in Everett, to bolster production of its 90-ton plant in Bellingham and its 50-ton plant in Anacortes. In 1932 the firm divided its properties, releasing the new Everett plant and its Snohomish County timber holdings. The Everett mill later emerged as Scott Paper Company, whose mill in that city became the largest sulphite pulp mill in the world. These changes in the business also maintained Puget Sound Pulp and Timber's financial equilibrium during the tough Depression years.

Feeding the remaining Puget Sound Pulp and Timber plants, Clear Lake Division went into the 1930s logging six days a week on a one-shift basis. The log dump on the Skagit River at Mount Vernon was reactivated having previously been used primarily before completion of the new mill in Clear Lake. Now surplus logs were dumped there, round-boomed and taken to the mouth of the river to be rafted for the general market. Logs sold were generally Douglas fir, cedar being run at the Clear Lake shingle mill and hemlock going for pulp at the Anacortes or Bellingham plants.

Puget Sound Pulp and Timber had been spending large sums of money revitalizing Clear Lake, the railroad and their logging operations. Yet profit margins were slim. New policy concepts and truck logging were constant reminders of a changing industry. By 1935 the Clear Lake sawmill sat idle, and was dismantled by 1938. Activities began slowing down in Clear Lake. In 1938 the shingle mill was sold for $18,000. That same year the company obtained permission from the Interstate Commerce Commission for the Puget Sound and Cascade Railway to cease its 26 year operation as a common carrier, which placed an end to all non-logging traffic. It is said at the time that all freight "could have been taken care of on a hand car."

SHAY NUMBER FOUR and crew inside the Clear Lake enginehouse and shop. *D. Kinsey, Dennis Thompson Collection.*

The last railroad logging show for Puget Sound Pulp and Timber at Clear Lake took place on Quartz Creek. The railroad ended a few hundred feet beyond the creek and the last Camp 2 was located about one mile before the Quartz Creek trestle. The last logging here ended in December of 1939 and Camp 2 was razed by the company shortly thereafter.

During July 1939 the Interstate Commerce Commission ruled to allow formation of the Mount Vernon Terminal Railway Company, Incorporated. This firm was organized by F. J. McGuire, engineer for the Puget Sound and Cascade, Hugh Finner, head brakeman for the Puget Sound and Cascade and F. L. Arndt, accountant for Puget Sound Pulp and Timber. The three men foresaw the coming end to rail operations and acquired the trackage of the former Pacific Northwest Traction Company from Mount Vernon to North Mount Vernon, approximately 1½ miles. Also in the initial agreement was trackage rights over the Puget Sound and Cascade to Clear Lake for the purpose of prolonging log transportation from that town.

163

NEW SKELETON CAR FOR CLEAR LAKE LUMBER is seen at the factory in Seattle. In the early 1920s, Clear Lake ordered some 85 new cars such as this one. *PC&F photo, Dennis Thompson Collection*

PUGET SOUND & CASCADE RAILWAY log car No. 601. *PC&F photo courtesy John Taubeneck.*

THE NEW CLEAR LAKE MILL IN 1919. This was said to be the largest inland sawmill in the region at the time. It made heavy use of Allis-Chalmers equipment, modern in every way. The mill boasted steam turbine generators to produce electricity - enough power, in fact, to run the mill and the town with power to spare.

Some 85 miles of railroad were operated using 8 locomotives. In 1924, the entire operation went into receivership. It was sold at public auction in 1927. *All photos Cress-Dale, courtesy Mrs. Frederick G. Brown*

166

MILL INTERIOR VIEWS

(right) **PUGET SOUND PULP AND TIMBER COMPANY** Shay No. 2 works a landing in the latter days of the railroad. *D. Kinsey, courtesy Whatcom Museum of History & Art*

80-TON SHAY NUMBER EIGHT in 1924. She carried shop number 3260. *Allen County (Ohio) Historical Society*

The portion of railroad purchased by Mount Vernon Terminal was acquired for the sum of one dollar. Operating rights over Puget Sound and Cascade provided fifty cents per carload and fifty cents per engine-mile to be paid to the Puget Sound and Cascade, with Mount Vernon Terminal maintaining the track to Clear Lake. A 20-ton Whitcomb gasoline locomotive was obtained by the new terminal railroad to serve Mount Vernon industries.

At Puget Sound Pulp and Timber, "By resolution by the Board of Directors the railway property was abandoned during 1940, for the reason that it was no longer necessary or useful in logging operations." The woods rails were removed in 1940 and 1941, while the mainline east up the Skagit River was left for a short time, then scrapped. A substantial amount of the old mainline there is now the South Skagit Highway. Puget Sound Pulp and Timber still ran occasional trains from Clear Lake to Mount Vernon after this time. Mikado No. 101 was seen pulling logs from Clear Lake to the dump as late as the summer of 1942, however, even this line was pulled out by 1946. Mount Vernon Terminal retained their core of operations in downtown Mount Vernon and continue to interchange cars to the Burlington Northern to the present day.

(left) **PUGET SOUND PULP & TIMBER CLYDE CRANE No. 1.** A handy piece of equipment on the railroad, it could move about on its own power, and do a variety of work along the railroad. *D. Kinsey, courtesy Whatcom Museum of History & Art.*

In the summer of 1940, the Anacortes pulp plant of Puget Sound Pulp and Timber was sold and the proceeds used to improve the Bellingham facility. Between 1940 and 1958, the Bellingham plant became a modern pulp and paper manufacturing unit. In 1961,

RIDING TO WORK on a Clear Lake Lumber Company incline. This was a 48 percent grade. *Dennis Thompson Collection*

Puget Sound Pulp and Timber acquired Columbia Valley Lumber Company, a retail lumber business which itself was an outgrowth of Bloedel-Donovan Lumber Mills. In 1963 Puget Sound Pulp and Timber was merged into Georgia-Pacific Corporation, with headquarters in Portland, Oregon, and later in Atlanta, Georgia. Georgia-Pacific now operates in 49 states and maintains offices and facilities in a number of foreign countries. It also retains a timber management office in Clear Lake and timber holdings throughout Skagit County.

The sole operating physical remains of the firm's once vast Skagit railroad network is seen now on the Mount Vernon Terminal Railway as their Baldwin V0-1000 diesel switches cars in North Mount Vernon. Using a little imagination the logging and interurban electric heritage can still be envisioned as you follow the

CLEAR LAKE ANNUAL COMPANY PICNIC, May 10, 1919. Hundreds attended and the highlight was a train ride up into the hills for a meal in one of the logging camps. Even a band was aboard the train. *Cress-Dale photos courtesy Mrs. F. G. Brown*

KEY MEN AT CLEAR LAKE LUMBER COMPANY, standing, L to R: Arthur Lewis, Byron Rutheven Lewis, president of the company, and Sidney B. Lewis, vice-president and general manager. Locomotive is 2-8-2 No. 200 with fireman Ed Wanes looking on. *Mrs. F. G. Brown*

FROM THE HILL looking south over Clear Lake. This was the appearance about 1920. Clear Lake was an industrial center in the area. *D. Kinsey, courtesy Mr. & Mrs. Jack Turner*

track along the riverbank and through the streets of Mount Vernon in 1989.

173

PUGET SOUND PULP AND TIMBER Number Six came to Skagit County from the Lake Stevens holdings of the Company. She had been built new as Cavanaugh Timber No. 3. She finished her days at Clear Lake. *Albert Farrow*

PUGET SOUND PULP AND TIMBER No. 8 in front of the Clear Lake shop September 7, 1938. She had worked for Puget Sound Sawmills and Shingle Company in Concrete until that firm went out of business. Puget Pulp picked her up for $4,500 in April of 1936, and brought her to Clear Lake. This is not the same shay as No. 8 pictured previously which was repossessed when the Company went into receivership in 1924. *Albert Farrow.*

CABOOSE No. 101 sits alongside the Company shops at Clear Lake. *Albert Farrow*

IN CLEAR LAKE, Mike No. 101 looked like this in later years. Here she is seen behind the shops at Clear Lake. The date is September 7, 1938 and the end is near for the railroad. *Albert Farrow*

(right) **BEFORE HER ARRIVAL IN CLEAR LAKE**, 2-8-2 No. 101 worked for the Smith-Powers Logging Company in Oregon. Puget Sound Pulp and Timber brought her to Washington State to do mainline duty on the Puget Sound and Cascade Railway. *Railroad Museum Of Pennsylvania (P.H.M.C)*

175

MOUNT VERNON TERMINAL's current power is this Baldwin VO1000 seen here in the shadow of I-5 freeway at the railroad's enginehouse in the fall of 1987. *Dennis Thompson*

176

THE FOREST AND THE RAILROAD SWITCHBACK, a scene repeated countless times in Washington timberlands. This view is of Clear Lake Lumber Company. *Cress-Dale photo, Dennis Thompson Collection.*

PUGET SOUND PULP AND TIMBER. When the railroad from Clear Lake was abandoned, this scene became common at the old railroad log dump at Mount Vernon. *Courtesy Georgia-Pacific Corp.*

Lbr Co.
Big Lake

CHAPTER 7

THE HEYDAY OF BIG LAKE

Day Lumber Company

In the 1890s, Shrewsbury and McLain operated a mill on Big Lake. In May of 1899, they sold out to Parker Brothers. Following only seven months operation, J. H. Parker was found completing what was called *one of the biggest transfers of property that has ever taken place in Skagit County...the sale of all the interests of Parker Brothers, including the sawmills and lumber camp, as well as stock on hand to Joe Day Lumber Company.* The price tag was $100,000, which was a large sum of money for its day. J. H. Parker then moved to Pilchuck to form Parker Brothers and Hiatt Company.

Joseph D. Day came to Washington State from Rhinelander, Wisconsin. On July 11, 1900, J. D. Day filed Articles of Incorporation in the Skagit County Court House with capital stock of $100,000. First trustees were: J. D. Day, now of Big Lake; George W. Maguire and Charles S. LaForge, both of Rockford, Illinois.

The new firm evidently overhauled the mill, for by summer they had installed new machinery and were ready to take car orders for finished lumber.

For the first two years, all their logging was done close around the lake near the mill. In the spring of 1902, the Company built a steamboat for use on the lake towing log rafts. She was launched that summer.

That same year Joe Day sold the operation to two other Rhinelander men but retained an interest and stayed on as manager. The new owners were J. C. Wixon and C. C. Bronson.

The little steamboat was busy on the lake for four years until the nearby timber was exhausted. Later, she did some work for other firms, such as Nelson-Neal Lumber Company. A fire loss of $3,000, in 1905, was the only break in the routine of business.

In 1906 new transportation was required to reach fresh timber. A railroad was begun leading out of the mill yard to the northeast. A Porter 0-4-0 tank locomotive with a single-truck tender was obtained from an unknown source to work on the railroad.

By 1907, steel rails had been extended some two miles and the Company had two donkey engines pulling logs out of the woods. A fleet of nine flatcars hauled the logs to the mill.

Business continued about the same until 1911, when a major purchase was made in the form of a brand new

DAY LUMBER COMPANY pile trestle east of Big Lake. As the company pushed steel into the hills near Walker Valley their grades cut through coal deposits. This caused considerable interest and limited development was attempted. *D. Kinsey courtesy Whatcom Museum of History and Art*

BEGINNINGS OF DAY LUMBER SAWMILL activities looked like this - including help from "horse" power. *D. Kinsey courtesy Josephine Hoffman*

locomotive from the Baldwin Locomotive Works. She was a 2-6-2 and was numbered "2" on the Day Lumber roster. The railroad by this time extended into the area east of Big Rock and across this flat valley floor to the lake ran the Baldwin.

Within a span of two years the flatland logging had finished and eyes were cast to the foothills of Cultus Mountain for more timber. In 1913 the almost new Baldwin was traded in on a new Shay locomotive in anticipation of future logging over steep grades. The Shay was construction number 2708, a 3-truck machine carrying road number 3. The Baldwin was resold by the Lima Shay agents to the Columbia and Nehalem River Railway as their No. 119.

By the summer of 1913, Day Lumber had completed their new barns and the July 31, 1913, **Mount Vernon Herald** reported, *Frank Roberson, foreman of the Day Lumber Company's ranch says he has just completed harvesting 280 tons of A-1 hay.* Also that year the sawmill received a new re-saw, planer, matcher, surfacer and sizer.

More news of Day Lumber was printed in the **Herald** of July 9, 1914: *J. C. Wixon, president, stated, "Two new veneer kilns have been built and a water tube boiler with a capacity of 800 h.p. has been installed. The boiler stands 37 feet high."*

THE ONE SPOT. Day Lumber Company's first locomotive; little is known about where she came from. Standing in gangway to cab is engineer James A. Barringer; on rear of tender tank is Pete Osborn and Mr. Layhe sitting on log. *Josephine Hoffman*

A new 80-ton Climax locomotive was purchased in 1916. Her spot plate displayed road number 7 on the Day roster; there appear no reasons why numbers 4, 5 and 6 were not used.

The Timberman for 1917 reported four miles of railroad in use and two geared locomotives (these would have been numbers 3 and 7). The disposition of the little Porter engine is unknown.

In 1919, Joseph D. Day passed away. The vacancy caused by his death was filled by Frank F. Day on December 31, 1919. Trustees for the firm on January 21, 1920, were J. C. Wixon, F. F. Day and R. R. Clark.

POST CARD VIEW of the left side of No. 1 with crew. *Rod Crossley*

By 1921 Day Lumber Company had twelve miles of railroad and the two geared locomotives in use.

Eight donkey engines were hard at work in the woods the following year and the Company employed 125 men logging fir, spruce and hemlock. In April of that year the firm purchased new railroad logging cars from Pacific Car and Foundry with a price tag of $19,300.

EARLY RAILROAD LOGGING near Big Lake covered relatively flat lands allowing use of rod locomotives. This photograph by Darius Kinsey show the area as well as Day Lumber's first two steam locomotives. As timber here was quickly cut out, loggers were left to face the steep country to the east where motive power such as these were of little use. *Josephine Hoffman.*

RARELY PHOTOGRAPHED was Day Lumber's Shay No. 3. She was captured here about 1917. *John Labbe*

A fire in 1923 destroyed a good part of the mill and surrounding buildings. This closed the plant for almost a year and during that time E. L. Conner purchased C. C. Bronson's share of the Company.

When they reopened in 1924, another Shay had been added to the roster, a used locomotive which came from Oregon. She was only four years old and was construction number 3144. It is not known what road number she carried at Day Lumber.

The Company was now at its all-time peak of activity on its railroad with twenty miles of logging railroad laid with 56 to 66 pound rail. Grades ran as

Map No. 15 The Seattle, Lake Shore & Eastern RR was built through the Three Lakes area in 1891. It was briefly known as the Seattle and International RR before becoming Northern Pacific's mainline to British Columbia via Sumas in 1901. For the next 30 years the bulk of the traffic on this portion of the line came from the connecting logging companies as they cut away virtually all the merchantable standing timber on the western slopes of the Cultus Mountains.

By comparing this map with map no. 11 on page 149 one can note the changes occurring between 1911 and 1917. Day Lumber Company's logging railroad was probably the most complex (and redundant) of all Skagit County railroads. Its railroad is therefore highlighted on this and the following two maps.

During 1917, Day Lumber's principal activities were centered in Walker Valley where a cut for one of its spurs exposed a coal seam and spawned the Blumont Coal Company. *Map by RD Jost MD 1989*

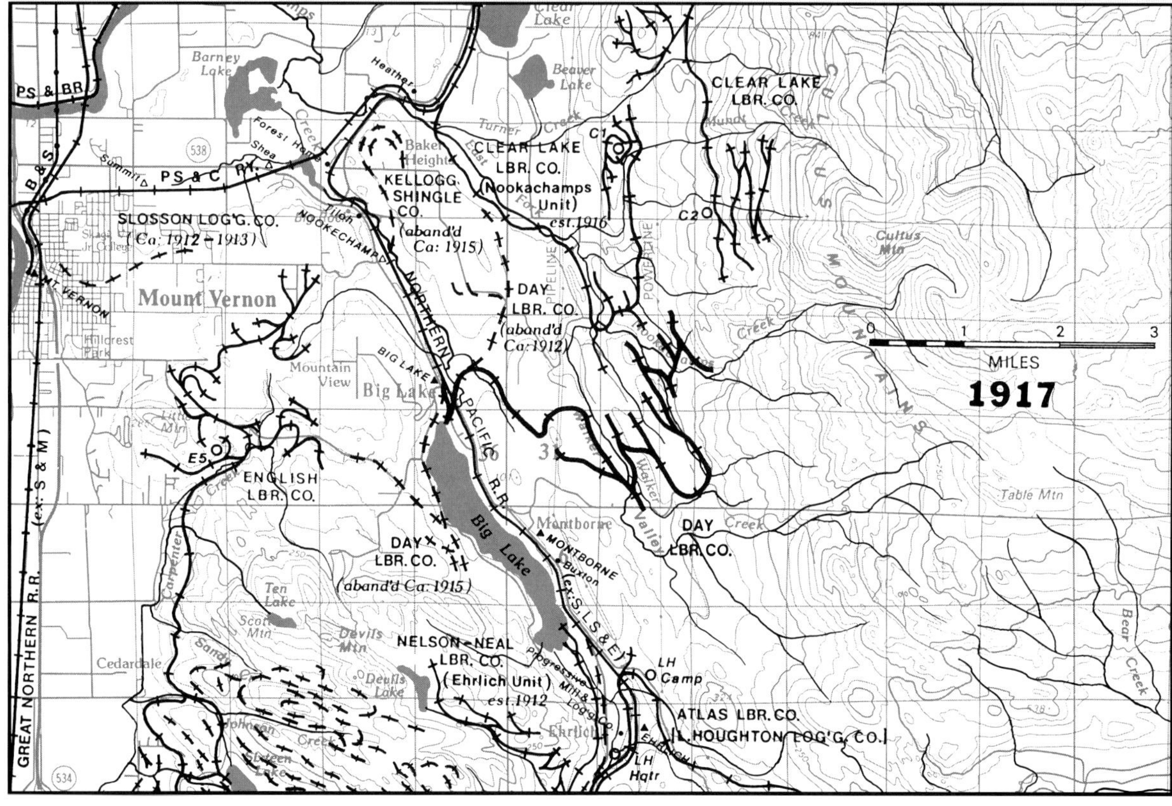

steep as ten percent. Logging cars numbered fifty with the new addition from Pacific Car and Foundry. They had three high-lead shows, electric lights, ten donkey engines and employed 125 men.

Big Lake was largely a "Company" town. The big red barns of the Day Lumber Company ranch were almost a trademark of the little settlement, and remain there today. There was a Company general store downtown. The mill was the major industry of the area and in peak years

DAY LUMBER'S ONLY ROAD LOCOMOTIVE, the two-spot, pauses for the photographer in the area north of Big Lake. She carried 3,500 gallons of water, 1,200 gallons of fuel oil and weighed 205,000 pounds. James Barringer standing in the gangway. She was traded in on a new Shay locomotive in 1913. *Art Barringer*

Map No. 16 Day Lumber Company gradually extended its Walker Valley operation southeast into higher country. 183
Some of the spurs built by Day were utilized for the mainline of Nelson-Neal's Montborne unit. At this time English Lumber Co. was building a new mainline into the Pilchuck watershed and the focus of activity for Clear Lake Lumber Co. had shifted further east along the south bank of the Skagit River.
Map by RD Jost MD 1989

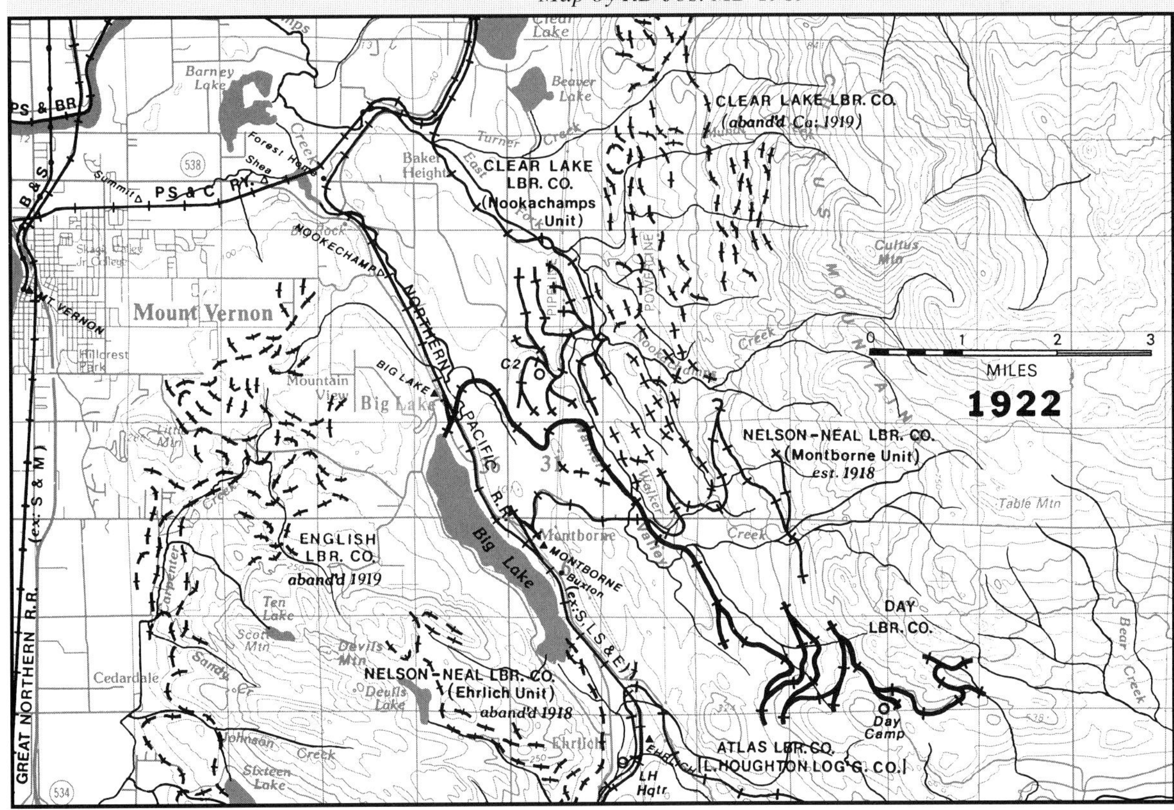

produced as much as 21,452,600 feet of lumber and 60,000,000 shingles per year.

An accident in the spring of 1924, derailed the Oregon Shay and received this mention in **The Timberman**: *Operations at the Day Lumber Company's camp were handicapped for a few days when its 110-ton Shay locomotive was derailed on a 4% grade, three miles from camp and 11 miles from Big Lake, where the company's mills are located. There were 11 cars of logs in the train but only one was ditched. A broken rail caused the accident. The locomotive was practically undamaged.* The locomotive gained a reputation of being rough on track.

(above) **THE COMPANY STORE** during the heyday of Big Lake. The maple tree in front provided a shady spot to visit during the summer. In modern times the maple trees are all that remain. The store dates to about 1925. *Dennis Thompson collection*

(right) **BOARDWALKS** link store, homes and sawmill in this early view looking down the road into the millsite. *Dennis Thompson collection.*

(below) **AT BIG LAKE DEPOT**, Ten-wheeler No. 342 waits for the high-ball. She is an 1889 Baldwin. Day Lumber Company's line passed under the N.P. near this location. *Josephine Hoffman*

184

Another accident occurred about this era, with Climax No. 7. Art Barringer remembers her starting out from camp headed towards Walker Valley with nine loaded log cars. She got out of control and the train crew jumped off. The train made it to the bottom of the grade, however, on a curve there the engine jumped the track and went into the woods. The nine loads stayed on the track and slowed to a stop on the upgrade. The 7-spot was loaded into five gondola cars and sent to Skagit Steel and Iron Works in Sedro Woolley to be put back together.

Even though the scope of Day's business was extensive in 1924, the health of the organization seemed questionable and the May issue of **The Timberman** carried a list of equipment offered for sale by the E. P. Jamison Company on behalf of Day Lumber. On the list was two 80-ton Shays and other various cars, steel and speeders. The article also stated that Jamison would operate the plant which indicates it was for sale as an operating unit. About this time Frank Day purchased property near Wenatchee and was said to be ready to leave this area.

DAY LUMBER COMPANY BARNS on the Company ranch are seen here. The main barn remains in 1988, as a local landmark of early days. *Josephine Hoffman*

In 1925 there was another fire in the mill and the Company went into receivership.

The mill was sold in April 1926, and most machinery went to Skagit Mill Company. Some also went to the Alpine Lumber Company and the rest went to dealers for stock. Frank Day sued the creditors, alleging mismanagement of the Company. He won a verdict of $105,000 in the Skagit County Court. The decision was appealed but the outcome is not now known.

DAY LUMBER COMPANY No. 2 and train drift across level land of the early days. *Josephine Hoffman*

186

SETTING UP CAMP ABOVE MONTBORNE at Day Lumber Company
Camp cars are brought in on the railroad and set into sidings. Small additions are built on site.
Next, steps are built and small buildings set onto skids. Even some electrical wiring is now in place.
Foundations are simple, but offer stability over railroad trucks. Camp is nearly ready for use. *All photographs courtesy Bert Kellogg*

DAY LUMBER COMPANY CLIMAX No. 7 new at the factory in 1916. "Comments on the Climax please me. And again, most men who worked with them will admit they could outhaul a Shay easily, even if they didn't like them otherwise. I am sometimes asked, 'where did they get so much power over the Shay and Heisler?' And really I am at a loss to give any reasons. They had the smallest piston displacement size for size of any of the three yet were much more powerful. And the gear ratio compares closely with Shay. Heisler though did have a lower ratio gears and compensated for it by larger cylinders. A Heisler of course could out-run a Climax or Shay in speed." *Photograph and comments: Walter Casler, past Climax Manufacturing Company employee and historian.*

PHOTO STOP IN THE TIMBER shows off Climax No. 7 early in her working career. She was the mainstay of Day's woods power. *John Wepler*

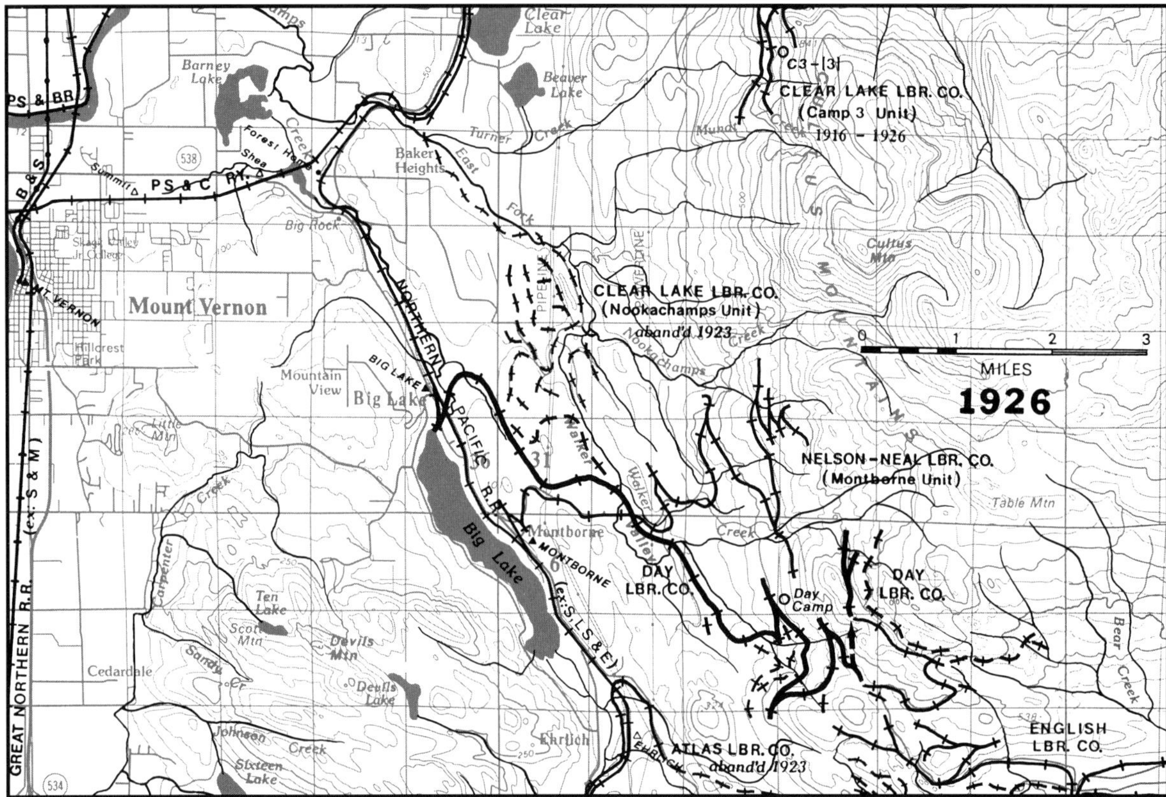

188

Map No. 17 Day Lumber Company appears to have built its railroad without due consideration for future operations. This map depicts the camp relocation, the incline and the realignments which were undertaken in an apparent effort to facilitate more efficient operations. The year is 1926; Day Lumber's last year.

By 1926, English Lumber Co. would be the only logging company which had its origins in the Three Lakes area to still be in business.

Montborne Lumber Co. took over the operations of Nelson-Neal Lumber Co. in 1927 and by then was the operator of the only logging railroad still active in the area covered by this map; it was, however, not the last. Montborne Lumber Co. ceased operations in 1930.

English Lumber Co. wrote the epilogue to railroad logging in the Three Lakes area when, for a brief period in 1931, it operated over the abandoned line of the Atlas Lumber Co. to log two quarter-sections of land to the south end of Walker Valley which was owned by Dempsey Lumber Co. *Map by RD Jost MD 1989*

THE TWO SPOT. Standing on the grounds of the Baldwin Locomotive Works, Philadelphia, Pennsylvania, Day Lumber Company No. 2 is fresh from the erecting floor and waiting shipment to Skagit County. The year is 1911. *Railroad Museum of Pennsylvania (P.H.M.C.)*

CHAPTER 8

TO DEVIL'S LAKE BY RAIL

Nelson-Neal Lumber Company

Campbell's Spur was located on the Northern Pacific Railway, 1½ miles south of Clear Lake where the Puget Sound & Cascade Railway crossed the NP. However, the PS&C is not there any more...and neither is the Northern Pacific. Nookachamps Creek still flows through the spot crossed by a new Highway 9 bridge and the home of Paul Wilcox, Sr. still rests on a little hill overlooking the area.

At this location in 1891, a shingle mill was erected on one side of the Northern Pacific. On the other side of the tracks a small settlement was established. A spur track led into the little mill and the place was named Campbell's Spur.

In 1893, the mill was sold to John Nelson and Frank S. Neal and the Nelson-Neal Lumber Company was born. Passing years provided expansion and in 1899, a son, Reid, was born to the Nelsons and mill production reached 25,000,000 shingles. When mill output climbed to 34,000,000 in 1901, the partners began to look for a new site for a larger mill.

The young company selected the town of Montborne as their new home and the old mill was sold to Snohomish gentlemen in the fall of 1902, for $15,000. Construction proceeded on the new mill and it went into operation July 1903.

The first logging to be done by the relocated firm was in the area around the south end of Big Lake. The logs were put in the lake and secured in small "tows." Assisted by a good south wind and a few strong hands the logs were moved to the mill by muscle power. An anchor was dropped in the lake a few hundred feet north of the waiting log tow and a hand winch used to move the logs. Step-by-step the one mile or so to the mill was traveled and with any luck from the wind the logs would drift the last quarter mile. The Company operated in this fashion through 1907, manufacturing both shingles and lumber in the new plant. By this date the Company was also operating a general store in Montborne.

Beginning new expansion, Nelson-Neal bought out Grammer's logging camp in May of 1906. Three months later, on August 14, Articles of Incorporation were filed in the Skagit County Court House for the Nelson-Neal Lumber Company. Capital stock was $200,000.

It followed within the year that ex-Governor Lind of

ON THE DEVIL'S LAKE line, Heisler and crew appear ready to leave camp. Train air brakes had been added to the little locomotive for the more severe grades Nelson-Neal now encountered. Unusual engine shed for the Heisler provided shelter with very minimal effort and cost. *Reid Nelson*

LINDWOOD The first railroad operation of Nelson-Neal began here near Bryant. *Reid Nelson*

Minnesota came into the Company and his son, Norman Lind, became secretary of Nelson-Neal Lumber Company.

Four new Sumner upright machines were delivered to the shingle mill in 1907, which improved operation. That year the Company officers were: John Nelson, Montborne, president; Frank S. Neal, Los Angeles, California, vice-president; Norman Lind, Everett, secretary/treasurer.

The Company obtained timberlands just north of Bryant and plans were made to move the logging to that location. It now became desirable to build a railroad to carry on the business. In 1908, track was laid from an interchange with the Northern Pacific at Bryant, north just over a mile to the new camp. The camp was named Lindwood in behalf of the gentleman from Minnesota.

Nelson-Neal purchased a shiny new Heisler locomotive in January of 1909; she weighed 42 tons, had 15 x 12 inch cylinders, was lettered No. 7 and was built under construction number 1152. To this day it is not known why Nelson-Neal's only locomotive was numbered "7." Perhaps it was meant to be good luck. The new locomotive arrived equipped with "steam jam" engine brakes only and was not equipped for train air.

Northern Pacific logcars were used at Lindwood, loads being sent via NP to Montborne.

The logging at Bryant lasted but two years, at which time the Company moved into newly acquired holdings at Ehrlich. Mr. Pingry, of the Pingry-Day Mill at Ehrlich, retired and their plant was closed. Nelson-Neal purchased their timber holdings which extended west from Ehrlich high into the Devil's Lake region. It happened that Northern Pacific had recently relocated their mainline and Nelson-Neal used their abandoned grade from Ehrlich across the flat valley floor to their old log dump at the south end of Big Lake. Today, Highway 9 is built on a portion of this old grade.

From Ehrlich, Nelson-Neal built south and west up the mountain using two switchbacks. The **Skagit County Times** of August 17, 1911 reported: *The grade stakes are all set for a logging road to be built up through Devil Creek Gulch and extending from Big Lake to Devil's Lake.* *(see map no. 15, page 182)*

John Nelson died in Seattle on November 15, 1913 at the age of 50; Frank Neal took over the Company.

About 1912, the heavy grade to the Devil's Lake country made it necessary to improve the brakes on the logging trains. This was accomplished by adding air

MILL SITE of Nelson-Neal Lumber Company at Montborne. Frank Day, of Day Lumber Company, eventually became president of this operation during its last years when the firm was succeeded by Montborne Lumber Company. *Inez Farmer*

equipment to the Heisler. An air tank was provided on each side of the smokebox and a single-stage air pump was mounted just ahead of the right side cylinder. Now each skeleton log car could be equipped with automatic air brakes.

During the days of the Ehrlich camp, log tows were sometimes moved up the lake by using Day Lumber Company's old steam tug boat.

Nelson-Neal management was in good spirit on May 28, 1914 for the **Mount Vernon Herald** of that date stated: *The Nelson-Neal Lumber Company shut down last Saturday to permit their employees to attend the circus at Sedro-Woolley.*

The Ehrlich camp finished in 1918 and the entire outfit returned to Montborne, this time to stay. A new railroad was begun running east from Montborne toward Walker Valley. One switchback took the new line from the mill to the top of the low hill on the east edge of Big Lake. The upper leg of this switchback was located approximately where the Walker Valley Road now leaves Highway 9 *(see map no. 16, page 183)*. The railroad was gradually extended east across Walker Valley and crossed the Day Lumber Company railroad at the east edge of the valley.

In 1924, the Company had one high lead setting and employed 75 men. Five miles of railroad were in use utilizing 56 pound rail, eight skeleton cars and two flat cars. Maximum grade was seven percent. Five donkey engines were in use and the firm was producing 60,000 feet of timber per day. Nelson-Neal's operation extended north to border Day Lumber Company's holdings and south to meet English Lumber Company.

Frank Neal died in 1924. His death left the Company in a state of turmoil. The situation continued until 1926, when on June 2 the Company sold its physical assets to a newly created firm, the Montborne Lumber Company. Price: $60,000. This marked the end of active operations for Nelson-Neal Lumber Company although the firm still operated for a time "on paper."

MONTBORNE LUMBER COMPANY

At the head of the new organization was John Nelson's old logging foreman, Ray Tippie, who with Thomas Smith filed Articles of Incorporation for Montborne Lumber Company on May 19, 1926. Capital stock was $40,000.

On August 5, 1927, Montborne Lumber Company purchased machinery from the Portland Machinery Company in the amount of $2,300. **Abbey's Register** in that year reports them running one side, employing forty men using four donkey engines and operating eight miles of railroad. They also had one speeder.

By this time the outfit was getting into rough country and climbing up Cultus Mountain *(see map no. 17 on page 188)*. To handle this terrain they purchased a used

3-truck Shay locomotive in June of 1928 for $5,000 from the Climax Manufacturing Company. It is thought this may have been Shay construction number 773 which came from Samish Bay Logging Company. The locomotive weighed almost twice that of the old Heisler and was purchased on contract which was paid off in May of 1929.

The future must have appeared bright for a second Shay was purchased in April of 1929. She was a large 3-truck machine reported to weigh 110 tons, obtained from a Portland dealer.

Misfortune followed rapidly. The Heisler was wrecked in February 1930. The damage was such that the insurance company wrote to the Heisler dealer in Tacoma for a repair estimate to determine if she was worth fixing.

During this time it is said the large Shay was found to be far too big for the railroad and spent more time on the ground than on the track.

Then the final blow came when a forest fire burned out the railroad. A sizeable amount of timber was left sound, however, the management elected to go out of business rather than rebuild the railroad.

Receivers were appointed the first of October 1930 for the Montborne Lumber Company, the company listing liabilities of $100,000.

When this happened a portion of the ownership reverted back to Nelson-Neal, although there is no evidence that the old company ever regained any active operations.

During later days of Montborne Lumber they had been using Northern Pacific cars to haul logs. Several of these cars were now stranded on the burned out railroad. Rex Everett, with three others, obtained a contract with the NP to bring out some of these cars in 1931. Delivered to the NP interchange at Big Lake, the logcars would bring $290 cash each.

The four men worked forty days on the project, slowly patching the old rails together just enough to roll each car down the hill as they were located. They camped where they were working. Rex recalls finding the big Shay locomotive sitting derelict, blocking their work by being precisely on the switchpoints of one of the switchbacks. After many hours of working and sweating they managed to nudge the huge machine far enough out on the tail track to be out of their way. Other derelict equipment was left in a gravel pit on the lower slopes of Cultus Mountain. Among this equipment was found the damaged Heisler. And here, in this gravel pit, sometime later, the scrap iron crew from Star Machinery performed their deadly work with the cutting torch.

Rex and his friends finished their "car collecting" and were rewarded at Big Lake when they presented Northern Pacific with 14 of their skeleton logging cars. The money collected from the NP amounted to a goodly sum for those depression days.

After a short time one B. H. Jones put together a shingle mill out of what was left of the Montborne Lumber Company property. Not being able to get the timber out he entered into an agreement with Reid Nelson whereby Reid would receive half the profit if he could deliver the shingle bolts. Reid Nelson then spoke

BUILDERS VIEW of Nelson-Neal Heisler No. 7. This 1909 model locomotive weighed in at 42 tons. *Courtesy Walter C. Casler*

A CRIB BRIDGE provides a location for photographs as well as a break in the day's work for this track gang working on the railroad. *Bert Kellogg*

to Sid McIntyre of Skagit Steel & Iron Works in Sedro Woolley and arranged to have them build a gas car with a flat bed trailer suitable to haul small logs and shingle bolts over the old Montborne railroad. The track was patched up once again and Reid operated his "gas car" business until about 1935 when he made an outright purchase of 26 million feet of timber wherein he was working. He then built a truck road from Montborne to Cultus Mountain.

The railroad was scrapped shortly thereafter.

BIG TIMBER, SMALL LOCOMOTIVES is a concept captured in this scene during early logging at Nelson-Neal Lumber Company. From an old photo postcard postmarked Nov. 1911. *Inez Farmer/Jack Turner.*

196

WOOD BURNING steam donkey belches smoke as the crew pauses in loading out the day's production. Nelson-Neal and their successor, Montborne Lumber Company, usually used Northern Pacific skeleton logcars for transportation. *Rod Crossley*

THE SEVEN SPOT and train of logs about 1910. *Bert Kellogg*

2033

AND BEHIND EVERY TREE

Thirty-Eight Logging Railroads

ATLAS LUMBER COMPANY

Today, the town of McMurray is a picturesque community nestled around the lake of the same name. Second growth timber covers the surrounding hills. Travel through McMurray is now limited to the asphalt path of Highway 9 and the contemporary visitor must look closely to detect that the little settlement once echoed to the whistle of no less than three distinct railroad companies.

When Washington was still a territory, Lake McMurray held fast to its share of thick spruce, fir and cedar timberlands. Long a somewhat isolated region, the eyes of industry fell on the area shortly before 1890. The entrepreneurs involved were James H. Farnsworth, Marcus Kenyon and James E. Houghton, who, after some consideration, incorporated the McMurray Cedar Lumber Company on August 14, 1890. Having secured about 100 million feet of standing timber, the trio set about constructing a large sawmill and shingle mill on the lake. The mill site selected was at the northwest end of the lake and construction began that fall. When it was completed in the spring of 1891, it was said to be the largest inland sawmill in the state.

Along the west side of the lake, the town of McMurray had grown to include several lively businesses. April 1890 found a plat being filed for a new town named Medina, at the south end of the lake. Although short lived, it added substantially to the excitement of these growing times.

Coincident with all this activity, the Seattle, Lake Shore and Eastern Railroad opened service through McMurray, with Seattle to Sedro operations beginning in November 1890.

Hard times arrived by 1893 and many of the some one hundred employees of the big mill were laid off. The situation not improving, McMurray Cedar Lumber Company shut down completely in the fall of 1894.

In April 1895 the mill changed ownership. For a consideration of $25,000, Pacific Cedar & Lumber Company, of Seattle, purchased the holdings. The new operation was named the Atlas Lumber Company, with A. B. Graham as president and Charles E. Patten as vice-president and general manager. The mill returned to operation quickly, cutting shingles during the day and

A BEAUTIFUL PORTRAIT OF SHINGLE BOLT TRANSPORTATION. Grandy Lake Shingle Company railroad with Fordson power operated here by Elmer Smith. *D. Kinsey courtesy Whatcom Museum of History and Art*

200 **L. HOUGHTON LOGGING COMPANY** operated the woods railroad for the Atlas mill. Here Shay No. 2 crosses a crib bridge northeast of Lake McMurray. *Hiram Fosnaugh*

lumber at night. Conditions seemed to stabilize and the firm added new cottages to their company housing, as well as other improvements.

The summer of 1898 found Charles Patten, with a Mr. C. L. Bergen, forming a separate company named the Skagit Logging Company. In December 1899, Patten purchased controlling interest in the Atlas Lumber Company and reorganized the firm. It now became the Atlas Lumber and Shingle Company, with Mr. A. B. Graham as president and Mr. Charles E. Patten as vice president, secretary, treasurer and general manager.

By 1901 Skagit Logging Company was doing the logging for the Atlas mill and a logging railroad was included in their future plans. Atlas purchased a Shay locomotive in January 1902, and the railroad was under construction

A PART OF THE ATLAS MILL and the town of McMurray. Little trace of industry is found today. *Inez Farmer*

north through the town of Ehrlich. There is some confusion at this point because Skagit Logging Company disappears from records about this time. (The same name was later used by a different company in Clear Lake.) A new name enters the story in 1902, in the person of Leland Houghton, who in February of that year, is found to be operating the railroad logging for Atlas under his own organization, L. Houghton Logging Company. It is probable that both of these logging companies co-existed for a time working for Atlas. It is said that Charles Patten was president of L. Houghton Logging Company as well as the earlier firm.

L. HOUGHTON LOGGING COMPANY Shay No. 4 was purchased new by the company in 1910. She was a 70-ton locomotive and was later used by Hogg-Houghton at Glacier, Washington. This photograph was taken at Ehrlich. *Bert Kellogg*

Japanese laborers were brought to McMurray in 1902, to build logging railroad for the Atlas operation. About fifty in number, they were housed in unheated bunkhouses by Atlas. Later, as the Japanese began to take jobs in the mill, considerable unrest began to take shape between them and the other workers. While labor tension increased, the company went on to improve the mill by adding a 1,000-horsepower Corliss steam engine. Other modernization was accomplished as well, however, it failed to stop the labor strike that arrived in 1906. Several of the strike related incidents between white and Japanese workers resulted in court action before the trouble healed some months later.

The Company took out a $250,000 mortgage in 1908, which was satisfied four years later. That fact may be the reason why, in 1912, the name changed back to Atlas Lumber Company.

The physical plant at this time was extensive, filling ten acres. Five water reservoirs fed the sprinkling system in the mill, two dynamos generated electric power, there were lumber kilns and a shingle kiln with a capacity of 5,000,000 shingles. Atlas owned a boarding house which would accommodate sixty persons. There were thirty company cottages for employees. The Company shipped 90 to 110 railroad cars of product each month.

Just when conditions seemed their best a train wreck claimed the life of Charles Patten. The accident happened in Sedro Woolley when a train collided with the Northern Pacific depot. Following his death, it appears Mrs. Patten retained E. R. Hogg to run the mill, with Leland Houghton closely involved in the logging operations.

The L. Houghton Logging Company continued as the supplier for the Atlas mill. The railroad reached about twelve miles in length using two coal burning Shays, twenty-four sets of logging trucks, on 56-pound rail with six percent maximum grade. The railroad logging was concentrated in the hills north and east of Lake McMurray.

By the early 1920s Atlas began to run short of timber to harvest. English Lumber Company had logged extensively to the west, and in fact, was building their new Lake Cavanaugh mainline through McMurray in 1921. To the northwest Nelson-Neal had cut sizable holdings, and in the southern Big Lake country, Day Lumber Company was also operating a railroad. Atlas found themselves surrounded by other logging railroads.

Consequently, in 1923, the mill closed forever. The equipment was sold at auction by the Union Machinery and Supply Company of Seattle.

Leland Houghton and Ed Hogg purchased a large portion of the logging equipment and traveled on to other areas as the Hogg-Houghton Logging Company.

The Atlas shingle mill was sold to two men who ran it as a small business. Continuing to diminish in size over the years, it was finally demolished in 1969.

3969
Shingle Co.

(left) **BALD MOUNTAIN MILL COMPANY** reveals their entire motive power roster in this scene. Bald Mountain is seen in the background. *D. Kinsey photo courtesy Whatcom Museum of History and Art*

BALD MOUNTAIN MILL COMPANY mill pond in 1929. This railroad was narrow gauge and in places operated dual-gauge with English Lumber Company's trackage. *Bill Mason*

BALD MOUNTAIN MILL COMPANY

In 1925, a few of the employees of English Lumber Company formed a business of their own and built a shingle mill ten miles east of Lake McMurray along the English Lumber Company railroad. Lying in the shadow of Bald Mountain, the men named the firm Bald Mountain Mill Company. James O'Hearne, English's superintendent and logging engineer, was president; Oscar Rose, vice president and Harry S. Eaman, secretary/treasurer.

The fascinating feature of the Company was their railroad. A narrow gauge Fordson siderod locomotive was purchased from Skagit Steel & Iron Works and track laid with 20-pound steel rail. Part of the little railroad shared English Lumber's mainline, by adding a third rail between the standard gauge rails. This was the only known dual-gauge track in Skagit County and would certainly be a novel prototype for the railroad modeler.

The company operated without incident into the 1940s, at which time a Burns Mill Company of Anacortes ran the operation for a short time. The entire operation closed down in 1944, when English Lumber Company sold out to Puget Sound Pulp & Timber Company.

BALD MOUNTAIN MILL COMPANY view of train dumping shingle bolts with mill in background. Date is 1929. *Bill Mason*

BAY VIEW'S RAILROAD
Ballard Lumber Company

The Ballard Lumber Company was incorporated in Seattle, in the summer of 1902. Capital stock was $100,000 and officers were: W. H. Stimson of Los Angeles, president; James Roe, vice-president; F. F. Fisher, secretary; and C. W. Stimson, treasurer - the last three gentlemen all residing in Seattle.

The firm located a sawmill at Ballard, just north of Seattle, hence the origin of the name. The company's object in Skagit County was to log about 1,700 acres of timberlands belonging to them on Bay View Ridge.

The Stimson family, well known in the timber industry, formed the Ballard Lumber Company and a good share of the Bay View timber had been held under the ownership of The Stimson Land Company.

Between August and December of 1902, Ballard Lumber Company constructed 3½ miles of standard gauge railroad commencing at the town of Bay View and threading its way east into the timber of the ridge.

Christmas of the same year found the company putting 55,000 feet of timber per day into the salt water at Bay View. Ballard never had a mill in Skagit County; all their logs were boomed and shipped to their King County mill or sold on the open market.

It is a mystery to this day what locomotive Ballard first used on the ridge, but she got into trouble on May 24, 1903. The locomotive was pushing three empty logging cars back to camp and on the train was the wife of the superintendent, Mrs. F. A. Doty, her two year old son and her sister, Mrs. Roland. Rounding a curve the brakeman, J. C. Martin, discovered a loaded logging car rolling unattended downgrade toward them. He signaled the engineer who reversed the locomotive and ordered the passengers to jump. This they did without injury and shortly the tramp car struck the train scattering logs and doing minor

BALLARD LUMBER COMPANY'S trim little Shay poses just south of Bay View about 1907. *Cecil Weyrick*

damage to the empty cars.

The company shut down that winter and idled some seventy employees.

Activities resumed in the spring with the Crescent Cannery sending its pile driver to Bay View to drive two hundred piles for the Ballard Lumber Company. The trestlework was built out into the water at the south end of town and here logs were dumped to be boomed.

The high point at Ballard Lumber in 1904 was the arrival of a new Shay locomotive in late February or early March. Built by Lima on the twelfth of February, she was delivered by rail to Whitney Station. The Shay's trip across the flats to Bay View with no railroad connection, must have been noteworthy, but unfortunately not preserved for posterity.

She was a pretty little Shay, sporting a diamond stack and an oil headlight. Her spot-plate carried no road number and her pilot was rigged for link-and-pin couplers. Her engineer said, "it was a fine engine."

Logging continued until the winter of 1906, when the railroad was extended and camp moved further back into the timber. About one mile east of where the Josh Wilson Road now intersects the Farm-to-Market Road, a well was drilled. It was here the little locomotive took on water for her boiler; probably the only engine in the area that fed on well water.

Tragedy struck the company on June 9, 1906. Superintendent Frank A. Doty was caught between two loaded logging cars as they coupled and was killed. He was 39 years old and left a wife and 5 year old son.

LOGGING ON BAY VIEW RIDGE in the days before Ballard Lumber Company built their railroad through the area. *Galen Biery*

Two months later, as the camp was operating about where Bay View Airport is now, fire broke out in timber owned by the Minnesota Lumber Company of North Avon. The blaze burned north to the edge of the Ballard Lumber camp and damaged some of the camp buildings, before running its course.

In 1906 the firm was dumping between 65,000 and 75,000 feet per day of cedar, fir and spruce. The operation reached its height about 1907 with production climbing to 130,000 feet per day at tidewater. The railroad had extended to some 5-$^{1}/_{2}$ miles in length. Two steam donkey engines were in use along with thirteen sets of disconnected logging trucks.

In January of 1909, the company moved its camp buildings to the

THE BALLARD SHAY WORKS in the woods on Bay View Ridge. She was issued no road number by the company. *Pearl Hector*

south end of the ridge near Fredonia and began drilling another well. Logging commenced at that location and continued into 1910. Most of the timber owned by the company was now cut and following 1910, history leaves no record until one lone item appeared in **The Timberman** magazine in September of 1912: *Ballard Lumber Company, Seattle, have gone out of business.*

BUTLER LUMBER COMPANY

The Butler Brothers Lumber Company began logging in the Belfast area in 1900. Their first operation was with a road donkey while plans were made to build a sawmill. The mill became reality and the year 1902 found the new plant had produced 600,000 board feet of lumber. The company was located about two miles north and east of Belleville Station.

The little company grew and on August 6, 1906, ordered a brand new locomotive from the Stearns Manufacturing Company, Erie, Pennsylvania. They were now in the railroad business and proceeded to file Articles of Incorporation on December 1, 1906 as Butler Lumber Company. Signing the papers were S.M. Butler, Curtis N. Butler and R. G. Butler. Capital stock was $30,000.

The new locomotive was shipped from the East in January 1907. She was a 28-ton Heisler. Three miles of railroad were built extending east and north of the mill into fresh timber. Butler Lumber Company had no railroad connection with the outside world and when the new Heisler arrived it had to be hauled cross-country some two miles to the mill site.

In 1912 the company opened a retail lumber yard in nearby Burlington.

The length of the railroad never grew much beyond three miles. Rolling stock consisted of three flatcars.

At the end of eleven years of operation the company closed down in 1918 and the railroad was torn up. The little Heisler was sold to a logger in Northern California.

BUTLER LUMBER COMPANY MILL. The firm was a family owned company throughout its lifetime. *Fred Butler*

BUTLER LUMBER COMPANY HEISLER No. 1 is seen in these two views during her younger years working about four miles north of Burlington. *D. Kinsey, Fred Butler*

206

D. J. CAIN

Dan J. Cain was a small businessman in Skagit County and the most fire-plagued logger in the region. He first appears in history running a shingle mill six miles north of Sedro Woolley in early 1898. Some addresses were given as Prairie - some as Thornwood. That July the mill burned, but within eight months he was operating again and had purchased six horses for getting logs to the mill.

He closed his mill in December 1900, to enlarge production to 50,000 feet daily, expecting employment to reach 65 men. Less than two years later the mill burned down again with an estimated loss of $35,000, of which $12,000 was insured. Before the fire he did manage to produce finished product - this time 8,000,000 feet of lumber.

He bounced back again in February 1903, ready to start cutting 24-inch shingles.

Business was quiet for a time and at the close of 1905, he bought a Shay locomotive. The following year his woods foreman was W. O. Brissendine and the company address was *Cain Spur Mill, Thornwood.* A short railroad was built south and east from Thornwood.

Another mill fire occurred in 1907, and on November 13, 1907, he was paid fire insurance losses in the amount of $34,369, by C. E. Bingham & Company of Sedro Woolley.

He next appears in Deming, in April 1909, incorporating as Cain Lumber Company, with capital stock of $25,000. Three months later he received another $1,800 for fire insurance losses, again from C. E. Bingham.

The final chapter for D. J. Cain appeared in **The Timberman**, April 1915:

A settlement has been made in the foreclosure suit brought against the Cain Lumber Company by C. E. Bingham, of Sedro Woolley, Washington. As a result of the settlement, unsecured creditors will realize probably about 50 cents on the dollar. Under the settlement all the company's property was conveyed to Bingham with the exception of two donkey engines, one locomotive and about 1800 feet of 56-pound rail. Bingham was required to pay Receiver Baldy $3,750 and release his claims against these items or personal property held under chattel mortgage. The total indebtedness of the company is estimated at $125,000; the original cost of its assets was approximately $100,000. The property of the company in-

BUTLER LUMBER COMPANY HEISLER in later days showed an unusual alteration, namely the sand dome moved to a location ahead of the stack. It seems reminiscent of a stocking cap pulled over the old girl's ears. *Stan Parker*

cludes 4½ miles of railroad, logging equipment, 1200 acres of timber lands and a shingle mill operated under the name of the United States Shingle Company.

COGSHALL AND METSKER

One of the pioneer mills of Sedro Woolley was built about 1891 by P. A. Woolley. A few years later it was sold and became the Frenzel-Heininger Mill which operated until the year 1905. A change of ownership again occurred in December of that year, this time transferring to L. A. Metsker of Tacoma and S. B. Cogshall, an eastern gentleman.

The mill was overhauled under the new management and in March of 1906, they incorporated with a capital stock of $28,000. First trustees were: S. M. Cogshall, L. A. Metsker, S. B. Cogshall and W. H. Morrison.

The little company put in a camp at Thornwood and 1½ miles of track the following year. They boasted two donkeys but listed no locomotive. Their daily production being only 30,000 feet, they could have had a tram road or gravity railroad, although by 1908, they were using Northern Pacific logging cars.

Business operated quietly until April 1910, when fire destroyed their dry kiln and about 500,000 shingles.

The following year in August, fire again struck - this time burning the entire mill to the ground. The company then appears to have gone out of business as no later evidence of them is found.

S. B. Cogshall appears again in 1921, as manager of the Grassmere Lumber Company, working in the Concrete-Hamilton area.

COWDEN LUMBER COMPANY

The Cowden Lumber Company built a small mill just above Sauk, Washington, in January of 1918. The next month they incorporated with a capital stock of $100,000. Signing the papers were Charles L. Riddle and A. Fitzhenry.

A railroad spur, 420-feet long, was built into the mill by the Great Northern Railway in June of 1918. Finished lumber was now shipped to market by rail. Logging was handled with a Washington road engine skidding logs in a straight line from woods to mill. As nearby timber was removed, materials were purchased to build a railroad to reach further into the forest. A 36-ton Heisler locomotive was purchased on contract with Hofius Steel and Equipment Company, September 29, 1919, for $5,000. The little railroad was built, switchbacking up the hill above Sauk, in a northeast direction. During the next three years it reached as much as two miles in length as logging extended to the boundry of state park land.

The little company soon fell on hard times and legal action was filed by Hofius in 1922, to reclaim the Heisler, as full payment had not been made. They succeeded in their desires and the locomotive was turned over to them by the Skagit County sheriff on March 24, 1922. This appears to have ended operations for Cowden Lumber Company. The Great Northern removed their spur in 1926.

DANAHER LUMBER COMPANY

Another eastern lumberman that moved west was Cornelius D. Danaher. He was, in 1891, president and general manager of both Danaher and Melendy Company and the North Branch and Sauble Railroad in

DANAHER LUMBER COMPANY Shay No. 1, c/n 2872 left the Lima plant in 1917. She was shipped to Darrington to work north into Skagit County. *Bert Kellogg*

THE BALD SIDE of Danaher's coal burning Shay. Interesting details include spark arrestor appliances, home spun lamp brackets, siphon plumbing and corrugated metal guard behind front truck. *Bert Kellogg*

Ludington, Michigan. By 1901, he was investing in northwest timber and looking for a permanent logging show in this region. In 1906, he purchased the plant of the West Coast Lumber Company in Tacoma and planned extensive improvements in the mill.

In 1910, C. D. Danaher was building a short logging railroad near Tacoma and was treasurer of the Skykomish Timber Company, president of the Diamond Mills Company in British Columbia, as well as president of the Danaher Lumber Company of Tacoma, Washington. At this time his activities became almost too numerous to trace. His investment in Skagit County came in 1916 when he opened a logging camp near Darrington and began building railroad north into Skagit County.

Late in 1916, Danaher's camp was operating and logging had commenced in the Sauk River Valley, two and one-half miles north of Darrington. Danaher was one of the first outfits to offer improved benefits and wages for loggers, and his camp was considered one of the best in the region. The camp employed 115 men in 1917 and was working two sides. Three Lidgerwoods were in use, one with a tower and two were tree-rigged. A Tacoma 10 x 15 machine was in use with a high lead. A Marion steam shovel was used to build railroad grade. Locomotives were three Shays, a 42-ton, a 70-ton and an 80-ton. The outfit lay alongside Sound Timber Company holdings and some of the railroad was operated jointly by both concerns. Danaher log trains ran into Darrington where loads were sent on to Everett on the Northern Pacific. They were then rafted and towed to the Tacoma mill.

A Sessoms lowering car was purchased in 1920, presumably for the Darrington camp. In 1921, another camp opened at Port Orchard.

Cornelius D. Danaher drowned in Puget Sound on March 17, 1921, under mysterious circumstances. Speculation ran that his support of labor movements of the time lead to his untimely death and perhaps of other than normal cause. Following his death the company went into receivership listing one million dollars in assets. The Darrington logging show was sold in mid-1922 to A. F. Anderson Logging Company of Seattle. Included were 45 million feet of timber, 10 miles of railroad, two locomotives and three Lidgerwoods. The Danaher/Anderson connnection to the Northern Pacific near Darrington became known as "Andron," an obvious contraction of the name Anderson. Railroads such as the Northern Pacific would frequently create such names for commercial spurs and their own use in timetables and milepost references. Anderson, or Andron Logging Company, as it eventually became known, left Darrington by 1930, their logging completed.

DICKEY AND ANGEL LOGGING COMPANY

When C. P. Dickey dissolved his partnership with J. C. Stitt in 1902, he immediately negotiated for more timber in order to remain in the lumber business. He entered into a new partnership, this time with R. L. Angel, and together they purchased the Ball timber near Fredonia,

DICKEY AND ANGEL began railroad logging at Fredonia. Their time there was short and they moved on to Machias, never to return to Skagit County. This little Climax went with them. *Stan Dexter*

in May of 1903.

Three months later, the new partners were laying railroad track into their timber in preparation for getting logs out to the Great Northern Railway, where they were to be shipped to Anacortes and boomed. If they employed the use of their own locomotive at the Fredonia camp, it has never been recorded.

The camp operated through 1904, when the company made plans to expand and move to another area. December 9, 1905, Articles of Incorporation were filed by C. P. Dickey and R. L. Angel for the Dickey and Angel Logging Company. Principal place of business was to be Mount Vernon. Capital stock was $20,000.

During the first three months of the new year Dickey and Angel moved from Fredonia to a new camp at Machias, in Snohomish County. Before leaving Skagit County they ordered a new 28-ton Climax locomotive, construction number 636, for the new camp, however, she was apparently broken in at Fredonia. Within a year a second locomotive was added to the little company's roster. They never returned to Skagit County.

ERICKSON AND FUHRMAN

In July 1925, two men purchased a 37-ton Shay locomotive on contract from Hofius Steel and Equipment Company of Seattle. The price was $6,750. The men were the team of A. H. Erickson and Frank Fuhrman and that September they began railroad logging for Jennings and Nestos at Rockport. They had two miles of track. In April 1926, they added $11,000 worth of logging equipment.

The following June they moved into the Mount Baker National Forest near Newhalem and began to remove the first of 11,000,000 feet of timber they had available. In August they lost a bunkhouse and a cookhouse in a fire.

In the spring of 1927, they obtained 100,000,000 feet of timber near the mouth of Ilabot Creek. A railroad was planned with a bridge to cross the Skagit River to connect to the Skagit River Railway east of Rockport. The bridge would have been an ambitious undertaking and it is doubtful it was ever carried out. However, in 1927, they were reported to be on the new site with an additional rod locomotive.

On April 22, 1929, Union Machinery and Supply sold to Frank Fuhrman a locomotive for $1,440.

After this date the two gentlemen dropped out of sight. Erickson & Fuhrman were generally known as contract loggers, working for other firms. They often joined forces with the Skagit River Railway, sometimes logging or hauling for them, on other occasions leasing motive power to them for winter snow removal.

THIS IS THE ONLY KNOWN PHOTOGRAPH OF FABER LOGGING COMPANY. This scene, with foreman Harry Powell, was taken at Van Horn. The photos tacked on the building are by the photographer, Darius Kinsey. He would often do this to show samples of his work. It was an example of early sales marketing. *Mary Larsen*

FABER LOGGING COMPANY

Robert R. Nestos, and others, first appeared in Skagit County doing some logging around the mouth of Day Creek. The enterprise became a fully developed business firm when they incorporated in April 1920, as Faber Logging Company. C. E. Bingham and J. J. Peth (of the LaConner Peths) were in the new company, however, the Articles of Incorporation were signed by G. W. Childs and E. E. Boyd. Capital stock was $50,000. R. R. Nestos was a stockholder and general manager. B. R. Lewis, of the Clear Lake Lumber Company, was another stockholder.

The firm moved their equipment upriver to Faber where they built a short spur track from the Great Northern to the river. The timber belonging to Faber Logging Company stood on the opposite side of the river. The loggers purchased a 45-ton Climax oil-burning locomotive through B. R. Lewis, loaded her on a raft and floated it across the Skagit River. There, some three miles of railroad were built into the forest.

By the spring of 1921, the little company was cutting timber. Nestos, being something of a pioneer in the art of long-span high-lead logging, strung a skyline across the river. Next, he converted a 11 x 14 Washington donkey into a high speed machine by changing gears. The result was a fast skyline system moving logs across the Skagit where they were loaded out on the Great Northern. A turn of logs required about five minutes to make the trip across the river and be deposited on the spur. The skyline was 1,400 feet long.

During the summer of 1921, the company closed down. In October they resumed operation for a short time. Conditions were not in their favor because by year's end, Faber Logging Company went broke.

The Climax was returned across the river, delivered to the Great Northern interchange and sold for $5,000.

Two years later Bob Nestos joined forces with William Jennings and began logging near Marblemount.

FOREST MILL COMPANY

About 1918 or 1919, Lyle McNeill ran a small logging operation at Birdsview. Working with him was James O'Hearne, better known for his association with English Lumber Company. A spur from the Great Northern Railway was built from a point one mile west of Birdsview, south to the river. A small rod locomotive was purchased which is said to have been an ex-mainline, four-coupled engine dating from the 1880s. After 160 acres were logged, the enterprise moved to Ingersol's Crossing, two miles east of Birdsview.

A mill was erected back of Ingersol's, about one-quarter mile north of the Great Northern Railway. The operation was incorporated by A. R. Burtt, E. D. Gowdy, W. T. Garthley and Jos. Satterthwaite in 1921, under the name Forest Mill Company. A mill spur was built by Great Northern to serve the facility. Official Great Northern maps gave the spur the title: "McNeill and O'Hearne Spur, known locally as Forest Mill Spur."

FOREST MILL COMPANY made use of early Bulldog Mack motor trucks. This scene was taken on the south side of the Skagit River about one-half mile upstream along Loretta Creek in 1929. Trucks were snubbed down a "timber road" with a piece of skyline cable. As the truck wheels rolled down the hued timber road, lateral movement was prevented by a wooden "bull-rail" spiked along the timber inside the wheels. Lyle McNeill is seen on ground with his pipe. *D. Kinsey courtesy Dick Taylor and Ed Marlow.*

211

The old rod locomotive was brought up to the mill. She steamed occasionally for switching duty but soon found herself derailed in the mill yard and left to sit.

Simultaneous to the operation of Forest Mill Company, McNeill and O'Hearne created a separate entity, McNeill & O'Hearne Timber Company to function as contract loggers in the upper Skagit Valley. Forest Mill apparently consumed the output of this second firm but did so only on a very marginally profitable basis. Thus Forest Mill Company encountered difficulty by 1923. In that year, the Bank of California obtained a judgement of $58,588 against the firm and it was ordered sold at public auction. Then, July 7, 1925, the plant burned. Loss was $75,000, of which $19,161 was covered and paid through insurance with C. E. Bingham and Company, Sedro Woolley.

During the fire, the cab was burned off the old rod engine. John Pinelli recalls walking through the ruined mill many times in his youth and looking at the forlorn old locomotive rusting in the weeds...still on the ground.

In 1926 the Great Northern removed the spur into the old mill.

Sam Beck purchased the mill property in the 1920s and the locomotive was scrapped.

WILLIAM GAGE

A good example of a small businessman making history is found in the person of William Gage who operated a logging camp just up the Skagit River from Mount Vernon.

In 1882, Gage was busy building a logging tram-road adjacent to the river using 3 x 5 inch maple rails. Not satisfied to use animal power for his long range plans, he located a most interesting machine for sale in Snohomish County. It was the first locomotive entirely built in Washington Territory. Only a few months old, it was the creation of the Blackman Brothers who operated a logging railroad at Mukilteo. Having been builders of Blackman logging cars for some time, the firm had designed their own locomotive. The prototype left North Pacific Iron Works in Seattle in August 1881. Patents were issued in August 1883. The new locomotive was placed in service at Mukilteo on eleven percent grades which proved a bit severe and Blackman's attention shifted to producing a more powerful locomotive. It was at this time that William Gage seized the opportunity to introduce steam power to his Skagit County railroad, and outright purchase of the machine quickly

THE FIRST STEAM LOGGING LOCOMOTIVE IN SKAGIT COUNTY must be credited to William Gage. This Blackman creation and its style of operation is seen in these three views taken in Snohomish County just before the machine was sold to William Gage.

See Appendix B for patent drawings of this unusual locomotive. *Courtesy Walt Taubeneck and Marysville Historical Society.*

followed.

The locomotive was rated at ten horsepower and weighed 6,000 pounds. Gage seemed pleased and was heard complaining that he could not yard out timber fast enough for it to haul.

The railroad of William Gage was known to be about 1½ miles in length. Evidently only the one tract of timber was logged for by 1885 the little line disappears into history. One of the most obscure railroads in Skagit County, Gage deserves credit for having the first locomotive in the county and also the first locomotive built in Washington Territory.

GALBRAITH BROTHERS

On the south side of the Skagit River, about one quarter mile west of Pressentin Creek, a small operation existed for about one year. One of the Galbraith brothers from Acme built a quarter mile of track south into a small block of timber in 1938.

The firm leased Shay No. 4 and some logging cars from Puget Sound Pulp and Timber Company and went into business. The Shay brought loads out to the Puget Sound and Cascade Railway which was the common carrier name for Puget Pulp's railroad. Galbraith would take the loads an additional mile downstream to Camp 1 of Puget Sound Pulp and Timber where they were set out for the mainline train to market.

In the woods logging was carried out with crawler tractors. Head loader was Ernie Parker. Logging lasted only a short time and Galbraith finished in this location about 1939, just before the end of the Puget Sound and Cascade itself.

GRANDY LAKE SHINGLE COMPANY

A little-known shingle bolt railroad was that of the Grandy Lake Shingle Company. Incorporated in March of 1920, principals were John Nicoll, Thomas Nicoll, G. Pierce and L. Pierce. Capital stock was $20,000 and the place of business was listed as Grassmere.

This was the second of three narrow gauge lines in Skagit County, all of which were Fordson-powered and carried cedar blocks. The company operated near Grandy Lake for less than five years. *See chapter 9 introduction photograph, page 198* .

CHARLES JACKSON

Another obscure logger in Skagit County was Charles F. Jackson who operated an oxen-powered tram road about a half mile east of Burlington. Jackson must have kept close company with the camp of Millett and McKay as both loggers seemed to have been in the same neighborhood at about the same time.

In operation by 1882, Charles Jackson soon considered steam power and is reported to have ordered a Blackman locomotive in April 1883. Evidently he reconsidered because a year later he was still using ten yoke of oxen and no locomotive appeared forthcoming. His logging cars were Blackman cars running on 100-inch gauge wooden track, considered the widest track gauge in the region at that time. Logs were dumped in the Skagit River and taken to market.

The little tram continued to haul logs into the late 1880s before disappearing into history.

JENNINGS AND NESTOS LOGGING COMPANY

The Jennings and Nestos Logging Company was organized in early 1923. Following the failure of Faber Logging Company about a year earlier, Robert Nestos and William Jennings, both of Concrete, set up the new firm with A. Elfendahl, of Seattle, as president.

It has not been established whether or not Jennings and Nestos ever finished any of the logging first started by Faber Logging Company. It remains a glaring possibility as Robert Nestos was greatly involved in both organizations. Another close parallel is that both companies owned Climax locomotives, however, the fragments of history that have survived indicate they were not the same machine.

Facts show Jennings and Nestos obtaining 4,000,000 feet of cedar and fir from the government shortly after the new company's formation. The holdings were located beyond Marblemount, near Bacon Creek. It was in this area the firm began logging with a 60-ton Climax purchased from Superior Portland Cement Company in Concrete. The locomotive weighed 15 tons more than the Faber Logging Company Climax.

The company continued to log several small tracts between Bacon Creek and the Newhalem region in the years that followed. Most of the work was done with the Climax although it is said some truck logging was included. The timber was delivered to the Skagit River Railway, which transported it to Rockport. The final leg of the journey was over the Great Northern Railway to market.

JENNINGS AND NESTOS CLIMAX is seen here during her last days. This location was along the Skagit River Railway above Marblemount, about one mile downstream from where the logging line crossed the Skagit River. The year is 1940. *Dennis Thompson collection.*

A steam donkey was added to the equipment list in April 1925, purchased from Union Machinery and Supply Company for $1,750.

Jennings and Nestos continued in operation into the 1930s. Eventually the Climax came to be derelict along the Skagit River Railway and was later scrapped by Monte Holm.

McCOY AND PULLMAN PALACE CAR LOGGING COMPANY

One of Skagit's most colorful lumbermen was the Honorable Patrick W. McCoy, who did some pioneer "woods work" in the northwestern part of the county. Of Irish descent, McCoy displayed spirit and innovation. He established some of the earliest log drives on the Samish River and built a logging camp along that river by 1882.

As of the turn of the century McCoy had diversified his interests as well as his logging camps. He became president of the Bald Mountain Mining Company and expanded his logging operations to Edison where he employed some 45 men. He floated his logs to the bay where they were formed into booms and towed to market. The bulk of his output went to the Whatcom Falls Mill Company of Whatcom.

Around 1901, Pat McCoy distinguished himself by importing an elephant to enhance his production in the woods. The effort, though notable for inventiveness, was less notable for getting out logs. He was very quickly heard giving the order, "get rid of it as soon as possible." Further details of the venture were not made available.

McCoy did find success in another modern improvement however, it was in the form of a steam railroad. He began building a new camp one mile south of the new settlement of Bow, and railroad grade between that point and Edison. The year was now 1902. McCoy ran for a seat in the legislature and formed a new name for his logging firm in that year. Both efforts were successful. His new railroad became the McCoy and Pullman Palace Car Logging Company. There was no contest; this had to be the most eloquent name for a logging railroad in all of Skagit County!! He evidently had an agreement with Pullman to provide car building materials for this well-known railroad coach and car builder. Details, again, never seemed to be mentioned.

McCoy's railroad was constructed from a log dump on the Samish River just south of Edison, east directly alongside what is now the Sunset Road. Some eight miles of track were ultimately in use, with logging being done in the low hills northeast of Bow.

The new camp was of sufficient size to accommodate one hundred men, and was ready by December of 1902. During the same winter McCoy arranged for a diamond crossing to be laid by the Great Northern thus giving him rail access to the hills by crossing directly over that mainline carrier.

Now in the market for motive power, McCoy negotiated with A. J. McCabe, a used locomotive dealer. McCoy came up with a Baldwin 4-4-0 which had seen service on the Oregon Railway and Navigation Company. The deal was executed on Valentine's Day of 1903, but the old iron horse must have been a lame duck because

BEFORE PAT McCOY brought railroad logging to the Edison area, the firm of Howard and Butler was hard at work using four-legged power in the woods. Team, crew and skid road is seen here at the H&B operation on July 12, 1892. *Ruth Foster and Bert Kellogg*

within two weeks McCoy had traded her back for a different 4-4-0 - again a Baldwin.

Thus in April of 1903, all requirements were met and the McCoy and Pullman Palace Car Logging Company began running trains into Edison.

Over the next year McCoy's high-drivered locomotive gave the same performance as similar types had with other loggers; too slippery for grades and lack of power on woods rails. So McCoy ordered a new Shay which was subsequently built in 1904.

DURING PAT McCOY'S early railroad ventures he was known to have done some locomotive trading. This classic 4-4-0 was part of one deal, and she likely came to Skagit County, at least for a short time. *John Labbe*

For the duration of the railroad's life, operations were uneventful. McCoy was, in fact, considered to be a good employer who ran a consistently good operation. He was also known for having in his employ, according to Herb Neises, "some of the best poker players in the county."

The Shay usually made three trips per day from the woods, until the timber was logged out in 1910. At that time the little locomotive and all the logging equipment was sold to the Filion Mill Company of Port Angeles for a consideration of $50,000.

McCoy's interests now turned to other areas. In 1915, he had purchased 640 acres of timber along the newly relocated Northern Pacific just north of Sedro Woolley. There he put in another logging camp as a joint venture with George W. Loggie of Bellingham. The new partnership was known as McCoy-Loggie Timber Company. They purchased three donkey engines from Washington Iron Works and built enough railroad to deliver the logs out to the Northern Pacific at Thornwood.

Simultaneously, McCoy-Loggie began developing operations in Whatcom County and built five miles of railroad from the end of the Milwaukee branch at Welcome up the middle fork of the Nooksack River. When the harvest at the Thornwood camp finished, the Whatcom operation was ready to begin. This was the summer of 1916.

The following year a total of eight miles of railroad was in operation using a brand new 90-ton Shay. To follow over the next three years were a 60-ton Climax and a 70-ton Climax. The company was very active in the Welcome-Kulshan districts of Whatcom County in the 1920s. At that time it was sold to the Nooksack Timber Company, a St. Paul and Tacoma Lumber Company firm. This marked the end of McCoy's railroad activities and formed the core of what was to be the Nooksack Camp of St. Paul and Tacoma Lumber Company.

PAT McCOY'S LOG TRAIN arrives at the dump near Edison. His use of link and pin couplers can be observed here as an extended link hangs out of the locomotive's front coupler pocket. Hanging under the running board can be seen a longer extension which could be used to provide clearance and distance for overhanging logs. *Arne Johnson*

McCUISH LOGGING COMPANY

On the northern fringe of Skagit County, William McCuish operated a logging railroad west out of the little settlement of Prairie, near the county line. McCuish had logged in various locations, largely in Whatcom County, beginning near Maple Falls in 1901. He was of Scottish descent, born in Ontario, Canada, in 1865, and coming to Whatcom in 1890. Sometime after his arrival in Washington, McCuish became a partner with Ernest and George W. Christie, to form the McCuish and Christie Logging Company.

By 1915 McCuish's logging camp was working at Wickersham, just north of the Skagit County boundry, building railroad grade northeast out of town. The Wickersham operation came under incorporation in 1917, as Christie Timber Company, with the same partners. However, it appears McCuish diverted his efforts following this event to begin an operation entirely on his own in Skagit County at Prairie. Here, he was running McCuish Logging Company in the early 1920s with its own railroad and Shay locomotives. To celebrate the opening of his new logging camp there, McCuish held a dance one evening, open to the public. A Shay locomotive and crew car were dispatched to the county road to pick up the party-goers and a fine time was had by all.

While devoting these years to the development of his logging enterprises, McCuish also found time to be one of the co-founders of the Bellingham National Bank in Bellingham. He remained active in the banking business throughout the rest of his life.

McCuish's railroad at Prairie seems to have had a rather uneventful life with the exception of one story which has survived through the years. It seems in 1922, that McCuish took advantage of the Christmas break in logging activities to send one of his Shays down to Sedro Woolley to undergo repairs at Skagit Steel and Iron Works. The holidays passed and the Shay was again healthy and ready for work. In the dark early hours of January 10, 1923, McCuish employees W. A. Painter and George Parrish were at Sedro Woolley to steam the Shay north back to Prairie. The Northern Pacific furnished Mr. R. B. Barber to ride the locomotive, while it operated over their track, as a pilot. W. A. "Rastus" Painter took the throttle, and with George Parrish as fireman, the locomotive left Sedro Woolley in a heavy rainstorm. The trip was uneventful through the darkness until the little group left the Northern Pacific at Prairie and began climbing the woods line toward the McCuish camp. Barber was still in the cab because he was scheduled to return from the logging camp with another Shay locomotive which had been there on a rental basis from Clear Lake Lumber Company.

Steaming around a curve and onto a trestle the three men were not able to see the washed out trestle bents which had submitted to the rain swollen waters.

Up in camp the foreman and timekeeper waited all night for the locomotive that would never arrive. About six o'clock the next morning two loggers started out from Wickersham to walk to work at the camp. When they came to the bridge, which was only a few hundred feet from the county road, they started walking across, their kerosene lights leading them through the early morning darkness. Shortly they noticed an alarming buckle in the track. Closer inspection revealed the center trestle bents were washed out and the track and ties were hanging in mid-air. The two men then climbed down into the canyon, went up the other side and on to camp, unaware of the tragedy that had occurred.

At camp they reported that the bridge was out. The foreman and timekeeper took lanterns and returned to the scene. There, the early morning light revealed the locomotive almost completely buried in the mud and sand after its fall of one hundred feet from the trestle. All three crew members were buried underneath the locomotive. The three lives lost weighed heavily on the little logging company's employees for a long time.

Following the costly accident, the company pressed on, but found themselves short of motive power. To fill the need, McCuish signed a contract for $20,000 to purchase a brand new 70-ton Climax locomotive.

The railroad reached a peak mileage of eight miles by the end of 1924. The logging camp worked at a good pace under the direction of a foreman known as "Jimmy-the-Bear."

Timber holdings at Prairie were evidently not extensive and in the late 1920s McCuish began selling off rail and machinery. The life of the railroad was rapidly coming to a close.

During this period McCuish succeeded to the position of president of the Bellingham National Bank in which position he remained until his death.

By 1930, his little railroad at Prairie was gone.

McNEILL AND O'HEARNE TIMBER COMPANY

Almost within the present eastern city limits of the town of Concrete, a railroad incline existed in the early 1920s. The men responsible for this notable work were James O'Hearne and Lyle McNeill. O'Hearne was a logging engineer and was involved in the management of English Lumber Company, and so the Concrete venture was for him a sideline effort. McNeill was the partner who undertook the logging and the firm was organized as McNeill and O'Hearne Timber Company in 1918.

The company immediately opened at least two camps in the Birdsview and Grandy Creek area, adjacent to the Great Northern Railway. By 1922, an incline was built just east of Concrete and Camp 3 established at the top of the incline near Lake Everett. Over one hundred men were employed running three sides. Nine donkey en-

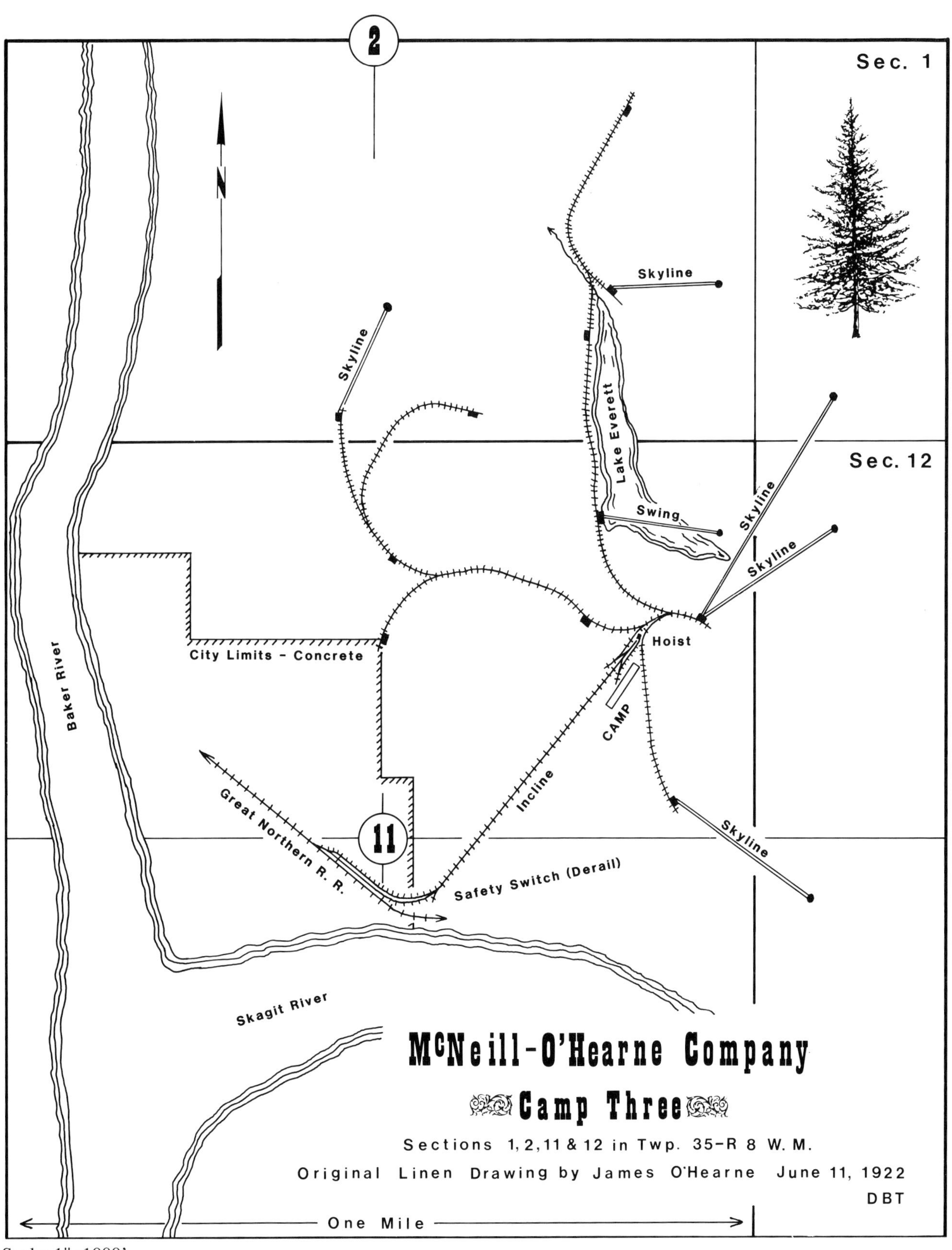
2
Sec. 1
N
Skyline
Skyline
Lake Everett
Sec. 12
Swing
Skyline
Skyline
Hoist
City Limits - Concrete
Baker River
CAMP
Incline
Great Northern R. R.
11
Skyline
Safety Switch (Derail)
Skagit River
McNeill-O'Hearne Company
Camp Three
Sections 1, 2, 11 & 12 in Twp. 35-R 8 W. M.
Original Linen Drawing by James O'Hearne June 11, 1922
DBT
One Mile

Scale: 1"=1000'

217

McNEILL AND O'HEARNE INCLINE at Concrete. Photo was from old county road overpass. *Al Gardinier*

gines puffed away in the woods and an unidentified coal burning locomotive brought loads the short distance to the Great Northern for shipment. In the summer of 1922, another locomotive was purchased from Fobbs-Wilson for the sum of $4,500, however, little else is known about her. She was evidently a geared engine and used on top of the incline.

By 1924 the Concrete operation was finished and removed. Puget Sound Sawmills and Shingle Company relaid steel over a portion of the old grade near Lake Everett for their line's relocation from Van Horn.

Camp 4 is thought to have been the last camp operated by McNeill and O'Hearne and was located on the Skagit River Railway just over the Skagit County line in Whatcom County. This camp cleared timber along the Skagit River line and was a short lived operation. The McNeill and O'Hearne company disappeared entirely by 1927. Lyle McNeill resurfaced in 1928, logging on his own in Whatcom County and using a pole road.

MILLETT AND McKAY

Credit for the first "railroad" in Skagit County is extended to the firm of Millett and McKay of Burlington. Arriving in Washington Territory in 1875, John P. Millett spent fifteen years in logging camps on Hood Canal and the Snohomish and Snoqualmie rivers. In 1881 he went into business under the name of Millett and McKay, located just east of what later became the town of Burlington. His partner was William McKay and together they built an 84-inch gauge tram railroad beginning on the Skagit River and running north up what is now the Gardner Road. They laid 3 x 5 inch maple rails and purchased two Blackman logging cars. The tram road eventually extended to the vicinity of the Cook Road and used horses for motive power.

After several years of operation, Millett retired from the lumber business and was elected Skagit County sheriff in 1896. Considerable credit is given to him for founding the town of Burlington.

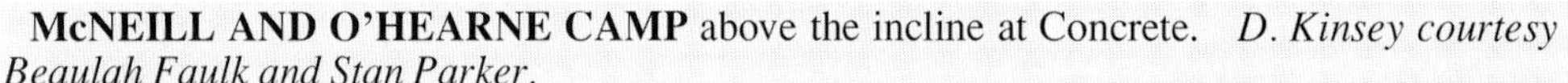

McNEILL AND O'HEARNE CAMP above the incline at Concrete. *D. Kinsey courtesy Beaulah Faulk and Stan Parker.*

MINNESOTA LUMBER COMPANY

During the earlier days of Skagit County the little town of Avon, on the bank of the Skagit River, was a pioneer settlement. By 1897, Avon sported its own broom handle factory and prosperity was in the air as well as talk of a railroad building through the area. The good news was that the Seattle and Montana Railroad did begin laying track east out of Anacortes a few months later. The bad news was that it missed Avon, passing a mile to the north of the town. However, a railroad station was built at the closest point and called North Avon. Soon a wooden boardwalk was established between the depot and town to encourage railroad business.

The railroad activity of 1899 brought with it a new lumber mill to North Avon. The Avon Lumber Company then began its own logging railroad and built northwest into the timber. By 1904 it incorporated as the Avon Mill Company with a capital stock of $3,000. Principals were H. W. Graham, Robert Wiley, John Wiley and H. M. Gibson. A saloon was built in North Avon for the entertainment of the loggers, a direct contrast to Avon itself, which was a dry town.

The Avon Mill Company soon fell to hard times and was in receivership by 1905.

Seattle investors purchased the property and incorporated under the new name of the Minnesota Lumber Company, in April of 1906. New figures in the business were Lewis Schwager, W. B. Nettleton and J. B. Price.

Four months into their new project a fire destroyed some of the firm's camp and burned north into the holdings of the Ballard Lumber Company on Bay View Ridge. However, logging continued unabated into 1907, at which time the company boasted three miles of railroad and one unidentified rod locomotive.

The company continued to operate until about 1910, at which time the timber apparently was close to being exhausted. The mill burned in a fire the first of June of the same year and active life for the business came to a close.

The Minnesota Lumber Company moved on to Mason and Kitsap Counties under the name Schwager-Nettleton Mills.

The old North Avon plant became a consideration for English Lumber Company in 1913, when the Puget Sound and Baker River Railway (49 percent English interests) built to within two miles of Avon. Serious thought was given to extending the new railroad on to the old Avon Mill site, but after 1913 the idea was evidently dropped and the lumber mill at North Avon died in peace.

MOSHER AND McDONALD

In the late 1800s, a Michigan lumberman by the name of Mosher purchased sizeable timber holdings in various locations throughout western Washington. The year 1890 found him beginning to develop his holdings and he set up a partner, Mr. McDonald, as the logger; backing him financially. By 1891 the firm was logging just north of Seattle.

In late 1895 difficulties between the two men developed. Mosher withdrew financial support and McDonald filed suit against his partner, asking for a receiver. At this time the company was worth some $500,000 and was considered one of the largest logging businesses in the state.

The company continued to operate under a receiver, and by 1898, had a large camp opened about two miles east of Sedro Woolley. Mosher and McDonald began building railroad to facilitate their business and this required crossing the Seattle and International track near town. In addition, it was necessary to rearrange one of Seattle and International's trestles to allow passage under. To this end the common carrier gave strenuous objection. A feud developed immediately between the now opposing forces, however, the loggers continued to approach the bigger railroad with their track. On a quiet Sunday the loggers appeared in force in the early morning hours and began to busily make changes to the trestle of the Seattle and International. Soon an army of sheriff's deputies were on hand to arrest several key loggers involved.

After things were sorted out the work in the woods

"AT WORK IN THE WOODS" often meant that anything goes, as men and tools were piled high as the train left for the day's labor. Here the Mosher & McDonald's *Belle* shows off her fluted domes and full gear covers. *Felix Minor*

MANY LOGGING SPURS were operated with little attention to preparation of road bed. In this Mosher and McDonald scene notice the rails bending under the weight of the loads. A mechanic's vise is thoughtfully mounted on the locomotive running board for "on the road" repairs. The little Shay was built in 1891 and named "Belle."
D. Kinsey courtesy Bill Mason

began again, however, the following year was marked by a major fire. At this point the organization of the company changed, emerging as McDonald and Cunningham, with plans to reopen the Sedro Woolley camp. This endeavor was short lived and they moved to Hood Canal in 1900.

Tyee Logging Company, operated by Ed English, took over the Mosher and McDonald Sedro Woolley camp and quickly finished cutting out the remaining timber.

THE OLD COLONY MILL was a Bloedel-Donovan subsidiary and operated near Blanchard. Its close proximity to the one-time Socialist "Equality Colony" in that vicinity doubtless fostered the name. *D. Kinsey courtesy Phil Swanson.*

OLD COLONY MILL

The third narrow gauge Fordson-powered shingle bolt railroad in Skagit County was the Old Colony Mill near Blanchard. A Bloedel-Donovan subsidiary, it was in operation by the summer of 1921 and only operated a few years.

The siderod Fordson weighed in at 3½ tons with a 3,000-pound drawbar pull. It would pull 120-tons on good track.

Old Colony Mill's railroad reached a length of about two miles before it closed.

OLD COLONY MILL Shingle bolt train was powered by a converted Fordson tractor. This view shows a horse re-load to the Fordson railroad. *D. Kinsey courtesy Whatcom Museum of History and Art.*

PARKER-BELL LUMBER COMPANY

The southbound traveler on State Highway 9 passes out of Skagit County only about two miles before crossing over a small bridge over Pilchuck Creek. The stream flows west from the bridge into a shallow valley bottom. It is a quiet area with only an occasional house along the road. Few folks today would guess that here was once a large sawmill and a lively town of some five hundred residents.

Again, the story follows the lumbermen. Two brothers from the state of Maine, Joseph H. and W. A. Parker, came to Washington and settled in the late 1800s. In 1899 they purchased the old Shrewsbury and McLain sawmill at Big Lake, only to resell it within the year. They

PARKER-BELL'S Shay Number One was built new for Joe Parker. She was completed Christmas Eve in 1900. *Ed Marlow.*

PARKER-BELL LUMBER COMPANY mill and the town of Pilchuck. This is all gone today, including the Northern Pacific mainline seen here in the foreground. *Ed Marlow*

proceeded into business with another gentlemen from the East, G. K. Hiatt. The resulting firm was Parker Brothers and Hiatt Company, incorporated in the summer of 1900. Capital stock was $30,000. The place of business was just south of the Skagit County line at Pilchuck.

A new Shay locomotive was built for them in December of that year and the new company began building railroad northeast toward the county line. Logs were "trailed" between the rails by the Shay, on grades as steep as 10½ percent. The business expanded steadily, and they doubled their lumber production from 7,600,000 feet in 1902, to 14,913,000 feet in 1904. Annual shingle production from the new shingle mill ran at eighty million.

James Bell of Everett purchased an interest in the company in the fall of 1904, and became mill superintendent. A name change occurred in 1905, when Hiatt left the company. The new firm became Parker-Bell Lumber Company.

The mill continued to grow until in 1908, it reached a capacity of 100,000 feet of lumber and 250,000 shingles per day. The operation evidently attracted attention for that year brought another modification to the ownership.

C. B. Howard and Company, of Emporium, Pennsylvania, was a sizable logging concern looking to the Pacific Northwest for fresh timberlands. One of the principals in C. B. Howard was Joseph Kaye, whose son-in-law was James Norie. In 1908, Norie, representing the Kaye-Howard interests, purchased James Bell's portion of Parker-Bell Lumber Company. Three years later Kaye himself purchased the Parkers' interest of the firm and the Pennsylvania lumbermen controlled the entire operation. The company name, however, remained the same.

These same eastern gentlemen, with others of C. B. Howard and Company, also formed the Samish Bay Logging Company at Blanchard in 1912. It is interesting to note that both these companies then went exclusively to the use of Climax locomotives, Parker-Bell ordering a new 80-ton Climax in 1912.

The new owners worked hard at Parker-

PARKER-BELL Climax No. 3 gives the appearance of a single unit supply train in this scene taken at the Company mill at Pilchuck. *Ed Marlow*

Bell and the town bustled with activity. The company hotel at Pilchuck earned a new coat of blue paint and an accompanying nickname of Blue Goose. Salesmen, loggers and travelers came and went by way of the several Northern Pacific trains that passed through, stopping at Pilchuck, each day. Joseph Kaye, while not spending a lot of time in town himself, had his three sons, Ed, Bob and Joe, hard at work running the business.

The logging railroad operated up Pilchuck Creek Canyon to Pilchuck Falls, then north toward a spot in Skagit County where some 25 Finnish families lived in the midst of the virgin timber. While the mill and offices of the company were in Snohomish County, the majority of the logging was done in Skagit woods. The Pilchuck Canyon was a bad slide area and constantly threatened the railroad during bad weather.

Another new Climax was purchased in the summer of 1920, for a cost of $29,800. The custom of Climax Manufacturing Company in those days was to set up a new locomotive to be pulled in a train and a factory man would ride all the way out west with her. A small pot-bellied stove was even provided in the Climax cab for his comfort as he tended the new machine's bearings and fittings during the long trip. Parker-Bell's new Climax was "delivered" by Walter Casler and when they arrived at Pilchuck, Walt put her in running shape and remained until she proved satisfactory.

Even with shiny new equipment on the property, time was running out for Parker-Bell. In 1921 a massive slide in the Pilchuck Canyon closed the railroad. Kaye and the Howard interests were forced to consider their position. The firm had not been making money. To reopen their railroad would be very expensive. Soon, talks were under way with English Lumber Company who operated immediately to the north of Parker-Bell property. A sale to English was agreed upon and all the details were accomplished by the following year. Parker-Bell Lumber Company was out of business.

English purchased the timber, railroad and locomotives. The two Climax engines went for their own use, however, only the newest machine remained with them. She was renumbered "12" on the English roster and became a favorite for the rough, high-country camps. English's 9-spot Shay switched the Pilchuck mill during scrapping. English picked up some twelve miles of 60-pound steel from Parker-Bell's railroad.

The mill was sold to the Panama Equipment Company of Seattle and dismantled in 1922.

The company houses at Pilchuck were sold for $25 to $50 each to those local folks and former employees who were interested.

Then the town began to vanish.

PROGRESSIVE MILL AND LOGGING COMPANY

As early as 1902, Rufus H. Kellogg was cutting shingles near Big Lake. Located about a mile north of Big Lake, Kellogg Shingle Company had their small plant adjacent to the Northern Pacific on the valley floor.

The little mill was a consistent producer and by 1910, a short railroad was added to feed the operation. Little is known about the railroad itself, however, in 1911, they did make the local news when their locomotive and three flat cars "went into the ditch." Damage was repairable and no one was killed.

Kellogg soon went looking for new territory and began to develop interests near Wenatchee. He put his Big Lake mill up for sale. Buyers were found and Kellogg moved on in 1913. The new owners selected the name Progressive Mill and Logging Company for their property. The new firm was incorporated in December of 1912. The first trustees were D. E. Kellogg (who stayed on to retain his portion of the old family interest), of Startup; C. E. Sutherland of Sunnyside and A. L. Arneson. Sutherland was elected president and announced that one thousand acres of timber had been secured from the Atlas Lumber Company. Their plan was to use the cedar for shingles and log the remainder for Atlas.

The company constructed a spur from the Northern Pacific at Ehrlich, into their new timber, in 1916. They worked there without incident, or public record, until the early 1920s. In 1925 the spur was removed; the shingle mill had been dismantled, and the company disappeared.

PUGET SOUND SAWMILLS AND SHINGLE COMPANY

Up in Fairhaven, Whatcom County, 1899 was a banner year. It was then that Puget Sound Sawmills and Shingle Company broke the state production record for shingles, producing 117,402,000 in 292 days. The following year the company gained the title of top shingle producer in the world.

FORMER NEW YORK CITY ELEVATED RAILWAY locomotive has made her way west to the city of Concrete, Washington to work on the Baker River and Shuksan. The little 0-4-4 Forney spent many days working the Baker River Gorge just above town. *Lloyd King*

(facing, right)
CAMP ON STILTS. Puget Sound Sawmills and Shingle Company camp northeast of Concrete. *D. Kinsey courtesy Whatcom Museum of History and Art*

Bellingham, in general, was beginning to develop a core of top notch lumber and shingle plants, a business network that was destined to remain for many years.

To supply their mill, Puget Sound Sawmills and Shingle Company invested in timberlands in various locations. After a few years one of these new holdings came to be located north of Concrete, in Skagit County. This acquisition was made by 1918 and involved areas along the Baker River and east of what is now Lake Shannon. Hydroelectric power development was underway and timber was made available to

SUPERIOR PORTLAND CEMENT COMPANY Climax No. 3 eases across the Baker River. The engine went on to work for Jennings and Nestos at the close of her career here. *Dennis Thompson collection*

(left) **EARLY VIEW** of the Baker River Bridge as originally built, Forney locomotive and the bridge gang. Before logging trains could be operated over the bridge in later years, a Howe truss was placed in the bridge as a center span. *Dorothy Hansen and Stan Parker*

(below) **WATER LEVEL VIEW** of the Baker River Bridge shows the changing construction features. This could be a modelers delight!. *D. Thompson collection*

OTHER QUARRY AND CEMENT PLANT CHORES were performed by this 0-4-0 saddletanker under the employ of parent Superior Portland Cement. *Dennis Thompson collection.*

THE BAKER RIVER GORGE about 1918. This canyon, as well as the Baker River and Shuksan railroad bridge seen in the background, were flooded with new lake water at the building of the Lower Baker Dam in 1924. *D. Kinsey courtesy Whatcom Museum of History and Art*

clear the land.

The most convenient transportation route into the area north of Concrete was the Baker River and Shuksan Railroad, which had been built by the Superior Portland Cement Company about 1908. For several years quarry trains had been operating in this area supplying lime rock for the cement plant in town. Their motive power ranged from an ex-New York City Elevated 0-4-4 to a 60-ton Climax. It was probably the most spectacular railroad in the county considering its short length. Within a mile of Concrete itself the track hung to the side of the gorge precariously. Some of the supports for the roadbed were "brackets driven against solid rock, holding the outer rail in position as a shelf is held against a wall of a house." The only part of the railroad even more impressive was the majestic Baker River Bridge itself, spanning the rocky gorge.

Puget Sound Sawmills and Shingle Company secured a joint-use agreement from the Baker River and Shuksan, provided the lumber company maintained the railroad. The first locomotive the loggers used on the line was a small Davenport leased from the cement company. Soon, however, larger power arrived. A 3-truck Climax was purchased in 1920, requiring the woods forces to strengthen the Baker River Bridge due to the weight of the new locomotive.

By 1922 logging was in full swing and the company boasted two sides in operation

THE THREE-SPOT at work in the cement plant at Concrete. *Charlie Bullock*

using eight donkey engines. There were 125 men employed. Nine miles of railroad was operated using three geared locomotives and a maximum grade of six percent. Logs were shipped from Concrete on the Great Northern to Anacortes where they were boomed for movement to Bellingham.

In 1924 the firm purchased a Washington Iron Works skidder for $19,500. Logging was now east of the present Lake Shannon and the railroad was eleven miles long.

The Baker River hydroelectric project was not only promising to change the face of the land but the logging railroad itself. The Lower Baker Dam under construction would soon flood and cover the big railroad bridge across the river. As the cement plant had just completed an overhead trolley system to haul in their lime rock, they no longer required a railroad. It was up to the loggers to relocate their railroad. This was accomplished in early 1925. The new railroad grade was several miles in length and connected the woods lines to the Great Northern at Van Horn. Construction was performed by contractors Parker-Schram of Portland. About 100 million feet of timber was being cut at this time on land soon to be flooded by the new dam. The new railroad provided for removal of this timber.

The year 1927 found the Van Horn operation at its height with 20 miles of railroad and 175 men employed. The railroad proceeded up the east side of Lake Shannon to a point about one mile south of Thunder Creek. This was as far north as the railroad ever got although bare grade was built almost to Thunder Creek. Just before Three Mile

THE LOWER BAKER DAM is seen here under construction in 1924. This is nearly the same location as the facing photo. Notice the Baker River and Shuksan railroad trestle clinging to the cliff on the left. This was one of the most spectacular pieces of railroading in the county prior to its inundation by lake waters after completion of the hydroelectric dam. *Dennis Thompson collection.*

Creek, three or more switchbacks were built up the hill to the east and the railroad operated to, or possibly just beyond, Jackman Creek.

The Bellingham plant had installed a new log dump and logs were now shipped direct to Bellingham from the woods. The mill had also been modernized with a new boiler and turbine in the sawmill, new dry kilns, new steel burner, storage sheds, transfer sheds, office and other general improvements.

Alas, with the expansion came immediate financial trouble. In April 1927, all of the firm's operations closed. Due to market conditions reopening was not advised. Instead, a half million dollar refinancing of the company was recommended. Trouble compounded with the advance of the Great Depression. Time passed and nothing operated...locomotives sat idle at Van Horn and the great mill was silent. Finally, in 1930, W. B. Hopple was appointed receiver and a year later he petitioned, and received, from the court a permit to "junk the plant." Mill equipment and logging machinery were put up for sale. Considerable mill equipment was purchased by Bloedel-Donovan Lumber Mills.

Hopple was authorized in 1932, to "recondition the company's logging railroad in Skagit County either for operation or removal of logging and railroad equipment, which is valued at $203,661."

The railroad did not operate again, and the steel was pulled up almost immediately. For the next few years

bits and pieces of remaining equipment were sold.

The railroad enginehouse and shop, which was located approximately in the northwest corner of section 11, was retained for a truck shop after the railroad was abandoned. It was used until about 1970.

Another picturesque railroad became history.

RUCKER BROTHERS

Another timber company headquartered outside of Skagit County was Rucker Brothers. The firm incorporated a subsidiary, Cavanaugh Timber Company, in 1906, and built a modern sawmill in Snohomish County. By 1917 they were running ten miles of railroad north out of Cavano into Skagit County timberlands. Cavano was located on the Northern Pacific's Darrington branch, a short distance east of Arlington. The logging took place around the south side of Frailey Mountain, east of territory owned and operated by Stimson.

There is a good chance that when Ed English secured large holdings in the Lake Cavanaugh country it edged the Ruckers out of their long range plans for the area. Cavanaugh Timber Company finished in the area before the Depression. Occasional maps still show a few old grades marked *Rucker Railroad.* Company properties became Puget Sound Pulp and Timber Company in 1929, and one Shay and a number of logging cars were transferred to Clear Lake for use on the new firm's last logging show there.

SCOTT BROTHERS LOGGING COMPANY

A very obscure operation, Scott Brothers is known to have been doing business near Concrete in the 1920s using a pole road with a Skagit Steel and Iron Works Fordson locomotive conversion.

They appeared to favor quaint equipment and techniques and show up again in 1934, in Alger. At this time they were trying to repair an old Tacoma steam donkey for their use there.

The last appearance of Scott Brothers was in 1936. At that late date they had gone back to using a four-horse team and were skidding logs for the Bellingham Sash and Door Company.

SEVERSON LUMBER COMPANY

Loggers sometimes appear, then vanish, like ships in the night. Such was the case of Severson Lumber Company, whose owner was, of course, Ole Severson. He was also manager, superintendent and purchasing agent. He built one mile of railroad near Lake McMurray and set up logging with one donkey.

The year was 1924. After doing a little business and being recognized as a functioning lumberman, he disappeared from public records.

SKAGIT MILL COMPANY

Immediately to the northeast of Sedro Woolley lies a significant hill of some 4,100 feet of elevation. This lofty landmark remains known today as Skagit Mill Hill, named for the last logger to lay steel rails high in its timber.

Skagit Mill Company began corporate life February 10, 1906. At that time the business filed for incorporation, listing the following trustees: C. R. Wilcox, E. G. English, J. T. Hightower, W. M. Kirby and E. C. Million. An interesting sidenote is that in the same month the same five businessmen also incorporated the Highland Timber Company. The principal place of business for both

THE BOYS AND THE TANK CAR at Skagit Mill Company.
Dennis Thompson Collection

SKAGIT MILL COMPANY SHAY NO. 1 with train of disconnected trucks. The locomotive was nicknamed *The Goat.*
Clark Kinsey courtesy University of Washington

MAP No. 19 **EARLY SKAGIT MILL COMPANY.** From the company's inception, railroad logging was conducted here until 1923, when the firm relocated their railroad some four miles to the west . In 1927-28, Dempsey Lumber Company re-laid steel over Skagit Mill's old right-of-way to access timber higher on the mountain. *See map no. 8, page 109.*

About two miles of the old grade north out of Lyman has been converted and named Pipeline Road.

Tyee/Mosher & McDonald grades are undocumented and therefore only location points can be noted.

At Prairie (north of Thornwood), the horse tram of Hoyt Lumber Co. is shown. *Map by RD Jost MD 1989*

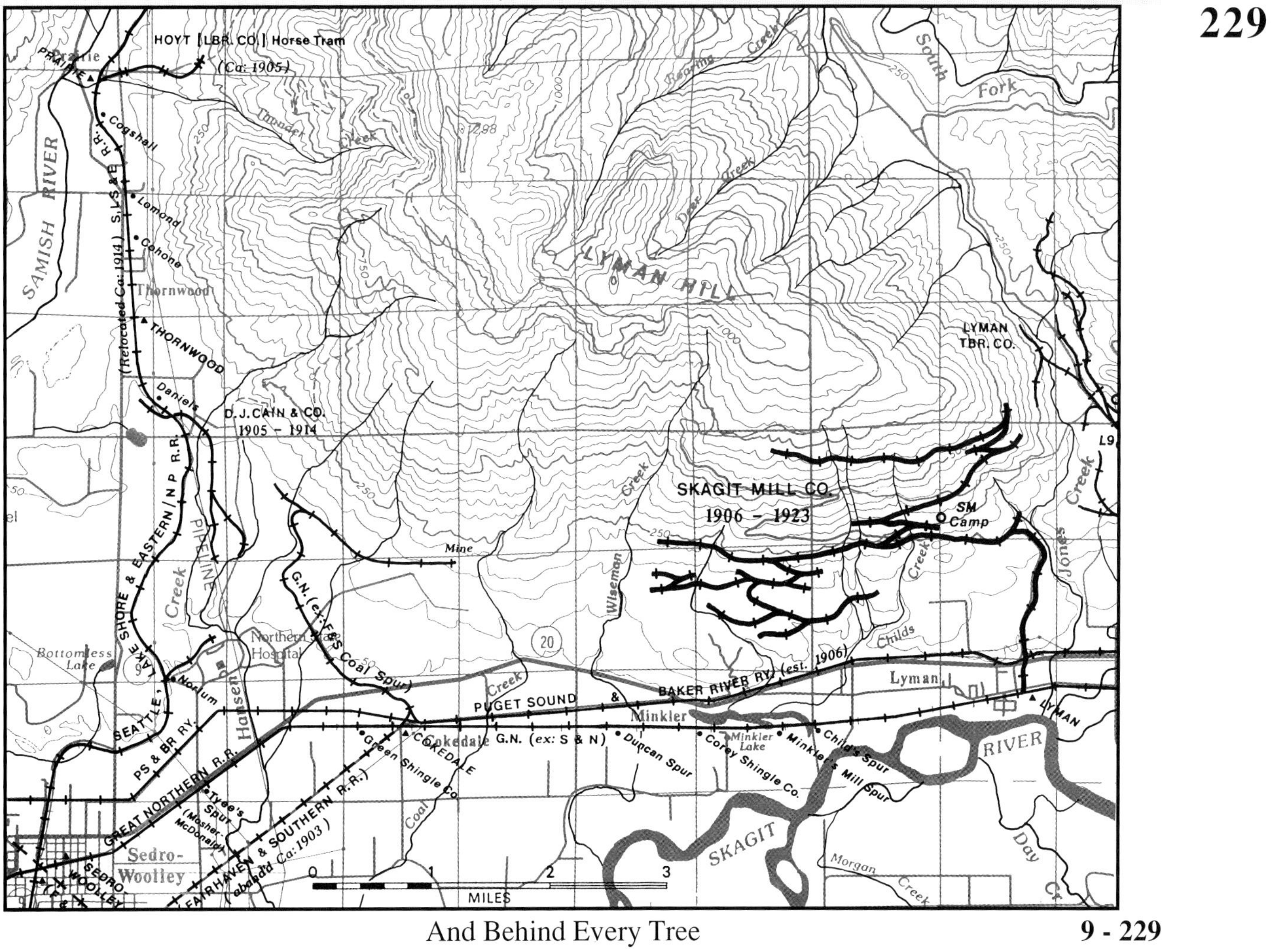

SKAGIT MILL ONE-SPOT taken in early days when she still retained her oil headlamp. The Skagit Mill shop seems to have had a practice of discarding the running board over the top of the cylinders. *Al Hodgin*

manner: "A few hundred yards beyond the lumber mills, the road enters a rocky gorge, and rises by marked degrees to the top of the extensive table lands, from which the timber had already been removed. Further progress, except for the genius of man, would terminate here, and that it is actually effected is a standing marvel to the timid novice. A series of switchbacks, however, solves the problem, and tracing their several legs back and forth the log trains may be daily observed from the streets of Lyman making their way up and down the precipitous mountain."

Skagit Mill gained considerable mention in the trade journals in 1917, when they purchased a McFarlane Sky Line donkey to work the high timber. This aerial cable yarding system became the only one of its kind in the state at the time. The mill did a large business producing turned wood columns on their five wood lathes. They also manufactured car building materials and their share of shingles.

The company operated north of Lyman until about 1923. The railroad had reached a peak of about 15 miles of track using 32 sets of disconnected trucks. William Kirby managed the affairs of the business at that time with Frank Gee as superintendent and Harley LaPlant as purchasing agent.

After the company holdings were logged out at Lyman,

firms was to be in Lyman. It is believed that Highland Timber Company was the timber holding company leaving Skagit Mill Company to be the operating company.

Following its inception Skagit Mill immediately began construction of a sawmill on the northeast edge of the town of Lyman, and John Hightower was named manager. During the next three years the bustling company built a logging railroad north from the mill into nearby timber. A 2-truck Shay locomotive was purchased in 1908, to work the railroad using "Snohomish" trucks from Seattle Car and Foundry. Another larger Shay was purchased the following year.

Otto Klement described the expanding railroad in this

SAWMILL OF THE SKAGIT MILL COMPANY. This impressive plant was located at what is now the intersection of Highway 20 and the Pipeline Road. *D. Kinsey, Steve Hauff*

the firm moved to fresh timber north of Cokedale. They began building railroad near Wiseman Creek northwest of the Puget Sound and Baker River Railway mainline, extending their rails toward the area around the old Cokedale coal mines.

In 1926 Skagit Mill purchased a large amount of mill equipment from the receivers of the Day Lumber Company sawmill at Big Lake. After this purchase, a new lathe mill was installed the following year in the Lyman sawmill.

SECOND LOCOMOTIVE in Skagit Mill's stable of power is seen here. This is Shay No. 2. In 1940, both of the firm's locomotives were up for sale. One gentleman, out shopping for engines, remarked of their Two-Spot, "Mr. LaPlant thinks it is a very valuable locomotive, but actually it is very poor, very old, and only worth $1500 to $2000." *Dennis Thompson collection.*

Over the next few years Skagit Mill logged steadily and their railroad grew at a complimentary pace. The tracks crossed the old Fairhaven and Southern grade as it marched up the hillsides. The railroad eventually reached high up on "Skagit Mill Hill," and a camp was built for the loggers.

In the spring of 1936, a wage dispute arose between Skagit Mill's sawmill crew and management. A five cent per hour raise was asked by the union and refused by the company. A union meeting was held, and although negotiations continued most

LOGGING CAMP DENTIST performs his work in Skagit Mill's camp about one mile north of Lyman behind Prevedell Hill. The "patient" in the wheelbarrow is Al Stendal, camp cook, who broke a tooth. The camp foreman brought up the dentist from Lyman and the scene here followed. The year is 1913. *Charlie Howard*

SKAGIT MILL COMPANY used these disconnected trucks until the end of their railroad. This view clearly shows the steep grade of this switchback and prompts one to remember....these log cars had hand brakes only! Also shown is the flexibility of disconnected trucks to easily haul loads of any length, particularly this long load. *Clark Kinsey courtesy University of Washington*

SKAGIT MILL COMPANY yarder in the woods. *Clark Kinsey courtesy University of Washington*

of the night, the confrontation ended in deadlock. The company then closed its sawmill, never to run again.

A labor agreement was reached, however, for Skagit Mill's railroad operation and for some 45 men at the Lyman shingle mill. The shingle mill continued to run for several months, then shut down itself as the company's cedar production dwindled.

The railroad remained for an additional two years, with the 2-truck Shay leaving each morning from Minkler Junction on the Puget Sound and Baker River Railway to take the crew to work in the woods. Outbound hemlock went to Hamilton Junction behind the 3-truck Shay No. 2. It was during this short period that skeleton cars were used for the first time at Skagit Mill due to the requirements of the Puget Sound and Baker River and the Great Northern to transport them on to market. Skagit Mill ran its last train in 1938, closing the railroad.

The big sawmill at Lyman was dismantled in mid-1939, erasing a major landmark for the town. In later years a relocation of State Highway 20 routed the highway through the old mill site.

Skagit Mill Company remained alive on paper until Harley A. LaPlant signed its dissolution December 29, 1942.

SKAGIT MILL COMPANY Shay No. 1 in the deep woods. She was built in 1908 as c/n 2107. *D. Kinsey courtesy Peter Replinger*

SKAGIT RIVER LOGGING COMPANY

One of the only companies in Skagit County to use electric logging machinery in the field was the Skagit River Logging Company. Organized in 1915, they controlled a small tract of timber on the south side of the Skagit River about one mile above Hamilton.

SKAGIT MILL COMPANY'S Lyman operations logged through what had once been the Cokedale Mines. This view of Cokedale dates from around the turn of the century. The railroad here is the Fairhaven and Southern. Almost all was gone when Skagit Mill arrived. *Dennis Thompson collection*

The firm built a short spur off the Great Northern near Hamilton, down to the river, directly across from their timber. They contracted with Williamette Iron and Steel Works for two electric engines. One to operate an electric overhead trolley and the second to function as a log loader. The system was put into use in the summer of 1915, bringing logs overhead some 2,000 feet across the Skagit River.

Within a few months the work was being done by the firm of Meiklejohn and Brown who leased the equipment from Skagit River Logging Company.

After an uneventful history of less than five years, the company finished logging and moved on.

SKAGIT RIVER RAILWAY

While not a logging railroad per se, the Skagit River Railway did handle a considerable amount of logging car traffic and thus deserves attention here. Begun in 1919, in conjunction with the Seattle City Light's Skagit River power project, the railroad was built to move

SKAGIT MILL COMPANY Loading donkey and crew. *Clark Kinsey courtesy Bert Kellogg*

FROM NEWHALEM EAST, the Skagit River Railway was electrified. In this scene, steam power takes over for the trip on to Rockport with 2-6-2 No. 6. Rolling stock consisted of a unique mix of steam and electric equipment. As seen here, some former electric interurban cars were converted to non-powered passenger cars. The little Prairie also hauled her share of logs, picking up loads along her route to Rockport. *D. Kinsey courtesy John Labbe*

materials over a rugged area of Skagit County to Seattle's future hydroelectric dam sites on the upper Skagit River.

The first portion of the railroad traversed relatively easy terrain to Newhalem, from its beginning at Rockport, eastern terminus of the Great Northern. The remaining seven mile portion of the railroad climbed through the rugged Skagit River gorge over grades as rough as four percent, crossing the river several times. This was one of the most spectacular pieces of railroad in the county, much of the right-of-way being blasted out of solid rock. Construction to Diablo was completed in 1927. The railroad length was 31 miles. Geared steam locomotives leased from local loggers furnished most of the early motive power on the line, along with an old 2-6-2 saddle tank engine. Details of these early engines are not known.

Considering the rugged nature of the last seven miles through the gorge and the abundance of electric power to be had, these last several miles were electrified and remained as an electric railway until the end of operations.

In 1928, older steam on the lower portion of the railroad received replacement power in the form of a new Baldwin 2-6-2, road number six. In addition to regular traffic on the line, the 6-spot hauled a respectable quantity of logs during her career. Several loggers operated reloads along the line and the 6-spot would pick up loads and deliver them to the Great Northern at Rockport. One of the most frequent log shippers was the firm of Jennings and Nestos, who had the contract to clear a power line from Rockport to Newhalem. They

OFFICIAL BUILDER'S PHOTOGRAPH shows how Skagit River Railway No. 6 appeared when new. When the railroad was abandoned in the mid-1950s, she was placed on display in Newhalem. In the early 1970s No. 6 was brought to Concrete and given a home in a newly constructed enginehouse. Other than some weather damage from almost 20 years of outside display, she was still quite sound and was placed in limited excursion service between Sedro Woolley and Concrete. While seeing her again in steam touched the hearts of many, high costs involved and other difficulties caused her excursion service to be short lived. Unfortunately, by 1987 she was removed from dry storage and returned to static display in Newhalem, again exposed to the elements. *Courtesy Railroad Museum of Pennsylvania, (P.H.M.C.)*

logged on their own using a Climax and a 2-6-2 Porter, moving from location to location and shipping logs out over the Skagit River Railway. At times Jennings and Nestos would send logs directly to Rockport behind their own rod engine. This continued for several years and certainly provided extra freight for an already busy railroad.

In addition to freight service and moving materials for hydroelectric projects, the railroad also carried a number of regular passengers, including employees, using a variety of interesting and unusual motor cars. City Light also assembled a train of passenger cars and in 1928, began offering public tours of their facilities. It was an overnight affair beginning in Rockport with a train ride up the Skagit River and returning the next day. This very popular feature continued for many years.

LOGGING WAGONS IN THE STREETS of Mount Vernon was not popular with city officials. This Slosson Logging Company photograph was taken looking north on First Street. *Ernie Rothrock*

By 1953, City Light was preparing to build a final dam at Gorge Creek, which would put much of the railroad under water unless it were to be rebuilt higher along the cliffs. Economic factors led to the decision to abandon the railroad. The last train ran in April 1954, after which all equipment was sold except 2-6-2 No. 6, which was placed on display at Newhalem.

The 6-spot was rescued from the elements in the early 1970s, restored and operated in the Skagit valley on numerous occasions between Sedro Woolley and Concrete. High operating costs soon found her in dry storage in Concrete, but in excellent operating condition. Unfortunately, in 1986, she was reclaimed by Newhalem for display and again sits mouldering in the weather.

SLOSSON LOGGING COMPANY

A small but innovative logging operation began unfolding in Mount Vernon in 1912, when Fred Slosson, with others, purchased 20,000,000 feet of standing timber on Lincoln Hill. The firm was incorporated in January of 1913, by Fred Slosson, M. N. Hawley and A. McLeod. Capital stock was $18,000.

The spring of 1913 found the new company having almost four miles of railroad on the hill. The timber stood in an area not excessively rugged and a small 0-4-0 locomotive was sufficient to get the logs as far as the edge of Lincoln Hill overlooking Mount Vernon. Getting the logs down the hill was something else. It was decided to reload the logs from the railroad to horse drawn wagons at the brink of the hill. The wagons were fitted with a steel wheel block called a "shoe," which was

THE ONLY LOGGERS in the area to use a reload from railroad to horse drawn wagons was Slosson Logging Company. Here the team and wagon is about to deposit a log into the Skagit River. *Ernie Rothrock*

SLOSSON LOGGING COMPANY train working on the top of Lincoln Hill in Mount Vernon. The company seemed to use the bare minimum of equipment to get the job done. Locomotive is unidentified as to her ancestry. *Bert Kellogg*

wedged ahead of the wagon wheel to brake them down the steep hill. Once at the bottom the wagons were driven through the streets of Mount Vernon to the Skagit River where they were dumped.

The system seemed to work well although one accident was reported where a wagon lost its "shoe," and ran away down Lincoln Hill. The resulting wild ride ended in a collision with a telephone pole. One horse, "Old Dick," was killed. Others in the team, and the driver, lived.

Slosson's practice of hauling logs through Mount Vernon met some resistance from the city council in 1914. Considerable meeting time was devoted to the logger's "determination to use the city streets as a logging road." No course of action was decided.

By 1915, the Slosson Logging Company had finished logging their timber. The locomotive was sold to an unknown buyer and Lincoln Hill became quiet once again.

SOUND TIMBER COMPANY

In late 1899, the Sound Timber Company was organized by Weyerhaeuser to manage a tract of timber in the Skagit and Sauk River area, between Rockport and Darrington. Weyerhaeuser was looking ahead to the time when their holdings in the Lake States were exhausted of timber. The Skagit-Sauk property was their first investment in west coast lands. Sound Timber Company incorporated in Olympia on January 14, 1900. There was no activity until about 1915, when Weyerhaeuser began to transfer operations westward and the Darrington operation got underway. Their first camp was begun about four miles east of Darrington about that time.

In 1917 the company was busy building railroad north along the Sauk River and two sides were being operated about four miles from town. By the early 1920s considerable debate evolved concerning how best to bring out the timber located near Rockport. W. C. Harvie, Sound Timber's logging engineer, was given the task of decid-

SOUND TIMBER COMPANY'S Shay No. 2 poses new at the factory in this classic builders photograph. This 80 ton class 3-truck locomotive was built in 1920 with shop number 3057. *Peter Replinger Collection*

ing a transportation route. A bridge was considered over the Skagit River at or near Rockport to allow connection to the Great Northern. Or the company logging railroad could be completed out of Darrington. Harvie chose the latter.

Railroad construction proceeded and in 1927, trains were rolling into the Martin Ranch and Ilabot Creek area across the river from Rockport. Logging continued in this large area for several years with trains rolling into Darrington daily.

About 1938, the company turned their attention to the west bank of the Sauk and fresh timber in the east Finney Creek country. A new railroad bridge was built during the last six months of 1939, taking the railroad across the Sauk River for a second time at a point about four miles south of Rockport. The new structure was 1,023 feet in length including approaches and cleared the water by some 14 feet. After the river crossing the company expected to build some 12 additional miles of railroad.

SOUND TIMBER COMPANY'S M.A.C. 4-40 RAILCAR poses on the Company's Sauk River bridge south of Rockport. Crew is headed home after an overcast Washington day punctuated by rain showers. Bridge is over 1,000 feet in length including approach trestlework. *D. Kinsey courtesy Whatcom Museum of History and Art*

Finney Creek logging was busy by 1941, but this was to be the last of Sound Timber's operations. After about three years logging there the company finished cutting out their timber and sold out to Washington Veneer in September of 1944. Steel was removed and the railroad was gone by the end of World War II.

L. E. STEARNS

Another little known logger was L. E. Stearns. He was a small contract logger working in the Concrete and Grassmere area. In April 1916, he secured his biggest job - a contract with Superior Portland Cement Company to log 45 million feet of timber northeast of Concrete.

To obtain access to the timberlands it appears he negotiated use of the old Baker River and Shuksan Railroad out of Concrete, and he is known to have rebuilt existing trestles and laid about one mile of new track. Stearns obtained a locomotive to use and began hauling logs by the summer of 1916.

The work lasted less than two years and was uneventful. When Stearns finished this tract of timber he disappears from record.

J. C. STITT

My first memory of logging on rails was at Bay View, where a track came down to the mill site. Horses pulled loaded cars down logs, laid like rails. This outfit was known as Dickey-Stitt. It was in late 1890s. These words from pioneer Catherine Pulsipher, provide the earliest known reference to Joe Stitt's logging efforts at Bay View.

DICKEY-STITT HORSE TRAM along present Josh Wilson Road at Bay View. *Pearl Hector*

Dickey-Stitt was a substantial business firm operating in Bay View at the turn-of-the-century. They maintained a logging camp, horse-drawn tram road, mill and general store in the town. Logs not cut in their mill were boomed and towed to Anacortes to be sold on the open market.

Their camp was about a mile east of town on what is now the Wilson Road. For water, a well two hundred feet deep was established. A windmill pumped the water some forty feet above ground into a tank.

On August 4, 1902, C. P. Dickey and Joe C. Stitt dissolved their partnership, with Mr. Stitt purchasing Dickey's half-interest in the merchandise, logging and shingle business. Stitt planned to open a new camp to tap some 12,000,000 feet of timber.

During 1904, Stitt was using two donkey engines and a ten-horse team getting out 40,000 feet of cedar and fir per day. Ballard Lumber Company had arrived in Bay View, built a railroad and was using a Shay locomotive. By the latter part of 1904, Stitt was "hauling logs over Ballard Company's railroad," and putting in about 50,000 feet per day.

The company continued to operate until 1914, when the shingle mill at Bay View burned in September.

This event signaled the end of the operation and in the **Mount Vernon Herald** for April 13, 1916, it was reported: *The junk dealers from Anacortes are taking away the boiler and lumber from J. C. Stitt's old mill.*

In October 1916, J. C. Stitt filed *voluntary petition for bankruptcy.*

NEAR THE TERMINUS OF THE DICKEY - STITT HORSE TRAM in Bay View was this Company general store. The firm was one of the main stays of the community for several years. *Pearl Hector*

SULTAN RAILWAY AND TIMBER COMPANY

The first appearance of Sultan Railway and Timber Company was in their namesake settlement of Sultan, Washington, located in Snohomish County. Here they began logging with a Shay locomotive about 1907. Company president was Joseph Irving. The firm maintained logging activities in the Sultan area into the early 1920s when they departed that town permanently.

The company diversified operations about 1916 when they opened a camp at Oso, and built ten miles of railroad. By the early 1920s their railroad had extended north of Oso into Skagit County where two camps were operated. The company, at their peak, rostered five geared locomotives and shipped all their timber over the Northern Pacific from Oso and the Great Northern from Sultan.

Joseph Irving was also involved in the Lyman Timber Company, Monroe Logging Company, Sauk River Timber Company, Crescent Logging Company, Irving-

LIMA BUILDER'S PHOTO of Sultan Railway and Timber Shay No. 4. She was a 90-ton locomotive built in 1919. In 1930, she was sold to Lyman Timber Company where she carried road number 6. *Allen County (Ohio) Historical Society*

Hartley Logging Company, Security Timber Company, Standard Cedar Lumber Company and the Standard Railway and Timber Company. This last firm presented some confusion due to the similiarity in name with the Sultan Company. Indeed, locomotives were transferred from the Standard Railway and Timber Company to the Sultan Railway and Timber Company. It is suspected the two names were interchanged unknowingly by photographers and reporters of the period in spite of the fact that Standard Railway and Timber changed their name to Boulder Railway and Timber in 1910.

For the Sultan Railway and Timber Company, logging expired by the mid 1930s in Skagit County and the firm moved on to log further in Whatcom County near Deming and Lake Whatcom. The company finished logging there about 1941, using motor trucks. After selling their properties, Sultan Railway and Timber was dissolved in 1942.

SULTAN RAILWAY AND TIMBER HEISLER No. 2. *Madge Ewing*

SULTAN RAILWAY AND TIMBER GROUND LEAD YARDER at Irving Spur about 1908. *D. Kinsey courtesy Dale Thompson and the Dept. of Natural Resources.*

SULTAN RAILWAY AND TIMBER Shay No. 5 at Camp One. The year is 1922. *D. Kinsey courtesy Dale Thompson and the Dept. of Natural Resources*

SULTAN RAILWAY AND TIMBER High Lead Yarder at Camp 2, north of Oso in 1922. *D. Kinsey courtesy Dale Thompson and the Dept. of Natural Resources*

SULTAN RAILWAY AND TIMBER Shays on the trestle at Camp One in 1922. Road number 5 sits in front while the 4-spot waits behind. *D. Kinsey courtesy Dale Thompson and the Dept. of Natural Resources*

LOCAL BRANCH LINES of the mainline railroads also carried a large quantity of logging traffic on a per-car basis. The above view shows Seattle and Northern's high stepping 4-4-0 No. 2 tied onto a string of single log loads on disconnect truck log cars in the late 1890s near Sedro-Woolley. The locomotive was a product of the New York Locomotive Works in the summer of 1890, and she weighed in at a mere 39 tons. The little engine became Seattle and Montana No. 139 in 1902, and Great Northern No. 139 in 1907. Years later she blew up in Mukilteo and was scrapped in 1939. *D. Kinsey, Whatcom Museum of History and Art*

The Hazards of logging weren't confined to the woods railroads:

(below) A SEATTLE AND MONTANA freight train carrying log cars crossed the Skagit River bridge at Mount Vernon on January 16, 1903. The log cars caused some damage to the bridge which went largely undetected, except to the engineer on the next freight the following day. He refused to cross the bridge. His superiors did not agree and ordered the train across. The bridge collapsed killing the engineer in the wreck. This view shows the locomotive, no. 320, a Rogers product of 1887, as removal operations commence. *Courtesy Stacey's Camera Center*

LOGGING RAILROADS IN SKAGIT COUNTY

Alphabetical list

Company	Operating Dates (railroad)	RR Mileage built Skagit	Other	Total[11]
Alger Shingle Company	1910-1918	2.0		2.0
Andron Logging Company (note 7)	1922-(1930)	2.0		2.0
Atlas Lumber Company	1891-1923			
Skagit Logging Company (note 12)	1898-(1902)			
[L. Houghton Logging Company] (notes 2 & 8)	1902-1923	10.4		10.4
Avon Lumber Company	*(see Minnesota Lumber Company)*			
Baker River and Shuksan (see industrial RR section)	1908-1918			
Superior Portland Cement	1908-1918			
Puget Sound Sawmills and Shingle Company	1918-1932			
Bald Mountain Mill Company (36" gauge) (note 3)	1925-1944	1.2		1.2
Ballard Logging Railroad	1902-1910	4.0		4.0
Blanchard Logging Railroad	1886-1901	8.6		8.6
Bloedel-Donovan Lumber Mills	*(see Lake Whatcom Logging Co.)*			
Bratnober-Waite Lumber Company	*(see McMaster and Waite Lumber Co.)*			
Butler Brothers Lumber Company	1905-1906			
Butler Lumber Company	1906-1918	2.5		2.5
Cain, D. J.	1905-1914	2.2		2.2
Clear Lake Lumber Company	*(see McMaster and Waite Lumber Co.)*			
Cogshall & Metsker	1906-1910	.-not located-		
Cowden Lumber Company	1918-(1923)	2.3		2.3
Danaher Lumber Company (note 6)	1910-1923	7.1	1.7	8.8
Day Lumber Company	1900-1926	34.8		34.8
Day Creek Lumber Company	1906-1910	.-not located-		
Dempsey Lumber Company (note 9)	1907-1930			46.2
Birdsview unit[1]	1907-1926	35.9		
Skagit (Lyman) unit[1]	1927-1930	10.3		
Dickey and Angel (note 9)	1903-1906	.-not located-		
Dickey-Stitt (horse tram)	1890-1901	1.8		1.8
English Lumber Company (note 9)	1902-1944			298.3
Skagit Valley Railroad	1902-(1913)	7.5	5.6	
Tyee Logging unit[1] (note 2)	1905-(1913)	33.8	7.6	
Puget Mill Co. contract unit[1]	1917-1927	-	40.5	
in English timberlands	1901-1944	196.8	6.5	
Puget Sound Pulp & Timber	(see separate listing)			
Erickson and Fuhrman	1925-1929	.-not located-		
Faber Logging Company	1920-(1921)	3.0		3.0
Forest Mill Company	1921-(1926)			
McNeill & O'Hearne (second unit[1])(note 2)	1922-1925	0.2		0.2
William Gage	1883	.-not located-		
Galbraith Brothers	1928-1939	0.4		0.4
Grandy Lake Shingle Company	1920-(1924)	unknown		
Hamilton Logging Company (note 8)	1907-1912	5.9		5.9
Lyman Timber Company	1917-1937			84.4
Hamilton Logging unit[1]	1912-1919	18.9		
Lyman Pass unit[1]	1915-1937	57.1		
Camp 16 unit[1]	1928-(1930)	4.2		
Grandy Lake Extension	1930-1937	4.2		
Soundview Pulp Co. 3	1937-1951	3.1		3.1
Hoyt Lumber Company (horse tram)	1905?	0.9		0.9
Charles Jackson	(1882-1884)			

Dates in parenthesis are estimated.

LOGGING RAILROADS IN SKAGIT COUNTY
Alphabetical list

Company	Operating Dates (railroad)	RR Mileage built Skagit	Other	Total[11]
Jennings and Nestos	1923-1927	1.5		1.5
Kellogg Shingle Company	1910-1912			
Progressive Mill and Logging Company	1912-1915	2.3		2.3
Kennedy and O'Brien	*(see McMaster & Waite Lumber Co.)*			
Lake Whatcom Logging Company	(1903)-1913	7.7		7.7
Bloedel-Donovan Lumber Mills	1913-1942			72.3
Alger unit[1]	1913-(1924)	36.2		
Delvan unit[1]	1916-(1922)	13.2		
Saxon unit[1]	1921-1937	22.9		
Lyman Timber	*(see Hamilton Logging Company)*			
McCoy & Pullman Palace Car Logging Company				
Pat McCoy Logging RR	1902-1910	5.2		5.2
McCoy-Loggie Timber Company	1915-(1916)	0.8		0.8
McCuish Logging Company	1923-1926	9.4		9.4
McMaster and Waite Lumber Company	1898-1899			
Bratnober-Waite Lumber Company	1900-1903			
[Kennedy and O'Brien]	1899-1902			
Clear Lake Lumber Company	1903-1929			
(Original unit[1])	1903-1913			
[Skagit Logging Company]	1910-1913			
Clear Lake Lumber Company (B.R.L.)	1913-(1917)	18.0		107.2
Nookachamps unit[1]	1916-(1922)	24.8		
Camp 3 unit[1]	1917-(1927)	14.9		
Camp 1 unit[1]	(1918)-(1927)	9.1		
Day Creek (Camp 2) unit[1]	1922-1927	5.2		
Day Creek (Camp 4) unit[1]	1922-1927	15.1		
Puget Sound Pulp and Timber Company	*(see separate listing)*			
Pressentin Creek unit[1]	1923-1927	11.4		
Finney Creek unit[1]	1924-1927	8.7		
McNeill and O'Hearne Timber Company	1918-(1927)			4.1
1921 unit[1] (camp 1)	1921-(1922)	0.6		
1922 unit[1] (camp 2) *(see Forest Mill Co.)*	1922-1925			
Camp 3 unit[1]	1922-1924	2.5		
Camp 4 unit[1]	1924-1926		1.0	
Meiklejohn and Brown Company	1917-1920	.-not located-		
Miller Logging Company	1910-(?)	1.4		1.4
Millett and McKay (horse tram?)	1883-1889	2.9		2.9
Minnesota Lumber Company	1906-1911	1.2		1.2
Montborne Lumber Company	*(see Nelson-Neal Lbr. Co.)*			
Mosher and McDonald	1898-1901	.-not located-		
Nelson-Neal Lumber Company (notes 9 & 5)	1908-1926			24.1
Bryant unit[1]	1908-(?)		1.2	
Ehrlich unit[1]	1912-1918	5.4		
Montborne unit[1]	1918-1927	10.3		
Montborne Lumber Company	1926-1931	2.4		2.4
Old Colony Mill	(1921)-(?)			
Parker Brothers & Hiatt	1900-1905			
Parker-Bell Lumber Company .... (note 4)	1905-1922	9.0	4.7	13.7
Progressive Mill and Logging Company	*(see Kellogg Shingle Company)*			

LOGGING RAILROADS IN SKAGIT COUNTY

Alphabetical list

Company	Operating Dates (railroad)	RR Mileage built Skagit	Other	Total[11]
Puget Sound and Baker River Railway	*(see Common Carrier section following)*			
Puget Sound and Cascade Railway	*(see Common Carrier section following)*			
Puget Sound Pulp and Timber Company	1929-1957			36.6
Day Creek unit[1]	1929-1938	11.0		
Finney Creek unit[1]	1929-1938	14.6		
Mill Creek unit[1]	1929-1938	8.5		
Day Lake Extension (English)	1944-1952	2.5		
Puget Sound Sawmills and Shingle Company	1917-1935	14.6		14.6
Rucker Brothers (note 7)	(1917)-1929	2.3		2.3
Samish Bay Logging Company (note 6)	1912-1928	21.0	1.4	22.4
Scott Brothers	1920s			
Scott Paper Company	1951-1960			
Severson Lumber Company (see UL-1)	(1924)-(1926)	-not located-		
Skagit Logging Company	*(see McMaster and Waite Lumber Co.)*			
Skagit Mill Company	1906-1938			34.5
First unit[1] (Lyman)	1906-1923	14.2		
Second unit[1] (Cokedale)	1923-1938	20.3		
Skagit River Logging Company	1915-1918	0.5		0.5
Slosson Logging Company	1912-(1913)	1.2		1.2
Sound Timber Company	1916-1942			134.4
Sauk River unit[1] (note 5)	1916-1942	99.2	2.8	
Camp 5 unit[1] (note 5)	1937-1942		17.6	
Camp 8 unit[1] (note 5)	(1939)-1942	8.1	6.7	
Soundview Pulp Company	*(see Hamilton Logging Company)*			
Stearns, L. E. (note 9)	1916-(1919)	-not located-		
Stimson Mill Co. (note 7)		10.4		10.4
Sultan Railway and Timber Company (note 5)	1907-1942	36.7	11.2	47.9
Tyee Logging Company	*(see English Tyee unit)*			
Total mileage built by Skagit County loggers		927.6		1,066.4

(note: mileage figures have been derived from various sources and may not agree or total)

LOCATED LOGGING RAILROADS of unidentified operators in SKAGIT COUNTY

	Location	Skagit	Total
UL-1	at McMurray - believed to be Severson Lumber Company	1.7	1.7
UL-2	at Van Horne	3.0	3.0
UL-3	at Nestos	2.4	2.4

LOGGING RAILROADS of other counties extending into SKAGIT COUNTY (shown in grey)

Company	Operating Dates	Skagit	Total
Andron Logging Company (note 7)	1922-(1930)	2.0	2.0
Rucker Brothers (note 7)	(1917)-1929	2.3	2.3
Stimson Mill Co. (note 7)		10.4	10.4

COMMON CARRIER RAILROADS IN SKAGIT COUNTY
Alphabetical list

Company	Operating Dates (railroad)	RR Mileage built Skagit	Other	Total[11]
COMMON CARRIER RAILROADS primarily incorporated to haul logs				
Puget Sound and Baker River Railway	1906-1960			25.3
Dempsey and English	1906-1930	22.0		
PS&BR log boom extension	1912	1.5		
Lyman Timber Company	1917-1937			
Soundview Pulp Company	1937-1951			
PS&BR Similk Bay log dump spur	1923-present	1.8		
Scott Paper Company	1951-present			
Puget Sound & Cascade Railway	1912-(1941)			27.6
Clear Lake Lumber Co/BRL	1912-1927	27.6		
Receiver	1927-1929			
Puget Sound Pulp & Timber Company	1929-(1941)			
INDUSTRIAL RAILROADS hauling logs				
Baker River & Shuksan Railroad	1908-1918			2.5
Superior Portland Cement Co.	1908-1918	2.5		
Skagit River Railway	1919-1954			25.5
City of Seattle (note 10)	1919-1954	17.8	7.7	

A-4

NOTES

See the end paper maps to locate the railroads shown in this listing.

Parens indicate an estimated date or date that could not be determined with reasonable confidence in accuracy.

1. A logging 'unit' is a separate and distinct operation as determined either by physical connection to a common carrier railroad or by legal separation (eg. - contract unit). Unofficial names of such units are shown in parenthesis.
2. Contract logging companies are shown in brackets. Those which held only cutting contracts are also shown in italics. All others contracted both for cutting and railroad operations.
3. Mileage constructed does not include 1.6 miles of ENGLISH mainline 3-railed (to 36" gauge) between mill and woods spur.
4. Mileage (total) is cumulative for all predecessor companies
5. Located in Snohomish County.
6. Located in Whatcom County.
7. Railroad mileage total omits operations in other counties.
8. Railroad mileage does not include "approximated" alignments.
9. The company operated one or more units at other locations in Washington.
10. Mileage total includes 2.7 miles of electrified railroad.
11. Mileage does not include double track, sidings or spurs less than 500 feet.
12. Not same as Skagit Logging Company of Clear Lake.

COMMON CARRIER RAILROADS IN SKAGIT COUNTY
Alphabetical list

COMMON CARRIER SUPPLEMENT

Chronological outline of individual common carriers operating in Skagit County

Steam Railroads:

FAIRHAVEN & SOUTHERN RR [F&S] (Woolley, WA to Bellingham)

1889 Bellingham to Woolley; 14 miles mainline in Skagit County with additional 8.3 mile spur to Cokedale mine.
1890 Bellingham to Blaine (New Westminster & Southern, New Westminster to Blaine)
1890/91 Woolley to Cokedale mines, coal spur
1891 Belfast to Burlington branch constructed (completed GN's route to Canada from Seattle over S&M/F&S rails)
1898 Acquired by SEATTLE & MONTANA Ry (GN subsidiary)
1900 Abandoned between Belfast and Woolley and between Woolley and Cokedale
1902 S&M 'Shortline Route' (Belleville to Bellingham) replaced F&S as mainline
1903 Abandoned Samish Lake to Fairhaven
1905 Cokedale Mine spur abandoned
1906 Bellingham to Belfast trackage leased to Lake Whatcom Logging Company
1913 Lease terminated
1917 Remaining Skagit County trackage (Belleville to Yukon) became abandoned and track material sold to B-D
1919 Cokedale Mine spur rebuilt, then abandoned again 1926

SEATTLE, LAKE SHORE & EASTERN RAILROAD [SLS&E] (Seattle to Sumas via Arlington and Woolley)

1890 Seattle to Woolley; 16.9 miles in Skagit County
1891 Woolley to Sumas; 11.6 miles in Skagit County
1897 Acquired by SEATTLE & INTERNATIONAL RR (controlled by Northern Pacific)

SEATTLE & INTERNATIONAL RAILROAD [S&I] (constructed no railroad/operating company only)

1901 Absorbed into Northern Pacific Railroad

NORTHERN PACIFIC RAILROAD [NP]

A-5

1912/14 Relocation of 13 miles (at Ehrlich and between Sedro-Woolley and Wickersham); 11 miles of original SLS&E grade abandoned
1969 Merged into BURLINGTON NORTHERN RR (see separate listing)

SEATTLE & MONTANA Ry (GN subsidiary, created in 1890 to establish Seattle to Canada route)

1891 Completed Seattle to Burlington line, 12.6 miles in Skagit County, and Belfast to Burlington; 5.8 miles.
1898 Acquired FAIRHAVEN & SOUTHERN RR
1907 Absorbed into Great Northern

SEATTLE & MONTANA RR (A "paper" company created 3-29-1898, all operations actually by GN Ry.)

1907 Absorbed into GREAT NORTHERN Ry. (see separate listing)

SEATTLE & NORTHERN RR (a property of the Oregon Improvement Co.)

1890/91 Anacortes to Hamilton via Burlington and Woolley; 32.7 miles
1900 Built Hamilton to Sauk, 18.84 miles.
1901 Built Sauk to Rockport, 2.36 miles.
1902 Acquired by Seattle & Montana Ry.
Burlington to Anacortes renamed 'Anacortes Branch'
Burlington to Hamilton renamed 'Hamilton Branch'

GREAT NORTHERN RAILWAY [GN]

1898 Assumed operations of SEATTLE & MONTANA RR
1901/03 Constructed shoreline route Belleville to Bellingham, 13.1 miles in Skagit County
1902 Assumed operations of SEATTLE & NORTHERN RR
1942 Anacortes Branch extended 3.5 miles west from Anacortes
1954 Extension west from Anacortes abandoned
1962 Abandoned Concrete to Rockport

1969 Merged into BURLINGTON NORTHERN RR [BN] (see separate listing)

BURLINGTON NORTHERN RR [BN]

1969 Created by merger of the properties of NORTHERN PACIFIC RR, GREAT NORTHERN RR, PACIFIC COAST RR, SPOKANE, PORTLAND & SEATTLE RR, and CB&Q RR
1973 Abandoned Bryant to Clear Lake
1982 Abandoned Clear Lake to Sedro Woolley

MOUNT VERNON TERMINAL RR [MVT] (operates switching railroad at Mount Vernon)

1939 Assumed operation of approx. 6 miles of former PACIFIC NW TRACTION CO. trackage in Mount Vernon.

Electric Railroads

FIDALGO CITY & ANACORTES INTERURBAN

1891 Constructed 13 miles between Fidalgo City and present day Dewey Beach. Exact alignment unknown.
1891 Abandoned and removed. Not actually placed in service.

BELLINGHAM & SKAGIT INTERURBAN RR [B&S]

1911 Bellingham to Mount Vernon, 22.2 miles in Skagit County
1912 Burlington to Sedro-Woolley, 4.8 miles; also graded between Mount Vernon and Skagit City.
1912 (by acquisition) became PACIFIC NORTHWEST TRACTION CO.

PACIFIC NORTHWEST TRACTION [PNT]

1912 projected completion to Skagit City and extension to Everett. Never undertaken.
1928 Passenger service discontinued due to Skagit River bridge poor condition. Bridge rebuilt and freight service continued to 6-1-30
1930 abandoned; removed except for trackage in Mount Vernon now operated as Mount Vernon Terminal RR see MOUNT VERNON TERMINAL RR

A-6

APPENDIX B

BLACKMAN LOCOMOTIVE and CAR PATENTS

B-1

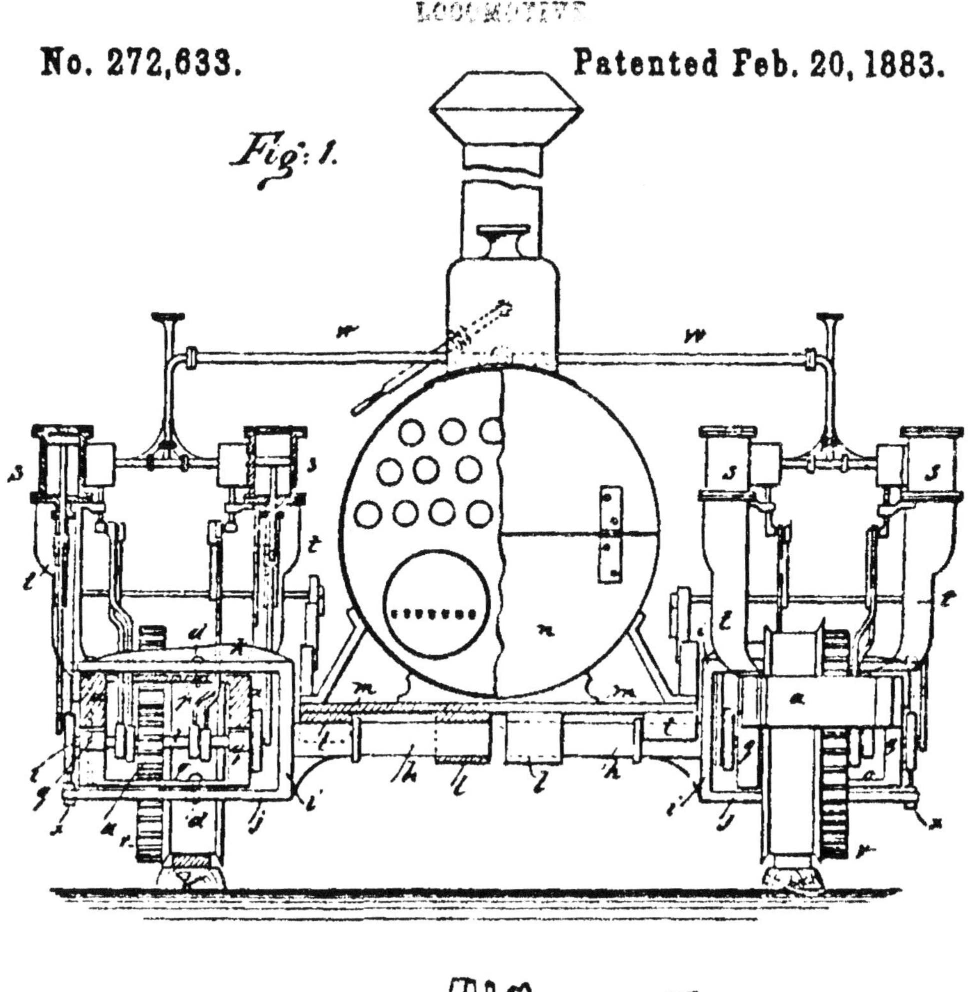

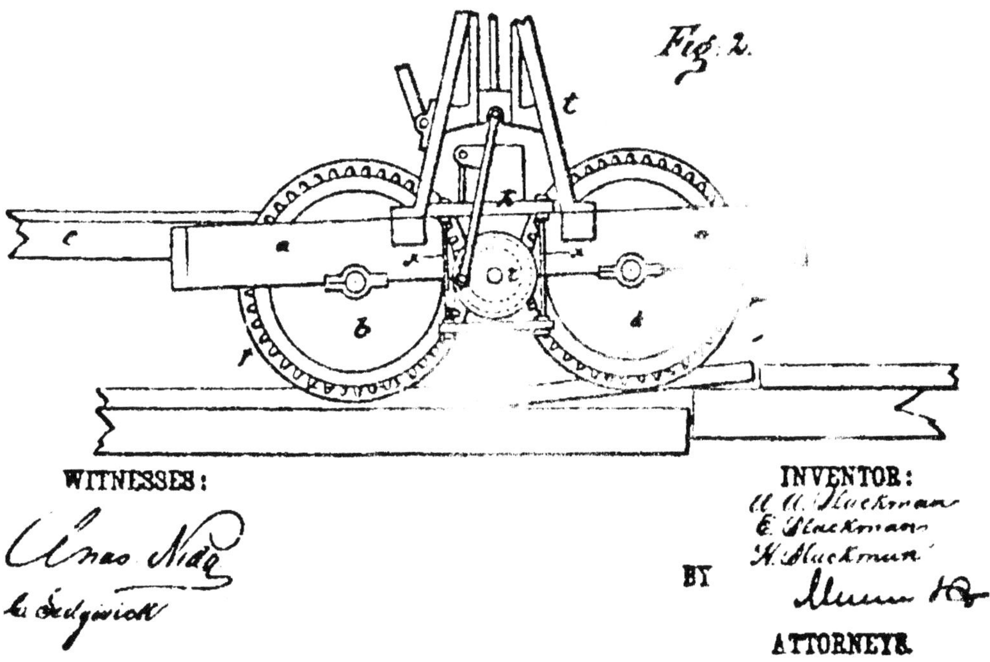

LOCOMOTIVE.

No. 272,633. Patented Feb. 20, 1883.

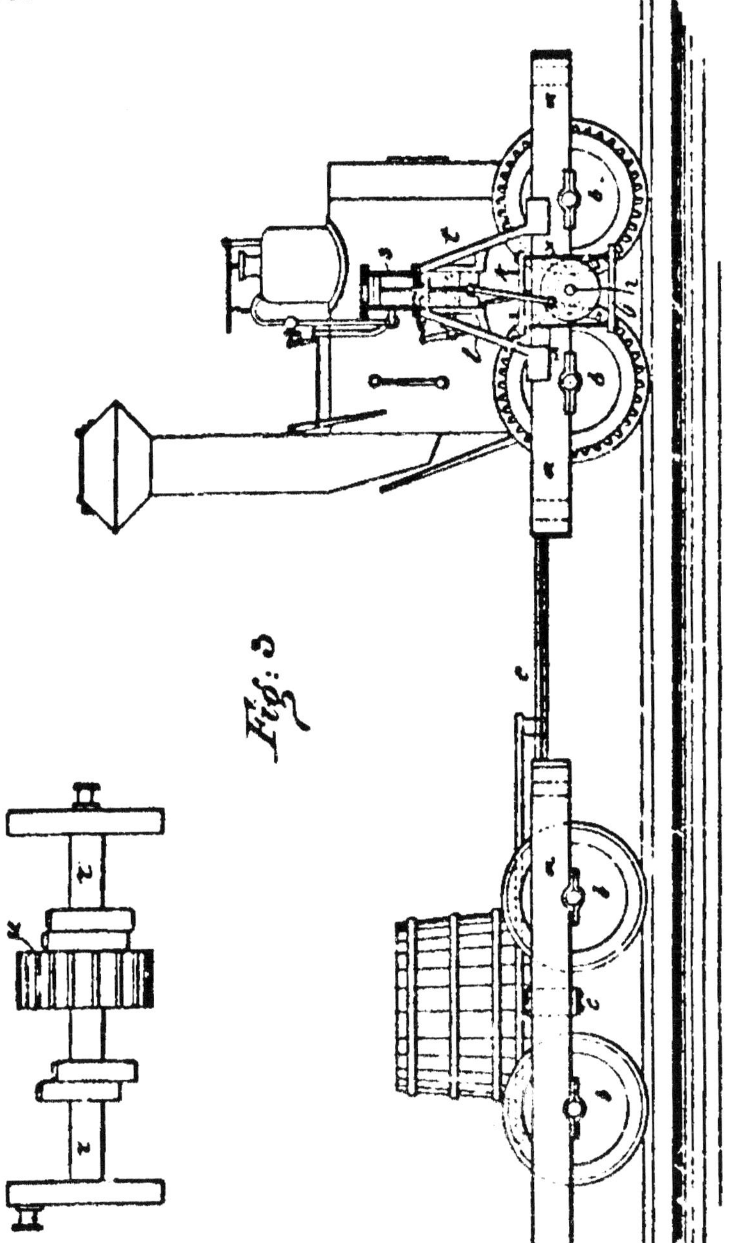

Fig: 3

Fig: 4.

B-2

WITNESSES:

INVENTOR:

A. A. Blackman

E. Blackman

H. Blackman

BY Munn & Co

ATTORNEYS.

(No Model.) 3 Sheets—Sheet 3.

A. A., E. & H. BLACKMAN.

LOCOMOTIVE.

No. 272,633. Patented Feb. 20, 1883.

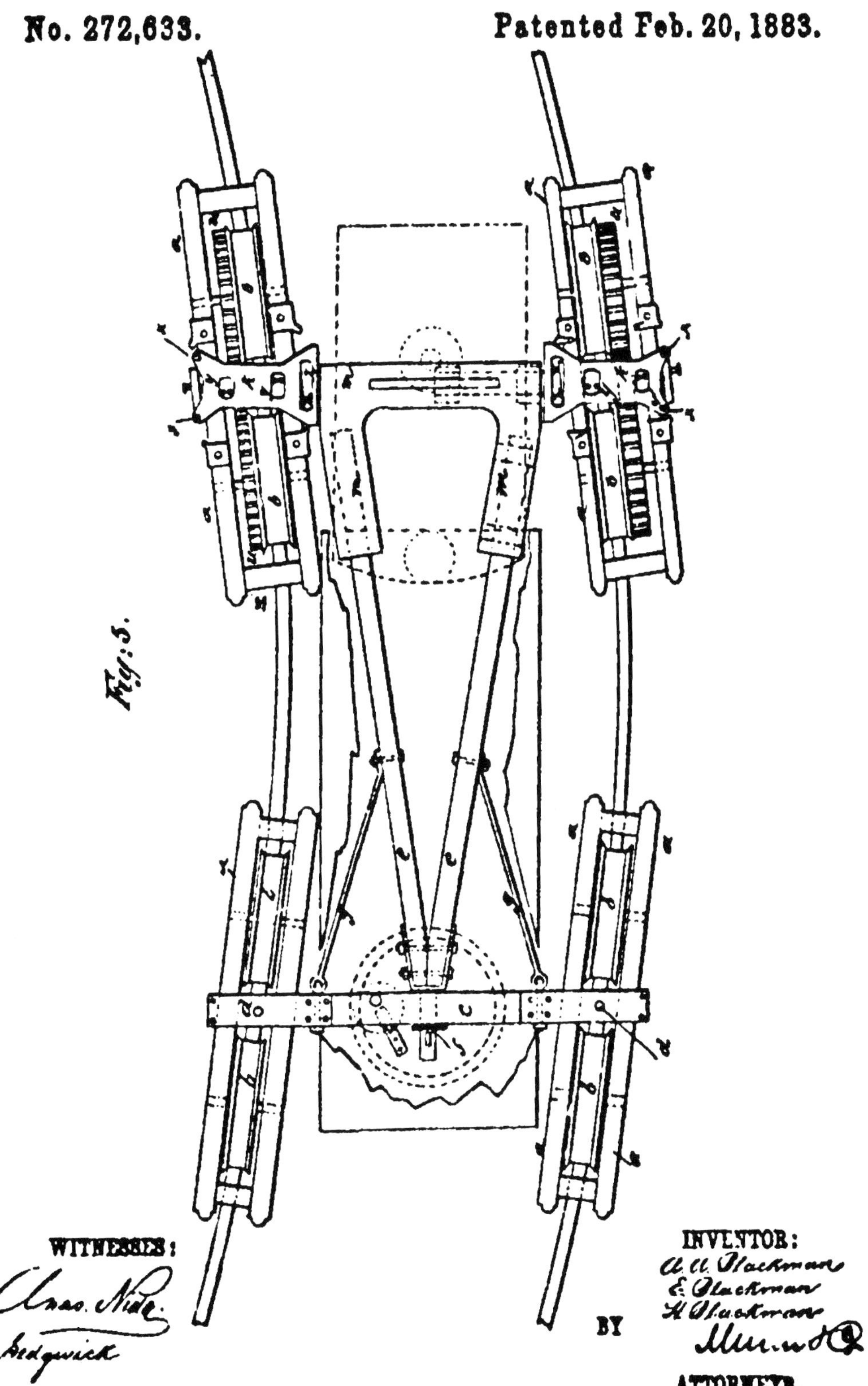

B-3

(No Model.)

A. A., E. & H. BLACKMAN.

CAR TRUCK.

No. 254,906. Patented Mar. 14, 1882.

B-4

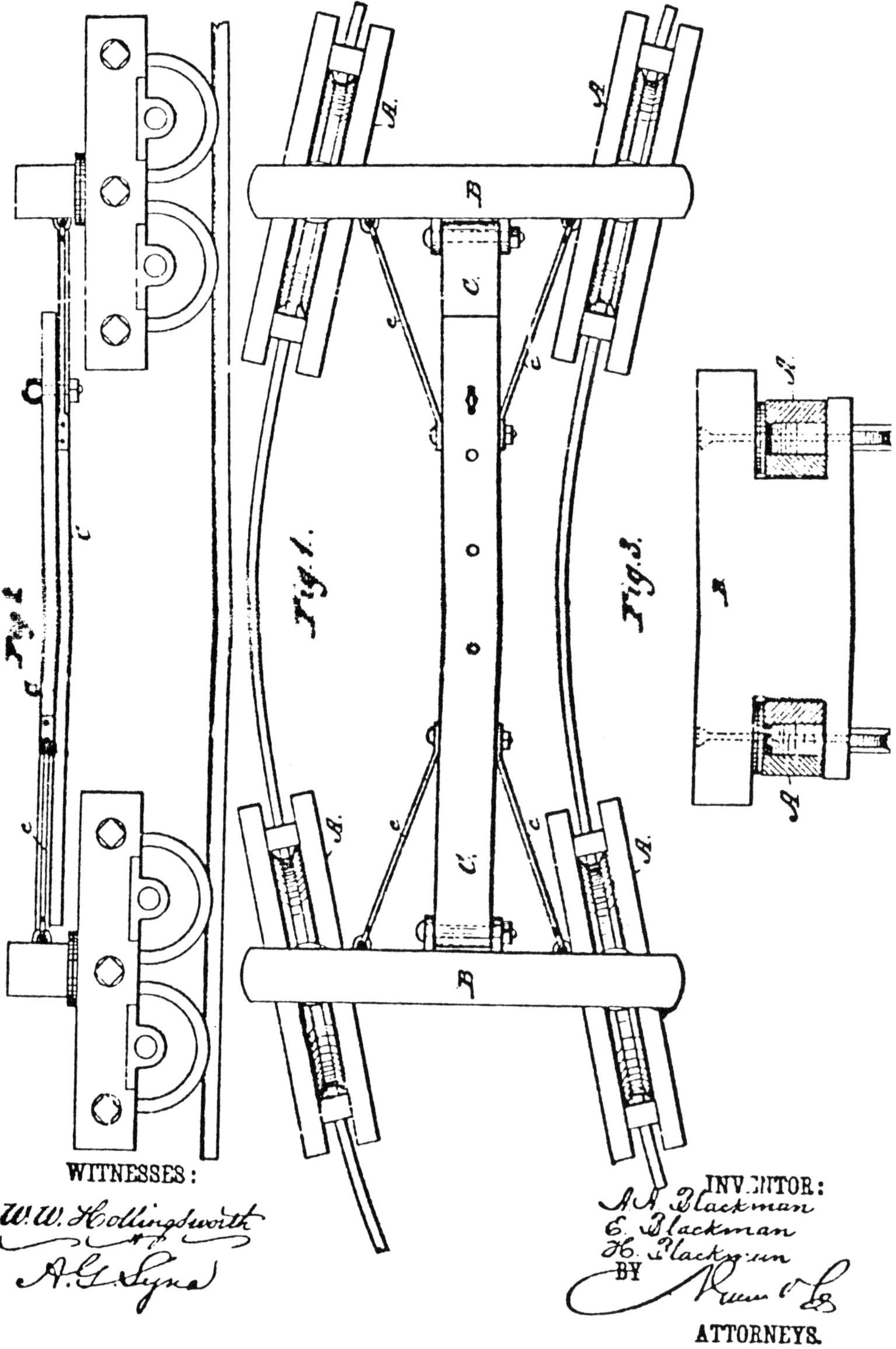

BLACKMAN LOCOMOTIVE

BLACKMAN locomotive with train on an unexpectedly sturdy and large but unusual design trestle for a logging railroad for the period - 1883. See page 212 for additional photographs of the locomotive. *Walt Taubeneck and Marysville Historical Society.*

B-5

M.A.C. speeders from Skagit Steel's Motor Appliance Company provided loggers with an economical power source for non-revenue jobs such as crew and supplies transportation as well as track building and maintenance illustrated in this deep woods scene of new trackage being pushed into fresh timberlands. This 6-60 Speeder has brought up the skeleton car load of ties to be distributed (manhandled) ahead in preparation for arrival of the rail (probably being picked up from an old side that has been cut-out). Occasionally a significant piece of equipment was accidentally stranded in such removals - one logger had to re-lay several miles of track when they looked around and found they had left their Lidgerwood skidder behind! *Skagit Steel and Iron Works*

APPENDIX C

SKAGIT STEEL AND IRON WORKS

Logging and Railroad Equipment manufactured in Skagit County

Within the borders of Skagit County a significant manufacturing company has existed for the past eighty-eight years. Located in Sedro Woolley the firm was founded by John Anderson in 1901, as a machine shop and foundry. First named Sedro-Woolley Iron Works, the company has been, and still is, a manufacturer of logging equipment.

In its early years the company found success doing all forms of repair work on logging machinery and logging locomotives. Sedro-

Woolley Iron Works began building single drum hoists for Alaska in 1908, and expanded steadily from that point. In 1914, the firm changed its name to Skagit Steel and Iron Works.

Skagit's reputation was usually associated with steam driven power - the standard of the day, including a number of Heisler conversions from steam to diesel, one a 2 trucker for the Yakutat and Southern Railway. However, Sidney McIntyre, one of the principals of the firm, was busy designing new uses for gasoline driven equipment and power plants. Uncertain of the market impact and public opinion of this new concept, it was decided to offer the new line under the name Motor Appliance Company, better known as simply M. A. C. (or MAC).

The first product was a hoist, or winching engine, using a modified Fordson farm tractor for power. This new unit was named the M.A.C. Little Tugger, and gained considerable popularity. McIntyre then designed a Fordson conversion that resulted in a small locomotive for use in small logging camps.

Fordson "locomotives" were available from 24-inch gauge to standard gauge. Pole road versions also appeared, and all varieties were in production from about 1921 into the early 1940s. Even in the early 1920s, these MAC units were sold all over the county and as far away as Japan.

SKAGIT STEEL AND IRON WORKS

Skagit Steel and Iron Works soon offered an extensive line of railroad equipment including speeders, rail cars of all sizes and even several small locomotives. MAC rail cars came into widespread use in the logging camps of the west coast.

C-2

Several small locomotives were produced in 1954 for the Taiwan Sugar Corporation. Skagit Steel itself retains a plant switcher in Sedro Woolley of its own creation, their model ZM10, built in July of 1951.

Skagit Steel and Iron Works is alive and operating at this writing, although a number of ownership changes have occurred. It is presently known as Skagit-LTV Energy Products. During the past two decades goods produced have covered a wide range from shell casings for military contracts, to shipboard winching machines, to the "true" Skagit line of modern tower logging systems. There remains a local pride in the firm, and Company management and employees continue to make sizeable contributions to the community.

SKAGIT STEEL AND IRON WORKS

C-3

Views of various Skagit built equipment

These two pictures of Long-Bell Lumber No. 1 M.A.C. speeder show the versatility and economy these units could provide the logger by doing work that otherwise could require a somewhat more expensive locomotive with full crew. *Photographs courtesy Skagit Steel and Iron Works*

C-4

Some fine examples of low budget tram road logging with equipment from Skagit Steel and Iron Works - one of these locomotives (intact) and tram car components exist at a logging museum near the Longmire entrance to Mount Rainier National Park.

C-5

Other Interesting Scenes in the Woods
trucks making inroads on the domain of the steam machines

Truck turntable being turned by horse for this S. W. Barker logging operation using GMC trucks in 1919.

Hogg-Houghton operation just north of Lake Samish with Bulldog Mack trucks fitted with flanged steel wheels inside the hard rubber tires. They were lowered down a railroad incline after which they drove off over gravel roads to the log dump in the late 1920s. *(below)* unknown location or operator but a fascinating scene. *Dennis Thompson Collection*

SCALE DRAWINGS

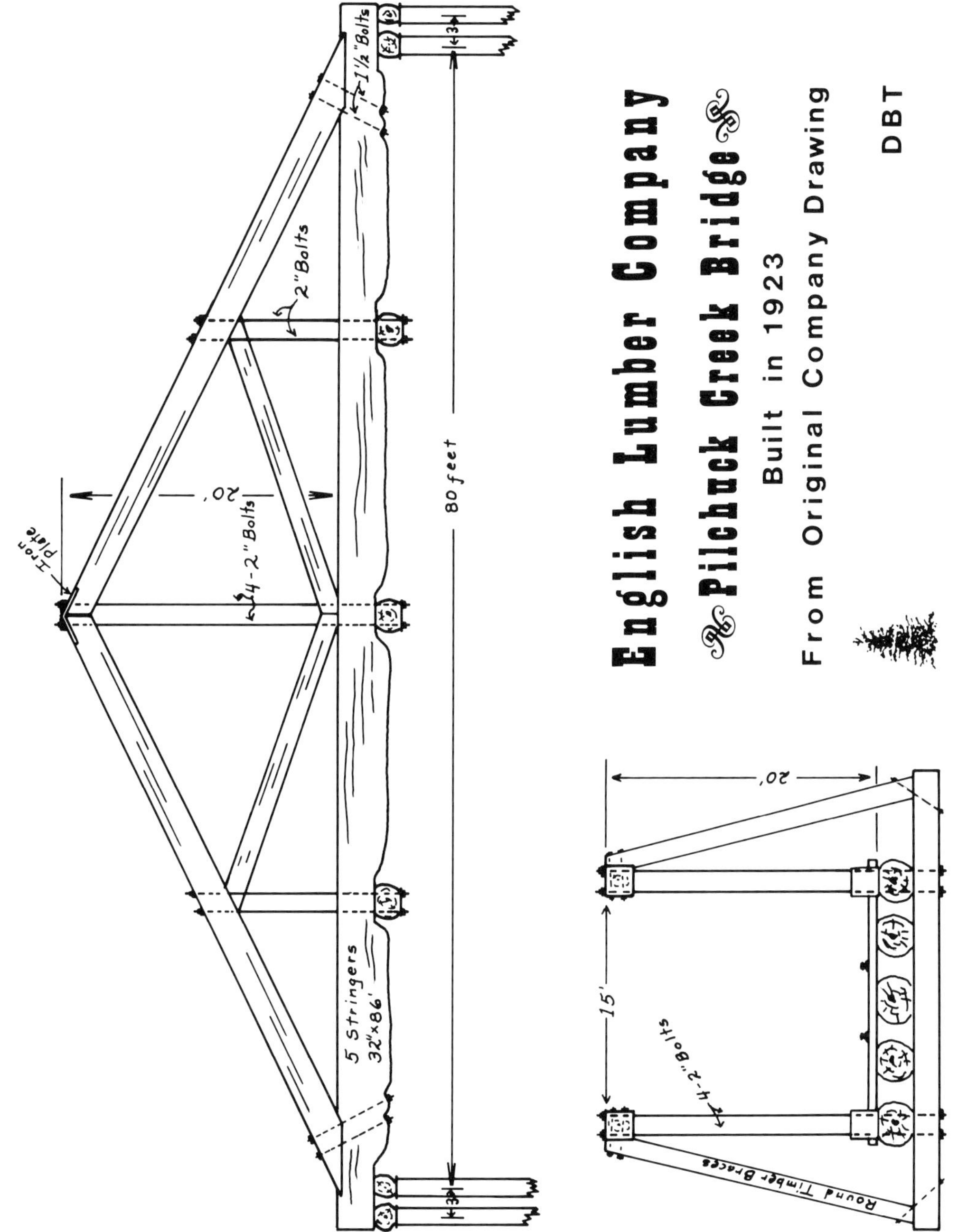

D-1

Full size for N scale (160-1 RATIO)

SKAGIT STEEL and IRON WORKS FORDSON LOCOMOTIVE CONVERSION

drawn by E. L. Hauff

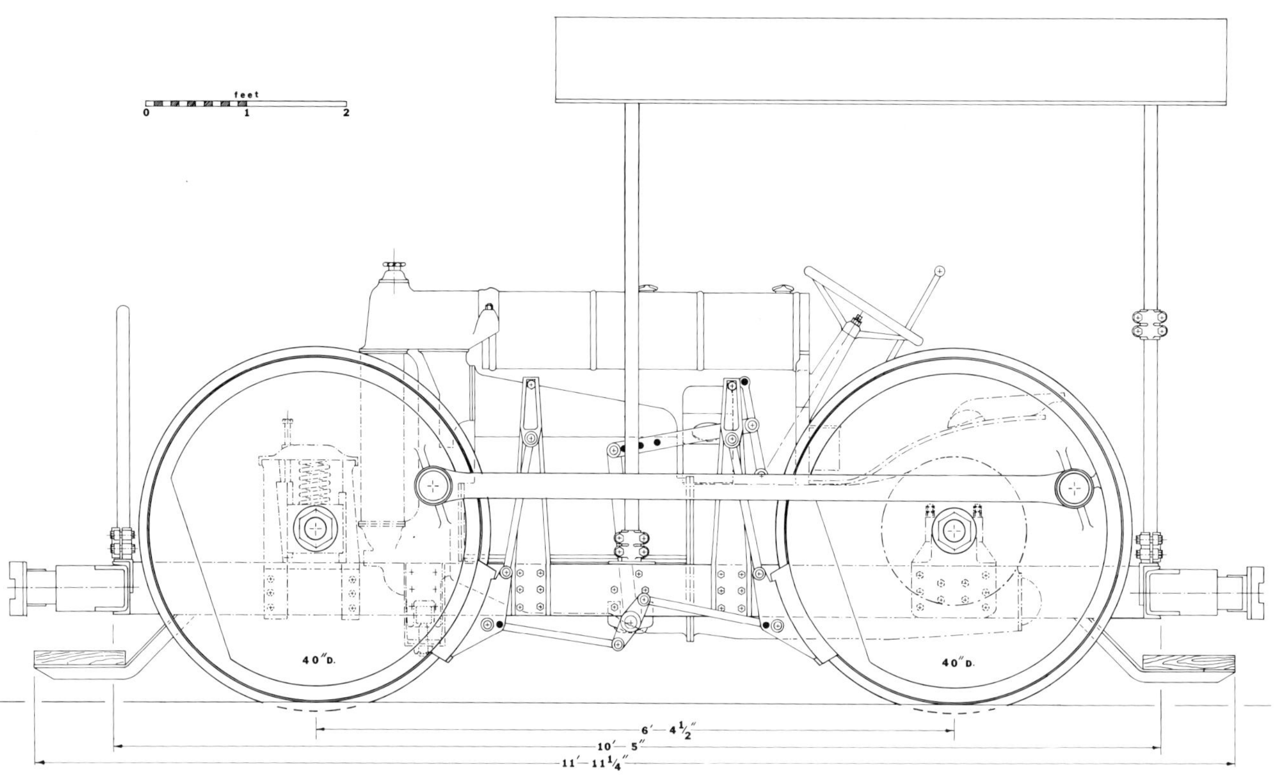

D-2 1/2" = 1' Scale

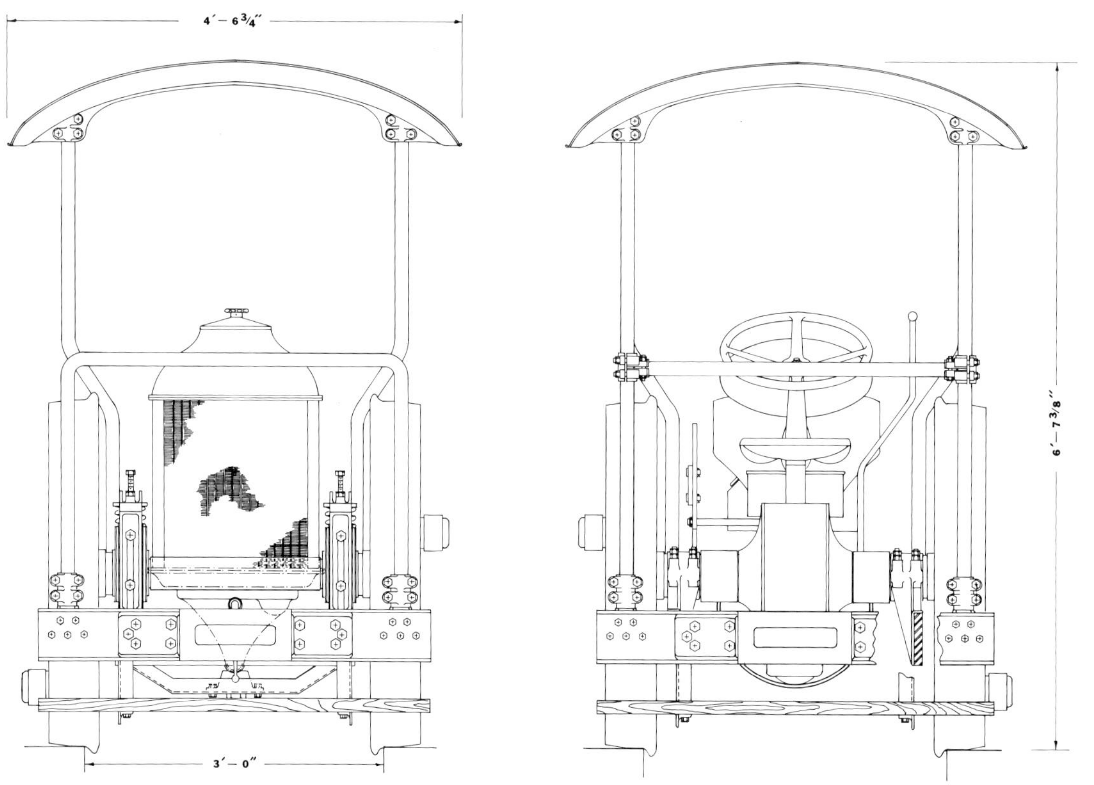

SKAGIT STEEL and IRON WORKS FORDSON LOCOMOTIVE CONVERSION

drawn by E. L. Hauff

D-3

SESSOMS LOWERING SYSTEM

D-4

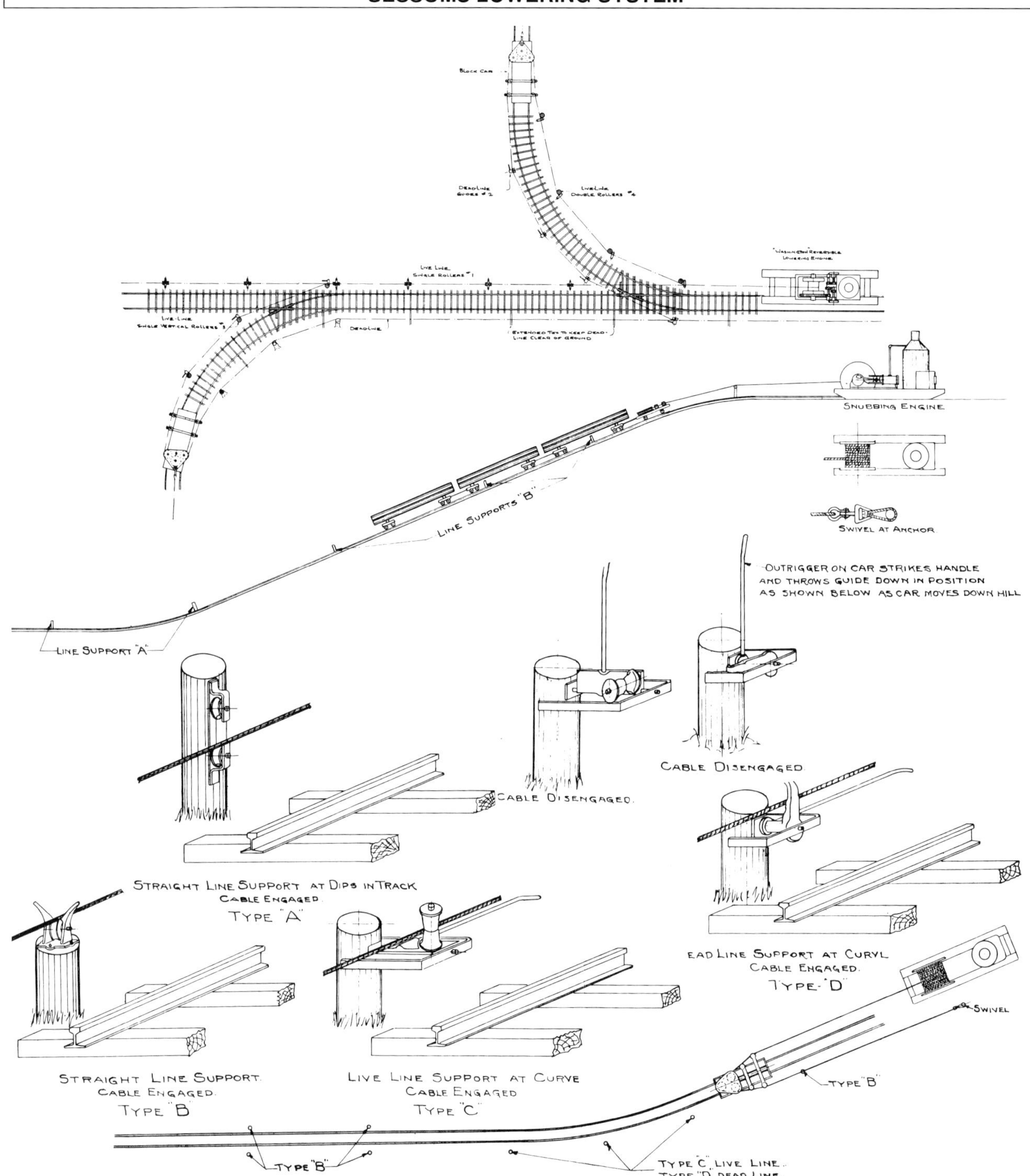

The Sessoms Lowering System was invented by Hugh Sessoms to provide more flexibility in laying out incline (or log car) lowering systems which previously were forced to be a straight drop due to the pulling cable. The Sessoms system had cable guides which restrained the lowering cable and a lowering (or block) car which guided (laid) the cable onto the guides and provided additional capacity due to 2-1 leverage provided by the lowering car pulley. The upper drawing from the Washington Iron Works 1921 catalog illustrates the lowering car, cable guides and the flexibility permitting turnouts to side spurs. The system equipment was built by Pacific Car and Foundry Company of Renton with Washington Iron Works offering a "Washington Improved Lowering Engine" snubbing engine to provide the power. The lower set of drawings are reproduced from a Pacific Car & Foundry Co. INSTALLATION and TRACK EQUIPMENT drawing of June 1, 1921. It incorrectly omits type "C" supports from the inside of the first curve - they should be on the live-line inside of the curve with the Type "D" on the outside as shown. See pages 106-107 and 171 for photographs of Sessoms systems in operation. *Ken Schmelzer Collection*

ANATOMY OF A LOGGING OPERATION

CLEAR LAKE LUMBER COMPANY INVENTORY (partial 1926 mortgage/bankruptcy list)

SAW MILL, containing amongst other equipment the following:

1 Cut Off Saw on mill pond
2 Log Decks fully equipped with log turner and kickers
2 Carriages - 1 four block carriage and 1 - 5 block both equipped with Front electric set works
2 Rock saws
1 11 ft. Allis Chalmers Band Mill
1 9 ft. " " " "
1 12x14 " " Twin Feed
1 14x16 " " " " Engine
1 16x20 Sumner Twin Feed Engine
1 16" Allis Chalmers Edger
1 14" " " "
2 20 Saw Allis Chalmers Air Trimmers
1 Pawling & Harnischfeger - 2 ton electric crane
1 14 x 18 Diamond Iron Works Gang
2 84" Merscoen Resaws
1 6" Diamond Iron Works Edger - Eastern Edger
1 12" Saw - Diamond Iron Works Trimmer
1 Yates Surfacer - 16x24" - Motor Driven
3 Yates Ready Sizer - 6"

POWER

3 1000 K.V.A. Transformers for Puget Sound Light & Power Company
3 800 H.P. Sterling Water Tube Boilers
1 400 H.P. Sterling Water Tube Boilers
2 250 H.P. Casey Hedges Horizontal Boilers
2 Platt Iron Works Oil Feed Pumps
1 500 gal. minutefire pump
1 1000 gal. minutefire pump
1 750 Kilowatt - Allis Chalmers Turbine
1 1000 " " " "
1 3200 " " " "
1 Motor driven exciter
1 12x12 Ingersoll-Rand Air Compressor
1 14x14 " " " "
1 Fuel house, including condensers, switch boards, sawmill and brick power house equipped with sprinkler system
Electric light system for mill and also for village of Clear Lake, including poles, wires and other equipment and apparatus.

DRY KILNS

17 Dry Kilns of the Grand Rapids and Moor type, equipped with trucks

PLANING MILL

1 Diamond Hog
1 Rip Saw
1 #10 Yates Surfacer
1 S. A. Woods combination and siding and planer machine.
3 Fast feed profile Yates Planers
5 Trimmer Saws
1 Yates sander
1 Clapboard machine
Filing room and other planing room equipment

SHINGLE MILL

18 Sumner upright shingle machines
2 Power Cut-offs
2 Power Splitters
1 Automatic splitter equipped with belt, saws, blow pipe system, filing room, conveyor chain, etc.
4 Grand Rapids Dry Kilns equipped with heat controls and kiln trucks
1 Shingle storage shed with storage capacity of 12,000,000 shingles

POWER

2 400 H. P. Sterling Water Rube (sic) Boilers
1 150 H. P. Sumner Horizontal Boiler
1 24x26 Ball Engine
1 10x12 Chandler Taylor Engine
2 6x4x6 - Prescott feed water pumps
1 500 gal. per minute fire pump
also automatic sprinkler system

WOOD DEPT.

2 48" Diamond Hogs
2 Wood Trimmers
Wood and Fuel Hog bunkers with filing room machinery and apparatus

YARD

Lumber Buggies and Lumber Trucks
1 - 3 ton G.M.C. Truck
5 - Ford Lumber Tractors
1 - Fordson Tractor
1 - Ford Gasoline Locomotive

MACHINE SHOP

3 - Blacksmith forges
1 - American bolt cutter
1 - Pipe and Bolt Cutter - Acme
1 - 6" Automatic Trip Hammer
1 - McCabe Lathe - 26", 48" - 2 spindle
1 - 10" Clauson Lathe
1 - Radical (sic) Drill - 48" - Bickford
1 - 14" Atkins Automatic Hack Saw
1 - 250 ton wheel press - Caldwell
1 - Shaper - 18" - American
1 - Gasoline electric welding machine
1 - Oxweld cutting torch and acetylene welding
1 - Oxweld generator
1 - 15 ton crane
2 - 5 ton cranes and car shop in conjunction

ROLLING STOCK EQUIPMENT

LOCOMOTIVES

2 - 50 ton Shay
1 - 60 ton "
1 - 80 ton "
2 - 80 ton "
1 - 70 ton Baldwin Side Tank
1 - 100 ton Baldwin Mikado
1 - Class 80 Standard Shay Geared Locomotive shop No. 3260 purchased by the Clear Lake Lumber Company under conditional sales contract from the Hofius Steel & Equipment Company under contract dated May 2, 1924, filed for record on May 10, 1924.
50 - Standard connected truck logging cars with U. S. Safety Appliance Platforms purchased

from Pacific Car & Foundry Company under contract dated February 27, 1925, filed by the Auditor of Skagit County March 6, 1925, being Auditor's No. 181486.

Certain electric equipment purchased from General Electric Company by Clear Lake Lumber Company under contract dated October 16, 1924, filed November 6, 1924, with the Auditor of Skagit County.

3 - Logging camps, being numbered 1, which is situated on Section 25, Township 35 North, Range 7 East, W.M., No. 2 situated on Section 19, Township 35 North, Range 8 East, W.M., and Camp No. 4 situated on Section 4, Township 34 North, Range 6 East, W.M., and all equipment, apparatus, furniture, rolling stock, camp kitchen, bedding, furnishings, yarders, roaders, pile drivers, electric light plants, unloading engines, lines, cables, rollers, blocks, tackle, pumps, spikes, bolts, hooks, tongs and equipment used therein and steam shovels and general equipment and apparatus, in or used in connection with said camps or appurtenant thereto.

STEEL RAILS

3 miles of 60 pound steel rails purchased from the Great Northern Railroad Company

6 Miles of 60 pound steel rails held under lease and contract of purchase from the Great Northern Railroad Company.

18 miles of 60 pound steel rails

6 miles of 66 pound steel rails held under contract of purchase and lease from the Northern Pacific Railroad Company. These rails being in part laid in track and in part in storage, together with all ties, spikes, switch blocks and other rail and track equipment and all other rails, spikes, bolts, switch box and railroad equipment owned by the said defendant company. All side tracks, spurs, sidings, and switch tracks belonging to the Clear Lake Lumber Company connected with its mill or yards, camps or the main line of the Puget Sound & Cascade Railroad Company, together with all the rails, ties, spikes, bolts, switch blocks and other track equipment appurtenant thereto. All logging roads and skid roads or timber felled and bucked in the woods, on the cars or in the yards or log pond and all lumber cut and manufactured in possession of the Clear Lake Lumber Company on the 1st day of August , 1925.

E-2

DONKEYS

2 - 9x10½ Three drum loader
2 - 11 x 13 Humboldt Yarder
1 - 12x12 Washington yarder - wood burner - in yard at mill
1 - 10x12 Washington roader - wood burner - in yard at mill
1 - 12x17 Washington yarder - 2 speed (new)
2 - 9x10¼ " duplex loaders (New)
2 - 12x14 - 2 speed Duplex Washington Aerial Yarders (New)
4 - 10x12 Washington Duplex loaders (new)
2 - 10½x10¼ " Com. Geared Yarders - wood burners
3 - 12x14 2 speed Washington Yarders (new)
1 - 11x11 Washington Comp. Geared Yarder
1 - 12x12 " Extension Fire Box Comp. Geared Yarder
1 - 12x14 Washington Snubbing engine - 72" Boiler
1 - 10½x15½x18 - C.C.R. Washington Snubber
2 - 7x9 Pile Drivers (fully equipped)
2 - 7x10 Pile Drivers (fully equipped)
1 - 9x10 Washington Unloading engine at dump at Clear Lake
1 - Fordson Gasoline donkey
Line, roller equipment, 2 lowering cars (Sesson's [sic - Sessoms] Type), water pumps, oil pumps, auxiliary electric light plants, and miscellaneous equipment such as railroad spikes, bolts, hooks, tongs, pipe, etc.

ROLLING STOCK

1 - 1500 bbl. capacity oil storage tank equipped with steam pump
2 - 100,000 capacity Donkey Moving Cars
1 - 200,000 " " " "
6 - Western side air dump cars - 80,000 capacity
3 - Center dump cars - 80,000 "
149 - Skeletons - Pacific Car & Foundry type. This figure includes the 50 cars which were bought from this company in 1925 under conditional sales contract.
5 - Log Flats
1 - 16" Wood rack
4 oil storage cars
3 Fire tanks
10 - 80,000 N. P. Box Cars purchased by Clear Lake Lumber Co.
185 - Total cars - 2 Kalamazoo Speeders

CAMP INVENTORY EXAMPLE

CAMP #4

Camp #4 - CAMP SITE -NE¼ SW ¼ Sec. 4 - Township 34 NR 6 E - Skagit County

Camp Spur graded off of Main Line of Logging road

1 Kitchen Car #1
1 - 3 oven Lang range
1 - Frick Ice machine
1 - Westinghouse motor - 1½H.P. #2416051
Sink, Dish up tables, cupboards, etc.
Dishes, cooking utensils, knives, forks, etc. to feed 175 men

2 Dining Cars #3 - #1

1 Store and Office Car #2
1 - Single bed
1 - Chair
1 - Table
1 - Wash bowl (modern)

1 Apartment Car #1
7 - Single bunks (Tiger)
7 - Tables
7 - Chairs
7 - Wash bowls (modern)

1 Combination Car #1
1 - 48" Upright Boilers
1 - Westinghouse D.C. Steam Turbine - 7½ K.W. #2304346
1 - Switchboard (Westinghouse)
Dry Room - 4 shower baths

5 Sleepers - #1 - 2 - 4 - 5 - 6
14 Double Deck Steel Tiger Bunks each car

1 Library Car #2
8 - Chairs
4 - Tables
1 - Drafting table
2 - Single Bunks (Tiger)
2 - Double " "

These camp cars are all on wheels, steam heated and electric lighted and modern in every respect.

1 Sanitary modern toilet on skids
5 - Bowls
1 - Urinal

1 Girls Shack on Skids 14' x 38'
3 - Single beds
4 - Chairs
2 - Tables
1 - Great Western Heater

1 Foremans Shack on Skids 14' x 36'
1 - Single bed
1 - Table
1 - Chair

1 Blanket House on Skids 14' x 40'
2 Great Western Heaters
1 Single Bunks
5 Double "
Mattresses, blankets and linen to accommodate 175 men

1 Blacksmith Shop 14' x 40' On skids
2 Homemade Yarding blocks
1 250# anvil
1 12" vise
7 pair tongs
1 Washington Haulback Block #2120
1 Buffalo Forge #200
12 Ft. 3/4" chain
7 1¼" choker thimbles
4 Homemade Butt lines
8 1¼" - D's
1 Champion Hand Drill Press
6 1¾" Shackles
7 Chokers without wire
8 Butt hooks " "
1 Toledo pipe stock and die - 3/4" to 1½"
1 Erie Manufacturing Co. "
1 Wylie & Russell " for bolts
3 Stocks and dies - 3/8" to 1½"
2 Adz
4 Swamping axes
2 8# Hammers
1 Champion Forge and emery wheel
1 Splicing frame
1 Babbitt Ladle
1 Complete set of Blacksmith tools, hammers, sledges, etc.
1 Steam pump - double action - 2 x 4

1 Filing Shack on Skids 14' x 36'
1 36" Grindstone
2 Saw filing benches
16 Wood bucking saws
2 6 ft. steam drag saw blades
1 11 ft. falling saw
2 12 ft. " "
3 8 ft. Bucking saws
45 7 ft. " "
19 8 ft. " " (new)
18 8# sledges and handles
40 Falling and bucking axes
3 8# Splitting wedges
100 Ft. 1" Rubber water hose
1 Artic heater
2 Single bunks - 2 chairs - 1 table
12 Spring boards
52 Falling & bucking wedges
6 Spring board irons
1 Buda Track Jack #2B1
40 Falling and bucking saw handles
6 Pipe wrenches - 12"
1 Oil House on skids 14' x 40'
72 Rd. Pt. #2 shovels
15 Picks and handles
5 Mattocks
10 Fire buckets
3 Swamping axes
2 Claw bars
4 Spike mauls
1 Track gauge
2 8# hammers
4 Bowser oil tanks #28750 - 100 Gal. capacity
#2C-53171
C-53171
C-53992
C-53970
5 1¼" Air hose
1 Steam drag saw
1 Toledo pipe stock and die 3/4" to 1½"
15 Stilson pipe wrenches - 12" - 14"
1 Monkey wrench
1 Scoop shovel
9 36" axe handles
1 6" pipe vise
Fittings, packing and misc repair parts for donkeys
1 Allis Chalmers Light Plant on Skids - 5 K.W. No. 1225
MK-4DK-1
1 Switchboard
1 Lining bar
1 Water tank on skids - 4x10x12 Wood
1000 ft. 1½" pipe to this tank
12 Houses at Potts on skids 14' x 40' with toilets -
Legal description - SW¼ SE¼ Sec 29 -Twp. 35 N.R. 6 E.
1 Water tank with spout on skids - 6'x12'x14' Wood
3500 Ft. 1½" pipe line to locomotive tank and houses
1 Push car (homemade)

Old Camp 4 Site

SW¼ NE¼ Sec. 10, Twp. 34, N.R. 6 E.
1 Sand House on skids 14' x 34'
1 Sand dryer
1 Locomotive water tank and spout - 6'x12'x14' - Wooden on skids
1800' - 1½" pipe line to supply this water tank

South Lateral Camp site

NW¼ NW¼ Sec. 15 - Twp. 34, N.R. 6 E
1 House on skids 14' x 36'
250 Ft. 1-1/8" Manila rope
2 8" Double blocks
1 6" " "
6 Mattocks and handles
5 Picks " "

E-3

1 Track jack - 6B1
8 Mattocks with handles
12 Picks with handles
1 2" Wood augur
20 Ft. 3/4" Drill steel
3 8# Sledges
3 Peavies
1 Round heating stove
3 Track mauls
1 Wheelbarrow
1 75# anvil
1 Forge, Lancaster geared #40
1 36" Grindstone
1 Shack on skids 14' x 36'
1 Pick
1 Peavy
2 Track tongs
1 Denver Rock Drill #27416
37 Ft. Bucking saws
20 Ft. 1½ hose

SW¼ NW¼ Sec. 10 Twp. 34 N.R. 6 E

1 10' x 16' House on Skids

Incline equipment

Fairleader and drum for Model 21 Steam Shovel
1 WaterTank and spout on skids - 6x10x14 - Wood
1500 Ft. 1½" pipe line to this tank

NE¼ NW¼ - Sec. 5, Twp. N.R. 6 E.

1 6'x12'x16' Locomotive water tank with spout
300 Ft. 2" pipe line to supply this tank with water

In Mill Yard behind Machine Shop -

SE¼ Section 1, Twp. 34, N.R. 4 E
1 Dry and bath house 14' x 36'

E-4

CAMP #4 - EQUIPMENT

NW¼ NW¼ Sec. 15, Twp. 34, N.R. 6E - South Lateral

1 Washington Chunk out donkey, on sled with roof, wood burner, steel tank - 9 x 10¼ #2248
1 Homemade yard block
1 Washington Haulback Blk #120
1 Shackle - 1½"
1 Pr. 1¾" Twin hooks
1 1¼" chocker
1 Rd. Pt. #2 shovel
1400 Ft. 3/4" line
700 " 3/8" "
3 Picks with handles
650 Ft. 1½" pipe line to this machine
1 Marion Caterpillar Steam Shovel - type 21 - #5017 - Wood Burner

Incline #1 - Camp 4 -

Bottom or Eastern endin center SE¼ NW¼ Sec. 10, Twp 34, 6 E
- Western endin SW¼ NW¼ Sec. 10 Twp. 34 - 6 E:

1 - 12x14 - 2 Speed Snubber engine on sled with snubber house 18' x 46' - Oil burner with steel oil and water tank - Engine #3408 Equipped with all oil cans, miscellaneous tools
1 2x4 Double action Steam Oil Pump brassbushed "The Dean of Holyoke"
500 Ft. 1" pipe to supply oil to snubber
1 150 barrel steel oil storage tank

1 crank shaft with pinions
1 Sessoms type lowering car, equipped with three sheaves and 4 outrigger sheaves - C.L.L. Co. #1
1 Home made Tree shoe line guide
1 Ball bearing swivel for lowering line #H-2
1 14" Sheave on shaft to spool lowering line
1 Hot water tank used for oil spray
4600 Ft. 1½" Lowering Line
4 16" Upright line guides
31 Fork type rollers
2 Trip line rollers
4800 Ft. 12 gauge telephone wire signal system
6 Battery boxes
1 Telephone
3 Shovels
3000 Ft 1½" pipe water line for operation of Snubbing Engine
1 Electric gong

Side "E" - Leg 2 Camp 4

SW¼ NE¼ - Section 9 - Twp. 34, N.R. 6 E

1 Spar Tree completely rigged
12 1-¼ Guy lines(All burned)
1 Washington 36-C High Lead Block
1 Lamb #1 - 14" Head Tree
4 Washington Loading Blocks #3140
2 Washington Loading Jacks #189
24 Ft. 3/4" chain
1 Washington Pass Block #780
1 Washington 12x14 - 2 Speed Yarder, on sled and roofed - #3530 - Exit. fire box oil burner, steel oil and water tank
1500 Ft. 1-3/8" Main line (poor)
4000 Ft. 7/8" Haulback line (good)
4000 Ft. 5/8" Straw line "
1 -Washington Yarding Block 4120B
1 Set Splicing tools
1 Peavy
1 Splitting maul 10#
2 Wedges
1 6x8x40 Wood water tank
1 1½ Yard Bagley Scraper
2 Pr. 1¾" twin hooks
1 Washington Haulback Block #212
1 " " " 120
1 " " " 2120 B
1 Willamette Yarding " #102
3 Clausen Butt lines
3 1¼" D chokers
1 Pair tongs

1 Washington - 3 Drum Duplex Loader - 10x12 Engine #3513 - on Sled with house; oil burner, steel oil and water tank.
700 Ft. 1" Loading line
500 " 1¼" Spotting line
3 Prs. Tongs
1 Washington Haulback Blk. #2120 R
1 " " " #120
3 Swamping axes
2 Hayes derails #285
11000 Ft. 2" water pipe connected with this side to supply it with water (Gravity system).

SW¼ NW¼ Sec. 9, Twp. 34, R. 6E.

1 Willamette - 11 x 13 Humboldt Yarder Engine #933 on sled and roofed, badly burned. Not in movable condition, wood burner, steel oil and water tank. Lines are all burned.

ANATOMY OF A LOGGING OPERATION

Camp 4

1	Washington Haulback Block #2120 R
1	" " " #120
2	" " " #212
1	" Hugh(sic) lead " 36-C
1000	Ft. 1½" pipe line to supply this yarder with water (gravity)

Side "F" - SE¼ SE¼ - Sec. 5, Twp. 34, N.R. 6E

1	Spar tree completely rigged with block
12	1¼" Guy lines (all burned)
1	Washington 36-C High Lead Blk.
1	Lamb Head Tree - Block #1
4	Washington Loading Blocks #3140
2	" " Jacks #189
1	Pass Block #780
2	Pairs Tongs
1	12x12Washington Compound, geared yarder Engine #2253,
	Wood burner - steel oil and water tank on sled, roof burned off.
1000	Ft. - 1-3/8" Main Line (poor)
2500	Ft. 11/16 Haulback "
3500	Ft. 3/8" Strawline (New)
1	Set Splicing tools
5	#2 Rd. pointed shovels
6	Fire buckets
1	150 bbl. round steel storage water tank
3	Washington Haulback Blks #120
1	" " " 212
3	Willamette Yard " 102
1	Pr. Tongs
1	Washington High Lead Blk. #30D
1	Hayes derail #285
1	Main Lead Block-Washington - #2480
1500	Ft. 1½" pipe water line to supply this donkey with water

RECAPITULATION OF DONKEYS

1	12x14	Washington	#3538	Camp #2
1	10x12	"	D-#3682	"
1	10½x10¼	"	1720	"
1	12x14	"	3340	"
1	9x10¼	"	D- 3351	"
1	9x10¼	"	2574	" (pile driver)
1	7x10½	"	1735	" "
1	12x17	"	3645	Camp #1
1	9x10¼	"	3359	"
1	12x14	" A.Y.	3601	"
1	10x12	"	D- 3684	"
1	10½x10¼	"	1000'	"
1	9x10¼	"	2106	" (Pile Driver)
1	10½x15½x18	"	3722	" (Snubber)
1	9x10¼	" Loader	2193	"
1	9x10½	" "	2554	"
1	9x10¼	" C.D.	2248	South Lat. Camp 4
1	12x14	" Snubber	3408	Camp 4
1	12x14	" Y.	3530	"
1	10x12	" D.L.	3513	"
1	11x13	Willamette Y.	933	"
1	12x12	Washington Y.	2253	"
1	10x12	" D.L.	3512	"
1	12x14	" A.Y.	3363	"
1	11x11	" Y.	2525	"
1	12x12	" Y.	1733	"
1	9x10¼	" L.	1424	Mill (Cherry Picker)
1	11x13	Willamette Y.	1022	Mill
1	9x10	Washington	539	Log Dump
1	12x12	Washington	1835	Mill
1	7x10½	"	1191	Mill
1	9x10¼	"	2575	Mill
32	donkeys total			
1	Marion. Cat. Steam Shovel 5017			
1	" " " " 5076			

The foregoing is a direct copy from court papers in the 1926 bankruptcy proceedings including word mis-spellings and period spellings. While the complete company inventory is not presented, these interesting portions are themselves complete. Dennis Thompson Collection

E-5

E-6

Pacific Logging Congress

WHISTLE SIGNAL CODE

HIGH LEAD SIGNALS

ONE SHORT	Go ahead on main line
ONE SHORT	Stop
TWO SHORT	Come back on haulback
THREE SHORT	Come ahead easy on main line
TWO SHORT AND TWO SHORT	Come back easy on haulback
FOUR SHORT	Slack the main line
TWO SHORT AND FIVE SHORT	Slack the haulback
THREE SHORT AND TWO SHORT	Tight line
THREE MEDIUM	Hooktender. Followed by three short, calls in crew
TWO LONG AND THREE SHORT	Donkey doctor
THREE LONG AND TWO SHORT	Climber
THREE LONG	Locomotive for switching
FOUR LONG	Foreman
TWO LONG AND ONE SHORT	Oil
ONE LONG	Stop oil
TWO LONG	Water
ONE LONG	Stop water
SIX LONG	Man hurt, locomotive and stretcher
FOUR LONG AND SIX SHORT—REPEAT	Fire
SUCCESSION OF SHORTS	Danger, blasting at landing
ONE LONG AND ONE SHORT	Starting and quitting

LOCOMOTIVE SIGNALS

FOUR LONG	Foreman
FIVE LONG	Section crew
SIX LONG—REPEAT	Man hurt, stretcher
FOUR LONG AND FOUR SHORT—REPEAT	Fire

BUTT RIGGING SIGNALS AT TREE

TWO SHORT	No choker
THREE SHORT	Strawline
TWO SHORT AND ONE SHORT	One choker
TWO SHORT AND TWO SHORT	Two choker
ONE SHORT AND TWO SHORT	Bull choker

The above Logging Whistle Signal Code has been adopted by the Whistle Committee of the Pacific Logging Congress as standard for Pacific Coast Logging Operations

From the February 1930 issue of **THE TIMBERMAN**

LOCOMOTIVE ROSTERS

ATLAS LUMBER COMPANY (see L. Houghton Logging Company)

BALLARD LUMBER COMPANY

LOCOMOTIVE SPECIFICATIONS

Road#	Builder	Year	Type	Cyl.	Driver	Blr	Weight	TE	notes
?	Unknown								1
?	Lima #838	2-12-04	2T Shay	8x12	26½"		28T	16,000	2

NOTES 1. Prior to arrival of two-truck Shay, an unidentified locomotive was used on the railroad for a short time
2. New to Stimson Mill Co., Kamilche WA, shipping destination
to Ballard Lbr. Co., Whitney WA;
to South Tacoma Mill Co., South Tacoma WA;
to Anderson Twedt & Co., Mineral WA; wrecked 3-27-26, and scrapped. Built as woodburner (1½ cord capacity), water tank capacity of 1,000 gallons.

BAKER RIVER & SHUKSAN Railroad(Includes Superior Portland Cement)

LOCOMOTIVE SPECIFICATIONS

Road#	Builder	Year	Type	Cyl.	Driver	Blr	Weight	TE	notes
1	Manhattan		0-4-4T Forney						1
?			4 wheel gasoline						
3	Climax #1399	1916	B	13½x16	35"		60T	26,400	2
4	Davenport #1129	3-1911	0-4-4	12x18					
?			0-4-0ST						

NOTES 1. Probably ex-New York City Elevated Railway locomotive.
2. New to Moore-Keppel & Co., #5, Ellamore WV where she was wrecked and traded in;
Superior Portland Cement purchased her in April of 1920;
Became Jennings & Nestos #3.

BLANCHARD LOGGING RAILROAD

LOCOMOTIVE SPECIFICATIONS

Road#	Builder	Year	Type	Cyl.	Driver	Blr	Weight	TE	notes
1	Baldwin #9106	1888	2-6-0	14x18	38"				1

NOTES 1. Built new for Blanchard. Sold
to Lake Whatcom Logging Company about 1905. Disposition unknown, probably scrapped at Alger.

R-2

BLOEDEL-DONOVAN LUMBER MILLS (Alger, Delvan & Saxon Camps)

LOCOMOTIVE SPECIFICATIONS

Road#	Builder	Year	Type	Cyl.	Driver	Blr	Weight	TE	notes
	unknown		0-4-0 or 0-4-2						
1	ALCO #45896	2-1909	2-6-2	18x24	48"		138,000	24,790	1
1 (2nd)	Climax #1648	1-1924	3T	15¼x16	36"		80T	35,200	2
2	Heisler #1055	1-1902	2T				25T		3
3	Baldwin #9106	8-1888	2-6-0	14x18	38"				4
4	Lima #820	9-1903	2T Shay	11x12	32"		90,000	18,750	5
5	Lima #2855	6-1916	3T Shay	12x15	36"		70T	30,350	6
6	Heisler #1288	10-1913	2T	15x12	36"		44T	17,500	7
7	Lima #3012	4-1919	3T Shay	12x15	36"		70T	30,350	8
8	Baldwin #58064	1924	2-6-6-2T	17&26x24	44"		212,500	37,500	9
9	Baldwin #58065	1924	2-6-6-2T	17&26x24	44"		212,500	37,500	10
10	Climax #1641	6-1923	3T	15-¼x16	36"		80T	35,200	11

NOTES 1. Built new for Lake Whatcom Logging Company. Transferred with sale of that company to Bloedel-Donovan in 1913, Locomotive was designed by ALCO to be used with or without pilot and trailing truck. Disposition unknown.
2. Built new for B-D, Alger Camp; transferred to Olympic Peninsula operation; later Rayonier #1. Scrapped circa 1953.
3. Built new for Genessee Lbr. Co., Genessee LA;
to Lake Whatcom Logging Co.;
to Bloedel-Donovan Lbr. Mills, Marysville WA
4. Built new for the Blanchard Logging Railroad, Blanchard WA;
to Lake Whatcom Logging Co., 1901;
to Bloedel-Donovan Lbr. Mills, 1913, where it was used on the Yukon Branch between Burlington and Alger. Probably scrapped in Skagit County.
5. Built new for Chinn Brothers Timber Co. #1, Maple Falls WA;
to Lake Whatcom Logging Co. #4 in 1910;
to Bloedel-Donovan Lbr. Mills in 1913, Alger Camp; transferred to Olympic Peninsula operation; later Rayonier, not used and scrapped in 1945.
6. Built new for Bloedel-Donovan Lbr. Mills, Delvan Camp and was principal power for that camp. Transferred to Olympic Peninsula operation; later Rayonier #5 at Sekiu; scrapped circa 1946.
7. Built new for A. C. Manning Logging Co. #1, Lake Whatcom WA;

BLOEDEL DONOVAN LUMBER MILLS (Alger, Delvan & Saxon Camps)(concluded)

to Lake Whatcom Logging Co.; to Bloedel-Donovan Lbr. Mills #6 in 1913; transferred to Olympic Peninsula operation. Scrapped circa 1950.

8. Built new for Siems Carey-H. S. Kerbaugh Corp. #7, Bellingham WA;
   to Bloedel-Donovan Lbr. Mills, Alger Camp; transferred to Olympic Peninsula operation, Sekiu WA;
   later Rayonier #7; scrapped circa 1956.
9. Built new for Bloedel-Donovan Lbr. Mills, Alger Camp; transferred to Olympic Peninsula operation out of Sekiu WA;
   to Rayonier #8;
   to private ownership of Peter Replinger & Byron Cole 1965, Shelton WA. In storage.
10. Built new for Bloedel-Donovan Lbr. Mills. After initial break-in operations at Alger Camp, locomotive was transferred to the Olympic Peninsula operation;
    later Rayonier #9. Scrapped circa 1956.
11. Built new for Bloedel-Donovan Lbr. Mills, Alger Camp; transferred to Olympic Peninsula operation as #10;
    to Rayonier #10. Scrapped circa 1953.

BRATNOBER-WAITE LUMBER COMPANY

LOCOMOTIVE SPECIFICATIONS

Road#	Builder	Year	Type	Cyl.	Driver	Blr	Weight	TE	notes
2	Climax #209	4-1900	2T	12x14	31"		35T	64,000	1
?	Climax	1902	2T	12½x14	31"		40T	72,000	

NOTES
1. Built new for Bratnober-Waite Lbr. Co.;
   to Valley Supply;
   to Craig Taylor Lbr. Co.

BUTLER BROTHERS LUMBER COMPANY

LOCOMOTIVE SPECIFICATIONS

Road#	Builder	Year	Type	Cyl.	Driver	Blr	Weight	TE	notes
1	Heisler #1099	9-1906	2T	12½x12	33"		28T	11,000	1

NOTES
1. Built new for Butler Brothers Lbr. Co. #1; Company name was changed to Butler Lbr. Co.;
   to Northwestern Redwood Co, Sherwood CA

CLEAR LAKE LUMBER COMPANY

R-3

LOCOMOTIVE SPECIFICATIONS

Road#	Builder	Year	Type	Cyl.	Driver	Blr	Weight	TE	notes
1	Lima #1940	10-1907	2T Shay	11x12	32"		105,200	22,580	1
2	Lima #2837	6-1916	3T Shay	13½x15	36"		179,300	35,100	2
3	Climax #371	12-1902	2T	12x14	31"		35T		3
3 (2nd)	Lima #2643	7-1913	3T Shay	13½x15	36"		160,000	35,100	4
4	Climax #872	3-1908	2T				52T		5
4 (2nd)	Lima #2304	3-1910	2T Shay	11x12	32"		100,000	20,350	6
5	Lima #2315	5-1910	2T Shay	12x12	36"		120,000	23,850	7
6	Climax #1063	12-1910	2T				57T		8
7	Baldwin #57013	1923	2-6-2T	17x24	44"		137,050	24,787	9
8	Lima #3260	4-1924	3T Shay	13½x15	36"		204,600	35,100	10
200	Baldwin #44106	1916	2-8-2	20½x28			160,500		11

Rolling stock included: 85 connected trucks (skeleton cars) purchased new from Pacific Car & Foundry
2 Sessoms Lowering Cars
3 Marion steam shovels (one was a model 31)
1 MAC 6-61 Rail Car

NOTES
1. Built new for Curtiss Lbr. Co. #2, Mill City OR;
   to Union Tbr Co., Oakville WA;
   to Skagit Valley Lbr. Co. (unknown and undocumented company) #1, Clear Lake WA;
   to Clear Lake Lumber Co. #1.
2. Built new for Clear Lake Lbr. Co. #2;
   to Puget Sound Pulp & Tbr. Co. (English Lbr. Co. unit), Conway WA, #2 (2nd); scrapped in 1952.
3. Built new for Clear Lake Lbr. Co. #3;
   to Nippon Lbr. Co.;
   to Alpine Lbr. Co.
4. Built new for Skagit Logging Co. #5, Clear Lake WA (this was the first name for B. R. Lewis' logging venture at Clear Lake - actual operations emerged as a newly reorganized Clear Lake Lbr. Co.), became Clear Lake Lbr. Co. #3;
   to Puget Sound Pulp & Tbr, Co. (English Lbr. Co. unit), Conway WA, second #3; scrapped in 1952.
5. Built new for Clear Lake Lbr. Co. #4;
   to West Fork Logging Co., Mineral WA;
   to Stillwater Lbr. Co.;
   to Wickstrom Lbr. Co.
6. Built new for Miller Logging Co., Sedro Woolley WA;
   to Clear Lake Lbr. Co. #4;

CLEAR LAKE LUMBER COMPANY (concluded)

to Skagit Valley Lbr. Co. #4, Clear Lake WA;
to Puget Sound Pulp & Tbr. Co. #4, Clear Lake in 1929. Saw service in Clear Lake all her life until 1940, and the end of the railroad. Scrapped at Clear Lake about 1941.

7. Built new for Clear Lake Lbr. Co. #5;
to Skagit Valley Lbr. Co. #5, Clear Lake WA;
to Puget Sound Pulp & Tbr. Co., Clear Lake.
8. Built new for Clear Lake Lbr. Co. #6;
to Hoff & Pinkey;
to Fobbs & Wilson;
to C. H. Wilson.
9. Built new for Clear Lake Lbr. Co. #7, original price: $20,375.
to Coos Bay Lbr. Co. #7 in 1926, Coos Bay OR
10. Built new for Clear Lake Lbr. Co. #8, original price: $29,528. Dealer was Hofius Steel & Equipment Co., Seattle. Locomotive was repossessed in 1926 by Hofius and re-sold
to Phoenix Logging Co. #8, Hoodsport WA;
to White River Lbr. Co. #6, Enumclaw WA; scrapped in 1941.
11. Built new for Clear Lake Lbr. Co. #200, lettered for Puget Sound & Cascade Ry. and was used for mainline hauling. Superheated. Locomotive was repossessed by Baldwin in 1926 and re-sold
to Cowlitz, Chehalis & Cascade as their #15. After being on display for a number of years in Chehalis, she was recently removed and is being rebuilt by the Mount Rainier Scenic Railway shops for operation.

COWDEN LUMBER COMPANY

LOCOMOTIVE SPECIFICATIONS

Road#	Builder	Year	Type	Cyl.	Driver	Blr	Weight	TE	notes
?	Heisler #1124	2-1907	2T	15x12	36"		37T	14,000	1

NOTES
1. Built new for Peninsula Lbr. Co., Columbia City OR;
to Cowden Lbr. Co. Sept. 1919 - repossessed by Hofius in 1922 after Cowden defaulted on purchase contract;
to Coos Bay Logging Co., Marshfield WA

DANAHER LUMBER COMPANY

R-4

LOCOMOTIVE SPECIFICATIONS

Road#	Builder	Year	Type	Cyl.	Driver	Blr	Weight	TE	notes
1	Lima #2872	1-1917	3TShay	12x15	36"		146,000	30,350	1
2	Lima #1948	9-1907	2T Shay	11x12	32"		90,000	20,350	2
4	Lima #3148	12-1920	3T Shay	12x15	36"		167,500	30,350	3

NOTES
1. Built new for Danaher Lbr Co. #1, Darrington WA;
to Cavano Logging Co., Cavano WA;
to Andron Logging Co., Darrington WA;
to Skamania Logging Co., Skamania WA;
to North Bend Tbr. Co. #1 (2nd), North Bend WA; scrapped 8-1942.
2. Built new for Stacey E. Wright Logging Co. #2, Hartford WA;
to Anderson & Middleton Lbr. Co. #7, Oakville WA;
to Danaher Lbr. Co., Tacoma WA;
to Cavano Logging Co., Arlington WA;
to Andron Logging Co., Darrington WA; scrapped 11-1939
3. Built new for Danaher Lbr. Co. #4, Port Orchard WA;
to Cispus Logging Co., Port Orchard WA 7-1922;
to Columbia Construction Co. #4, Ilwaco WA 7-1936. (It is unlikely this locomotive operated at the Darrington unit.)

DAY LUMBER COMPANY

LOCOMOTIVE SPECIFICATIONS

Road#	Builder	Year	Type	Cyl.	Driver	Blr	Weight	TE	notes
1	Davenport #582	5-1907	0-4-0T	13X18					1
2	Baldwin #36044	3-1911	2-6-2	18X24	44"				2
3	Lima #2708	10-1913	3T Shay	13½X15	36"		179,300	35,100	3
7	Climax #1405	1916	3T	15¼x16	36"		80T	35,200	4
?	Lima #3144	11-1920	3T Shay	13½x15	38"		199,200	35,100	5

NOTES
1. Built new for Day Lbr. Co. #1, disposition unknown.
2. Built new as oil burner for Day Lbr. Co. #2, traded in on Shay #3 in 1913;
to Kerry Tbr. Co. #2, Kerry OR;
to Columbia & Nehalem River #119, Neverstill OR in 1916;
to K-P Tbr. Co. #119, Kerry OR.
3. Built new for Day Lbr. Co. #3;
to English Lbr. Co. #15 in 1926;
to Puget Sound Pulp & Tbr. Co. (English Lbr. Co. unit) in 1944; scrapped at Conway, date unknown. The following details apply to this locomotive as built new: built to Lima plan No. 909, 44'-6" wheelbase, fuel oil capacity 1200 gal., water

DAY LUMBER COMPANY (concluded)

tank capacity 3500 gal., Westinghouse A-1 air brake, wood cab, Pyle-National headlights, 5" whistle and 100 pound bell.

4. Built new for Day Lbr. Co. #7; disposition unknown, locomotive was not on property in 1924.
5. Built new for Booth-Kelly Lbr. Co. #7, Wendling OR;
   to Day Lbr. Co. in 1923;
   to Flora Logging Co. #8 (Carlton & Coast Ry. #8), Carlton OR;
   to Dulien Steel Products (dealer), Portland OR 1943

DEMPSEY LUMBER COMPANY

LOCOMOTIVE ROSTER

Road#	Builder	Year	Type	Cyl.	Driver	Blr	Weight	TE	notes
1	Heisler #1105	11-1906	2T	16¾x14	40"		52T	20,000	1
?	Heisler #1166	9-1909	2T	16¾x14	40"		60T	24,000	2
2	Heisler #1298	4-1914	2T	16¾x14	40"		62T	24,800	3
1 (2nd)	Heisler #1425	2-1920	3T	17x14	38"		75T	30,000	4

Rolling stock included but was not limited to the following:

PC&F Hercules disconnected trucks, later converted to connected (skeleton) cars using PC&F "conversion" kits.
One Sessoms Lowering Car (PC&F) purchased in 1922
1 MAC 4-20 Rail Car purchased in 1926
1 MAC 6-60 Rail Car purchased in 1928

NOTES

1. Built new for Dempsey Lbr. Co. #1, purchase price was $9,400;
   to Dept. of Public Works, Hetch-Hetchy Water Supply (Hetch Hetchy RR), Groveland CA about 1921;
   to Standard Lbr. Co. #7, Standard CA;
   to Pickering Lbr. Co. #7, Standard CA;
   to Macco Construction Co. #2062, China Lake CA;
   to Guy F. Atkinson Construction Co., Lathrop CA
2. Built new for Pittsburg Iron Ore Co. #1, Mountain Iron MN (Hanna Ore Mining Co.);
   to Whitney Engineering Co. (dealer), Tacoma WA;
   to Green River Lbr. Co, Baldi WA;
   to O. H. Wheeler Logging Co., Cochran OR;
   to Clearwater Tbr. Co. (leased), Clearwater ID;
   to Dempsey Lbr. Co. (leased 1924), Hamilton WA;
   to Manley-Moore Lbr. Co. (leased), Fairfax WA;
   to Ostrander Ry. & Tbr. Co. (leased), Ostrander WA;
   to Western Logging Co. (leased), Ocosta WA; seized for taxes and sold
   to Western Machinery Exchange (dealer), Aberdeen WA.
3. Built new for Dempsey Lbr. Co. #2, purchase price was $11,055;
   to Dempsey Lbr. Co., Ohop WA operation in the Fall of 1930. When Dempsey closed their business, locomotive was offered for sale to the War Department for $3,500. Offer was not accepted and locomotive was probably scrapped at that time.
4. Built new for Dempsey Lbr. Co. #1 (2nd), purchase price was $24,844;
   to Dempsey Lbr. Co., Ohop WA operation in the Fall of 1930. When Dempsey closed their business, locomotive was offered for sale to the War Department for $5,000. Offer was not accepted and locomotive was probably scrapped at that time.

R-5

ENGLISH LUMBER COMPANY

LOCOMOTIVE SPECIFICATIONS

Road#	Builder	Year	Type	Cyl.	Driver	Blr	Weight	TE	notes
?	Baldwin		4-4-0						1
?	Lima		2T Shay	2 cyl.					2
1	Lima #708	6-1902	2T Shay	11x12	33"		93,000	19,650	3
2	Lima #1878	3-1907	2T Shay	12x12	36"		110,000	23,850	4
3	Baldwin #2719	1871	2-6-0	16x24	48"		55,000		5
4	Lima #945	1-1905	2T Shay	11x12	35"		90,000	18,750	6
5	Rhode Island		0-4-0						7
5 (2nd)	Lima #1878	3-1907	2T Shay	12x12	36"		110,000	23,850	8
6	Lima #2251	1-1910	2T Shay	12x12	36"		138,500	23,850	9
7	Lima #2630	12-1912	2T Shay	12x12	36"		138,500	23,850	10
8	Heisler	2-1910	2T						11
9	Lima #2533	4-1912	3T Shay	11x12	32"		120,000	25,830	12
10	Baldwin #53255	1922	2-8-2	20½x28	48"		175,500	35,400	13
11	Climax #1081	1-1912	3T	16x16	36"		75T		14
12	Climax #1581	5-1920	3T	16x16	36"		90T	39,600	15
13	Lima #3198	1-1923	3T Shay	14½x15	36"		201,500	40,400	16
14	Lima #2704	2-1914	3T Shay	12x15	36"		140,000	30,350	17
15	Lima #2708	10-1913	3T Shay	13½x15	36"		160,000	35,100	18

ENGLISH LUMBER COMPANY (concluded)

Rolling stock included but was not limited to the following:

Purchases over the years from PC&F totaled 173 connected trucks (skeleton) log cars
one new caboose in 1921
1 MAC 4-40 Rail Car
various cars from foreign roads interchanged from Great Northern at Fir
Some forest products were shipped using foreign cars and various supplies received by same means.

NOTES

1. In May 1902, A. J. McCabe (dealer) sold ex-Oregon Railway & Navigation Company 4-4-0 #39 to "E. English, at Mount Vernon, Washington." It is likely English used this locomotive during his early railroad construction. No further records have been found.
2. Unidentified two-cylinder Shay involved in one of English's early enterprises. It is possible this locomotive was used in northern Snohomish County.
3. Built new for English Lbr. Co. #1, "Woolley, Washington," first used near Sedro Woolley (Tyee Camp), later at Conway; to Goodro Logging Co., Shelton WA 4-1920
4. Built new for Izett Logging Co. #2, Brinnon WA;
   to English Lbr. Co. #2, re-numbered to #5, sold in March 1923
   to Hofius Steel & Equip. Co, Seattle (dealer - may have been traded in on Shay #13);
   to Apex Tbr. Co., Pe Ell WA, 5-21-23;
   to Peterman Mfg. Co #5, Tacoma WA 5-1938.
5. Built new for Virginia & Truckee Railroad in Nevada as their #10 and named "Washoe." Sold
   to Oregon Ry. & Navigation Co. in 1881 for $9,500, became their #42;
   to Union Pacific as #1379; to OR&N again as #16; sold
   to English Lumber Co., Conway WA 2-1903 and became #3; sold
   to Mason County Logging Co, Belfair WA by 1908.
6. Built new for English Lbr. Co. #4 and lettered "Skagit Valley RR," sold in July of 1924 for $7,500
   to Maine Logging Co. Belfair WA #4.
7. This locomotive was ex-Seattle, Lake Shore & Eastern #5. It had been purchased and was in use by English about 1901. The engine did not remain long on the loggers roster. Disposition unknown.
8. English re-numbering. See note 2.
9. Built new for English Lbr. Co. #6, first used at Hamilton WA for Hamilton Logging Co. (owned by E. English). Locomotive spent only a short time there, the balance of her operating life at Conway. Scrapped late 1930s.
10. Built new for English Lbr. Co. #7. Worked all her life for English and was scrapped about 1942.
11. Locomotive #8 was a two-truck saddle-tank Heisler obtained by English between 1912 and 1914, and used at Camp 5. She was wrecked about 1916, after which she sat at Headquarters for some time. It is almost certain she was shop number 1189, which was built new for Johnson-Deane Lbr. Co. as their #101 at Robe WA. In any case, exact disposition is unknown.

R-6

12. Built new for Big Creek RR #100 (Stone & Webster Co. #100), Nopac Siding CA;
    to San Joaquin & Eastern RR #100, Auberry CA 1913;
    to Jardine Mach. Co., San Francisco CA (dealer) 1918;
    to English Lbr. Co. about 1918 as #9. Scrapped at Headquarters early 1940s.
13. Built new for English Lbr. Co. #10. Sold in May of 1943
    to Red River Lbr. Co. as their #105.
    to Fruit Growers Supply about 1945. Scrapped 1950.
14. Built new for Parker-Bell Lbr. Co., Pilchuck WA #4;
    to English Lbr. Co. in 1922 as their #11, but only used for a very short time;
    to Silver Falls Logging Co. in 1923;
    to Northwestern Logging Co., disposition unknown.
15. Built new for Parker-Bell Lbr. Co., Pilchuck WA #5;
    to English Lbr. Co. in 1922 #12;
    to Puget Sound Pulp & Timber, Conway WA in 1944; scrapped at Headquarters, early 1945.
16. Built new for English Lbr. Co. #13;
    to Puget Sound Pulp & Timber Co., Conway WA in 1944; scrapped at log dump Sept 1952.
17. Built new for Pine Belt Lbr. Co. #7, Fort Towson OK; Henderson Land & Lbr. Co., Fox AL;
    Birmingham Rail & Loco Co. (dealer), Birmingham AL;
    to English Lbr. Co., Conway WA in early 1924 as #14; wrecked in 1926 and rebuilt;
    to Puget Sound Pulp & Tbr. Co. in 1944; Scrapped about 1946
18. Built new for Day Lbr. Co., Big Lake WA #3; may have been used briefly by the receivers of Day Lbr. Co. before sale
    to English Lbr. Co. in Nov. 1926 as their #15.
    to Puget Sound Pulp & Tbr. Co. #15. Scrapped about 1946.

ERICKSON AND FUHRMAN

LOCOMOTIVE SPECIFICATIONS

Road#	Builder	Year	Type	Cyl.	Driver	Blr	Weight	TE	notes
?	Lima #2587	8-1912	2T Shay	12x12	36"		120,000	23,890	1

NOTES

1. Built new for Simpson Logging Co., Shelton WA #2;
   to Fredson Bros. Logging Co., Shelton WA; to Foster-Newbegin Lbr. Co., Frederickson WA;
   to Hofius Steel & Equip. Co. (dealer), Seattle WA ; to Erickson and Fuhrman April 1926 for $11,000;
   to Columbia Contract Co., Astoria OR 1-1932; to Winston Bros & Guy F. Atkinson Co. #44, Reedsport OR;
   to Willamette Iron & Steel Co. (dealer), Portland OR; scrapped 1939.

WILLIAM GAGE

LOCOMOTIVE SPECIFICATIONS

Road#	Builder	Year	Type	Cyl.	Driver	Blr	Weight	TE	notes
?	North Pacific Iron Wks	8-1881	Blackman	6x10			6,000		1

NOTES 1. Built new for Blackman Brothers, Mukilteo WA;
to William Gage by 2-1883. Cost of locomotive was $3,000. Operating speed 10 mph; rated at 10 horsepower. Disposition unknown.

HAMILTON LOGGING COMPANY

LOCOMOTIVE SPECIFICATIONS

Road#	Builder	Year	Type	Cyl.	Driver	Blr	Weight	TE	notes
?			0-4-2T						1
2	Lima #2574	7-1912	2T Shay	12x12	36"		120,000	23,890	2
3	Lima #1881	5-1907	2T Shay	12x12	36"		110,000	23,850	3
3 (2nd)	Lima #2618	11-1912	2T Shay	12x12	36"		120,000	23,890	4

NOTES 1. ex-J. A. Veness Lumber before coming to Hamilton Log. Co.; Burned in forest fire at Hamilton in 1912 and rebuilt. Disposition unknown.
2 Built new for Hamilton Logging Co. #2;
to Lyman Tbr. Co. in 1917 as #2.
3. Built new for Lyman Lbr. Co., Hamilton as #3;
to Hamilton Log. Co. #3;
to Lyman Tbr. Co. in 1917 as #3; scrapped 1936
4. Built new for Hamilton Log. Co. #3;
to Lyman Tbr. Co. in 1917 as their #4;
to Soundview Pulp Co. in 1937, at Hamilton WA as #4; scrapped at Hamilton in 1950.

L. HOUGHTON LOGGING COMPANY

LOCOMOTIVE SPECIFICATIONS

Road#	Builder	Year	Type	Cyl.	Driver	Blr	Weight	TE	notes
1	Lima #714	6-1902	3T Shay	12x12	32"		100,000	17,900	1
2	Lima #780	7-1903	3T Shay	12x12	32"		130,000	17,900	2
4	Lima #2222	1-1910	3T Shay	12x15	36"		140,000	22,580	3

R-7

NOTES 1. Built new for L. Houghton Log. Co. #1, McMurray WA;
to Eatonville Lbr. Co., Eatonville WA;
to Royce Lbr. Co., Eatonville WA;
to Wheeler-Reese Lbr. Co., Harding WA;
to Crocker Lake Log. Co., Crocker Lake WA;
to Buckley Log Co., Buckley WA;
to Raymond Foundry & Machinery Works (dealer), Raymond WA; (rebuilt after wreck);
to Pacific Cedar Co., Raymond WA;
to Case Shingle & Lbr. Co. #1, South Bend WA 1-1928;
to Case Cedar & Shingle Co. #1, South Bend WA.
2. Built new for Lyman Lbr. Co., Hamilton WA #2;
to Zimmerman, Wells & Brown (dealer), Portland OR;
to L. Houghton Log. Co., McMurray WA;
to Union Machinery & Supply Co. (dealer), Seattle WA ;
to Yeomans Lbr. Co. (Pe Ell & Columbia River RR), Pe Ell WA, 2-14-1924;
to Pe Ell Lbr. Co. #6, Pe Ell WA.
3. Built new for L. Houghton Log. Co., McMurray WA #4; also used by L. Houghton at Ehrlich WA;
to Hogg-Houghton Log. Co., Glacier WA 11-1930;
to Warnick Lbr. Co., Glacier WA.

JENNINGS & NESTOS LOGGING COMPANY

LOCOMOTIVE SPECIFICATIONS

Road#	Builder	Year	Type	Cyl.	Driver	Blr	Weight	TE	notes
3	Climax #1399	1916	2T	13½x16	35"		60T	26,400	1
8	unknown		rod engine						2

NOTES 1. Built new for Moore-Keppel & Co. #5, Ellamore WV;
to Superior Portland Cement Co. #3, Concrete WA in April 1920, (Baker RIver & Shuksan RR);
to Jennings & Nestos. Scrapped about 1942 by Monte Holm.
2. Jennings & Nestos, as contract loggers, were known to have had at least one rod engine, numbered "8", in use on jobs adjacent to the Skagit River Ry. Number 8 was in use during 1924 and 1925, and possibly longer.

KELLOGG SHINGLE COMPANY

LOCOMOTIVE SPECIFICATIONS

Road#	Builder	Year	Type	Cyl.	Driver	Blr	Weight	TE	notes
1	Lima #349	4-1891	2T Shay	9x8	26"		40,000	9,130	1

NOTES 1. Built new for A. B. Root, "Junior No. 1," Ostrander WA;
E. S. Collins & Co. #1, (Ostrander Ry. & Tbr. Co. #1), Ostrander WA;
to Kellogg Shingle Co., Big Lake WA;
to Bale Logging Co., Hoquiam WA;
to Ward-Sargent Tbr. Co. #1, Ocosta WA, 2-1923

LAKE WHATCOM LOGGING COMPANY

(see Bloedel-Donovan Lumber Mills)

LYMAN LUMBER COMPANY

LOCOMOTIVE SPECIFICATIONS

Road#	Builder	Year	Type	Cyl.	Driver	Blr	Weight	TE	notes
2	Lima #780	7-1903	3T Shay	12x12	32"		130,000	17,900	1
3	Lima #1881	5-1907	2T Shay	12x12	36"		110,000	23,850	2

NOTES 1. Built new for Lyman Lumber Co. (English interests) #2;
to Zimmerman, Wells & Brown (dealer), Portland OR;
to L. Houghton Log. Co. #2, McMurray WA;
to Union Machinery & Supply Co. (dealer), Seattle WA;
to Yeomans Lbr. Co. (Pe Ell & Columbia River RR), Pe Ell WA, 2-14-1924;
to Pe Ell Lbr. Co. #6, Pe Ell WA.
2. Built new for Lyman Lbr. Co. (English interests) #3;
to Hamilton Log. Co. #3;
to Lyman Tbr. Co. in 1917 as #3; scrapped 1936

LYMAN TIMBER COMPANY

LOCOMOTIVE SPECIFICATIONS

R-8

Road#	Builder	Year	Type	Cyl.	Driver	Blr	Weight	TE	notes
1	Lima #2107	8-1908	2T Shay	11x12	32"		100,000	20,350	1
2	Lima #2574	7-1912	2T Shay	12x12	36"		120,000	23,890	2
3	Lima #1881	5-1907	2T Shay	12x12	36"		110,000	23,850	3
4	Lima #2618	11-1912	2T Shay	12x12	36"		120,000	23,890	4
5	Lima #3143	11-1920	3T Shay	13½x15	36"		188,000	35,100	5
6	Lima #3038	10-1919	3T Shay	14½x15	36"		180,000	40,400	6

Other railroad equipment included, but was not limited to the following:
One MAC 4-40 Rail Car purchased in 1925 and sold in 1929
One MAC 6-61 Rail Car purchased in 1929 with hi-cab, 9' wide deck and 125 hp motor, price $7,505.83

NOTES 1. Built new for Skagit Mill Co. #1, Lyman WA;
to Lyman Tbr. Co. #1, Hamilton WA;
to Marona Mill Co. #1, Acme WA 8-1942; converted to gasoline-hydraulic power.
2. Built new for Hamilton Log. Co. #2, Hamilton WA;
to Lyman Tbr. Co. #2 in 1917;
to Soundview Pulp Co. #3, Hamilton WA in 1937.
3. Built new for Lyman Tbr. Co. #3, Hamilton WA;
to Hamilton Log. Co. #3;
to Lyman Tbr. Co. #3 in 1917; scrapped in 1936
4. Built new for Hamilton Log. Co. #3;
to Lyman Tbr. Co. #4 in 1917;
to Soundview Pulp Co. #4, Hamilton WA in 1937; scrapped at Hamilton in 1950.
5. Built new for Lyman Tbr. Co. #5, at a cost of $30,925;
to Soundview Pulp Co. #5, Hamilton WA; scrapped at Hamilton in 1950.
6. Built new for Sultan Ry. & Tbr. Co. #4, Oso WA at a cost of $26,675;
to Lyman Tbr. Co. #6 in 1930;
to Soundview Pulp Co. #6 in 1937; scrapped at Hamilton in 1950.

MILLER LOGGING COMPANY

LOCOMOTIVE SPECIFICATIONS

Road#	Builder	Year	Type	Cyl.	Driver	Blr	Weight	TE	notes
4	Lima #2304	3-1910	2T Shay	11x12	32"		100,000	20,350	1

NOTES 1. Built new for Miller Log. Co. #4, Sedro Woolley WA;
to Clear Lake Lbr. Co. #4, Clear Lake WA;
to Puget Sound Pulp & Tbr. Co. #4, Clear Lake WA in 1929; scrapped about 1941.

McCOY and PULLMAN PALACE CAR LOGGING COMPANY

LOCOMOTIVE SPECIFICATIONS

Road#	Builder	Year	Type	Cyl.	Driver	Blr	Weight	TE	notes
1	Baldwin #6033	1882	4-4-0	16x24	57"				1
?	Baldwin #6211	1882	4-4-0	16x24	57"				2
1	Lima #914	9-1904	2T Shay	11x12	32"		90,000	18,750	3

NOTES
1. Pat McCoy purchased c/n 6033 from A. J. McCabe (dealer) on 2-14-1903. Locomotive was ex-OR&N #33. Fourteen days later, McCoy traded her back to McCabe on c/n 6211, apparently unsatisfied with the first engine.
2. This locomotive was accepted from A. J. McCabe as usable;
   ex-Oregon Water Power & Ry. #111; ex-OR&N #38.
3. Built new for Pat McCoy Ry, Bow WA;
   to Filion Mill & Lbr. Co. #1, Port Angeles WA by June of 1910;
   to Klement & Kennedy Lbr. Co. #1, Fortson WA June 1920.

McCUISH LOGGING COMPANY

LOCOMOTIVE SPECIFICATIONS

Road#	Builder	Year	Type	Cyl.	Driver	Blr	Weight	TE	notes
1	Lima #2022	11-1907	2T Shay	10x12	29½"		84,000	16,900	1
2	Climax #1618	1-1923	3T	14½x16	35"		70T	30,800	2
3	Lima #2540	5-1912	2T Shay	11x12	32"		100,000	22,580	3

NOTES
1 Built new for Balcom-Riley Log. Co. #1, Seattle WA;
   to Bolcom-Vanderhoof Lbr. Co. #1, Lochsloy WA;
   to Dungeness Log. Co., Dungeness WA;
   to Crocker Lake Log. Co., Brinnon WA;
   to McCuish Log. Co., Prairie WA; sold by 1924
   to Hoevet Log. Co., Mohler OR;
   to Orvel Parks, Wheeler OR 5-1928.
2. Built new for McCuish Logging Co. #2, Prairie WA; price new was $20,000. Disposition unknown.
3. Built new for Brown Bay Log. Co. #3, Meadowdale WA;
   to Admiralty Log. Co. #3, Meadowdale WA;
   to McCuish Log. Co. #3, Prairie WA;
   to Galbraith Brothers Log. Co., Acme WA; 10-1929

R-9

McNEILL and O'HEARNE TIMBER COMPANY

LOCOMOTIVE SPECIFICATIONS

Road#	Builder	Year	Type	Cyl.	Driver	Blr	Weight	TE	notes
1	Climax #210	4-1900	2T	12½x14	31"		40T		1

NOTES
1. Built new for Mason County Log. Co. #1, Bordeaux WA;
   to Luedinghaus Brothers;
   to J. A. Veness Lbr.;
   to Fobbs & Wilson Co.;
   to McDonald Shingle;
   to McNeill & O'Hearne Co., Concrete WA on June 27, 1922 for $4,500. Disposition unknown.

MONTBORNE LUMBER COMPANY

LOCOMOTIVE SPECIFICATIONS

Road#	Builder	Year	Type	Cyl.	Driver	Blr	Weight	TE	notes
4	Lima #773	9-1903	3T Shay	14½x12	36"		150,000	27,155	1
7	Heisler #1152	1-1909	2T	15x12	36"		42T	16,800	2
151	Lima #2703	9-1913	3T Shay	14½x15	36"		180,000	40,400	3

NOTES
1. Built new for C. B. Howard & Co. #4, "Old Joe" (Emporium & Rich Valley RR #4), Emporium PA;
   to Samish Bay Log. Co., Blanchard WA;
   to Montborne Lbr. Co. #4, Montborne WA in June of 1928.
2. Built new for Nelson-Neal Lbr. Co. #7, Bryant WA;
   to Montborne Lbr. Co. #7 in 1926;
   Scrapped at Montborne about 1935. (Had been wrecked Feb. of 1930, and may have not been used since.)
3. Built new for Independent Coal & Coke Co. #151, (Kenilworth & Helper RR #151), Kenilworth UT;
   to Denver & Rio Grande RR #151 (leased), Kenilworth UT;
   to Kenilworth & Helper RR #151, Kenilworth UT;
   to Pacific Equipment Co. (dealer), Portland OR, 9-1928;
   to Montborne Lbr. Co. #151, Big Lake (Montborne) WA April of 1929;
   scrapped at Montborne in October of 1937; boiler to Willapoint Oyster Co., Bay Center WA.

NELSON-NEAL LUMBER COMPANY

LOCOMOTIVE SPECIFICATIONS

Road#	Builder	Year	Type	Cyl.	Driver	Blr	Weight	TE	notes
7	Heisler #1152	1-1909	2T	15x12	36"		42T	16,800	1

NOTES 1. Built new for Nelson-Neal #7;
to Montborne Lbr. Co. #7 in 1926; scrapped at Montborne about 1935.

PARKER-BELL LUMBER COMPANY

LOCOMOTIVE SPECIFICATIONS

Road#	Builder	Year	Type	Cyl.	Driver	Blr	Weight	TE	notes
1	Lima #611	12-1900	2T Shay	11x12	32"		80,000	17,485	1
?	Climax		2T						2
?	Lima		3T Shay						3
3	Climax #680	6-1906	2T	13x16	31"		50T		4
4	Climax #1081	1-1912	3T	16x16	36"		75T		5
5	Climax #1581	5-1920	3T	16x16	36"		90T	39,600	6

NOTES 1. Built new for Joe Parker as #1, (Parker Brothers & Hiatt Log. Co. #1), Pilchuck WA;
to Parker-Bell Lbr. Co. #1, Pilchuck WA;
to Phoenix Log. Co. #4, Potlatch WA;
to Marys River Log. Co. #7, Philomath OR;
to Spaulding-Miami Lbr. Co. #7, Grande Ronde OR 11-1920;
to Oregon Coast Range Lbr. Co. #7, Grande Ronde OR 9-1924;
to Polk Operating Co. #7, Grande Ronde OR 1926.

2. Unidentified 2 truck Climax operated at Parker-Bell
3. Unidentified 3 truck Shay operated at Parker-Bell for a number of years. Very likely unit is Lima c/n 733.
4. Built new for Parker-Bell Lbr. Co. #3, Pilchuck WA; traded in on Climax #4 in late 1911;
to Index-Galena Co.;
to B&J Tbr. Co.
5. Built new for Parker-Bell Lbr. Co. #4, Pilchuck WA; went with sale of P-B holdings
to English Lbr. Co. #11 in 1922;
to Silver Falls Log. about 1923;
to Northwestern Log. Co.
6. Built new for Parker-Bell Lbr. Co. #5, Pilchuck WA, delivered to Pilchuck by Walt Casler of Climax Mfg. Co. late June 1920. Cost new was $29,800;
to English Lbr. Co. #12 in 1922;
to Puget Sound Pulp & Timber Co. #12 in 1944 (old English operation); scrapped there about 1945.

R-10

PUGET SOUND & BAKER RIVER RAILWAY

LOCOMOTIVE SPECIFICATIONS

Road#	Builder	Year	Type	Cyl.	Driver	Blr	Weight	TE	notes
1	Baldwin #31474	8-1907	4-6-0	16x24	44"		104,000	18,990	1
2	Baldwin #39058	1-1913	4-6-0	16x24	44"		104,000	18,990	2
3	Porter #6797	7-1923	2-8-2	20x24	46"		168,000	33,700	3
95	ALCO-GE #69045	1-1938	B-B				199,000		4

NOTES 1. Built new for PS&BR Ry. and worked her entire life there until cut up for scrap in 1956. Her tender was set aside and saved for display with locomotive #2. Cost new was $9,975. She was built with smaller cylinders and drivers than Baldwin's stock model. Her factory optional equipment was the following: larger boiler, $65; steel cab, $125; steel running boards, $35; steel tender frame, $75; syphon and hose, $65; additional sand box, $30. She came equipped with Westinghouse automatic air brakes and was able to operate on grades of 6% or less.

2. Built new for PS&BR Ry. and worked her entire life there until placed on display in Sedro Woolley WA in 1957 with the tender from #1. The tender from #2 was scrapped at Hamilton in 1956.
3. Built new for Monroe Logging Co.;
to PS&BR Ry. in 1938. Scrapped at Hamilton spring of 1958.
4. Built new for Chicago & Eastern Illinois as their #102 and their first ALCO diesel, model HH660. She was built at Schenectady NY. She was retired and sold from C&EI in August of 1949,
to a locomotive dealer.
She went to work for contractor Guy F. Atkinson on the Pine Flat Dam in California. In 1956, she was sold
to PS&BR Ry. as #95. In 1960, PS&BR's parent company, Scott Paper Co., closed the PS&BR and sent #95
to one of the firm's other operations at Chickasaw (Mobile) Alabama. The locomotive was scrapped there in 1971.

PUGET SOUND PULP & TIMBER COMPANY - CLEAR LAKE UNIT

LOCOMOTIVE SPECIFICATIONS

Road#	Builder	Year	Type	Cyl.	Driver	Blr	Weight	TE	notes
2	Lima #2837	6-1916	3T Shay	13½x15	36"		179,300	35,100	1
3	Lima #2643	7-1913	3T Shay	13½x15	36"		160,000	35,100	2
4	Lima #2304	3-1910	2T Shay	11x12	32"		100,000	20,350	3
5	Lima #2315	5-1910	2T Shay	12x12	36"		120,000	23,850	4
6	Baldwin #34840	6-1910	2-6-2	17x24	44"				5
7	Lima		2T Shay	12x12	36"				6
8	Lima #3171	8-1922	3T Shay	13½x15	36"		183,400	35,100	7
101	Baldwin #38271	1912	2-8-2	18x24	44"		141,100	28,375	8

NOTES

1. Built new for Clear Lake Lbr. Co. as #2; to PSP&T 1929;
   to PSP&T, Conway (English Lbr. unit) about 1945; scrapped there in 1952.
2. Built new for Skagit Log. Co. #5, Clear Lake WA;
   to Clear Lake Lbr. Co. #3;
   to PSP&T in 1929;
   to PSP&T, Conway (English Lbr. unit) about 1945; scrapped there in 1952
3. Built new for Miller Log. Co., Sedro Woolley WA;
   to Clear Lake Lbr. Co. #4;
   to Skagit Valley Lbr. Co. #4, Clear Lake WA;
   to PSP&T #4, Clear Lake WA in 1929. Scrapped in Clear Lake about 1941.
4. Built new for Clear Lake Lbr. Co. #5;
   to Skagit Valley Lbr. Co. #5, Clear Lake WA;
   to PSP&T #5, Clear Lake.
5. Built new for Rucker Brothers, as Cavanaugh Tbr. Co. #3, Hartford WA;
   to Hartford Eastern Ry. #6, Hartford WA;
   to PSP&T, Clear Lake WA in the mid-1930s; scrapped at Clear Lake about 1941.
6. to PSP&T in 1929, Clear Lake WA; offered for sale at Clear Lake in 1940 and described as "...in extremely bad condition, tires are sharp, gears worn out and boiler in need of extensive repairs." Scrapped at Clear Lake about 1941.
7. Built new for Security Log. Co. #1, Tolt WA;
   to Seattle Lbr. & Cedar Co. #8, Bellingham WA;
   to Puget Sound Sawmills and Shingle Co. #280, Concrete WA;
   to PSP&T #8, Clear Lake late in 1936 for $4,500;
   to St. Paul & Tacoma Lbr. Co. #8, Nooksack WA in 1941. **R-11**
8. Built new for C. A. Smith Lbr. Co., Coos Bay OR;
   to Coos Bay Lbr. Co., Coos Bay OR;
   to PSP&T, Clear Lake in mid-1930s; scrapped at Clear Lake about 1941.

PUGET SOUND PULP & TIMBER COMPANY - ENGLISH UNIT

LOCOMOTIVE SPECIFICATIONS

Road#	Builder	Year	Type	Cyl.	Driver	Blr	Weight	TE	notes
2	Lima #2837	6-1916	3T Shay	13½x15	36"		179,300	35,100	1
3	Lima #2643	7-1913	3T Shay	13½x15	36"		160,000	35,100	2
12	Climax #1581	5-1920	3T	16x16	36"		90T	39,600	3
13	Lima #3198	1-1923	3T Shay	14½x15	36"		201,500	40,400	4
14	Lima #2704	2-1914	3T Shay	12x15	36"		140,000	30,350	5
15	Lima #2708	10-1913	3T Shay	13½x15	36"		160,000	35,100	6

NOTES

1. Built new for Clear Lake Lbr. Co. #2;
   to PSP&T 1929;
   to PSP&T, Conway (English Lbr. unit) about 1945; scrapped there in 1952.
2. Built new for Skagit Log. Co. #5, Clear Lake WA;
   to Clear Lake Lbr. Co. #3;
   to PSP&T in 1929;
   to PSP&T, Conway (English Lbr. unit) about 1945; scrapped there in 1952
3. Built new for Parker-Bell Lbr. Co., Pilchuck WA #5;
   to English Lbr. Co. in 1922 #12;
   to Puget Sound Pulp & Timber, Conway WA in 1944; scrapped at Headquarters, early 1945.
4. Built new for English Lbr. Co. #13;
   to Puget Sound Pulp & Timber Co., Conway WA in 1944; scrapped at log dump Sept 1952.
5. Built new for Pine Belt Lbr. Co. #7, Fort Towson OK; Henderson Land & Lbr. Co., Fox AL;
   Birmingham Rail & Loco Co. (dealer), Birmingham AL;
   to English Lbr. Co., Conway WA in early 1924 as #14; wrecked in 1926 and rebuilt;
   to Puget Sound Pulp & Tbr. Co. in 1944; scrapped about 1946
6. Built new for Day Lbr. Co, Big Lake WA #3; may have been used briefly by the receivers of Day Lbr. Co. before sale
   to English Lbr. Co. in Nov. 1926 as their #15.
   to Puget Sound Pulp & Tbr. Co. #15 in 1944. Scrapped about 1946.

PUGET SOUND SAWMILLS & SHINGLE COMPANY

LOCOMOTIVE SPECIFICATIONS

Road#	Builder	Year	Type	Cyl.	Driver	Blr	Weight	TE	notes
280	Lima #3171	8-1922	3T Shay	13½x15	36"		183,400	35,100	1
290	Climax #1415	1916	3T	16x16	36"		90T	39,600	2

NOTES
1. Built new for Security Log. Co. #1, Tolt WA;
   to Seattle Lbr. & Cedar Co. #8, Bellingham WA;
   to Puget Sound Sawmills and Shingle Co. #280, Concrete WA;
   to Puget Sound Pulp & Tbr. #8, Clear Lake late in 1936 for $4,500 (road number change was made by grinding out the "2" and the "0");
   to St. Paul & Tacoma Lbr. Co. #8, Nooksack WA in 1941.
2. Built new for PSSM&S Co. #290, Concrete WA; disposition unknown.

SAMISH BAY LOGGING COMPANY

LOCOMOTIVE SPECIFICATIONS

Road#	Builder	Year	Type	Cyl.	Driver	Blr	Weight	TE	notes
1	Climax #1187	11-1912	3T	16x16	36"		75T		1
2	Climax #1593	3-1921	3T	15¼x16	36"		80T	35,200	2
4 (?)	Lima #773	9-1903	3T Shay	14½x12	36"		150,000	27,155	3

Rolling stock included, but was not limited to the following:
One MAC 4-40 Rail Car purchased in 1924
company used High-Hercules PC&F disconnected cars and later PC&F skeleton cars

NOTES
1. Built new for Samish Bay Log. Co. as #1, locomotive arrived in Blanchard December 12, 1912. Locomotive was scrapped at Blanchard when company ceased operations.
2. Built new for Samish Bay Log. Co. #2, cost was $27,400. Disposition unknown.
3. Built new for C. B. Howard & Co. #4, "Old Joe" (Emporium & Rich Valley RR #4), Emporium PA; C. B. Howard moved to Washington State and formed Samish Bay Log. Co. Locomotive became Samish Bay Log. in 1912.
   to Montborne Lbr. Co., Montborne WA in June of 1928.

R-12

SKAGIT MILL COMPANY

LOCOMOTIVE SPECIFICATIONS

Road#	Builder	Year	Type	Cyl.	Driver	Blr	Weight	TE	notes
1	Lima #2107	8-1908	2T Shay	11x12	32"		100,000	20,350	1
2	Lima #2236	10-1909	3T Shay	12x15	36"		140,000	29,800	2

Skagit Mill also operated two MAC Rail Cars, one model 4-20 and one model 4-30.

NOTES
1. Built new for Skagit Mill Co. #1, Lyman WA;
   to Lyman Tbr. Co. #1, Hamilton WA;
   to Marona Mill Co. #1, Acme WA 8-1942; converted to gasoline-hydraulic power.
2. Built new for Bolcom-Vanderhoof Log. Co. #2;
   to Skagit Mill Co. #2, Lyman WA;
   to Guy F. Atkinson Co. #2, Enumclaw WA 1-1940; later at Neah Bay WA.

SOUND TIMBER COMPANY

LOCOMOTIVE SPECIFICATIONS

Road#	Builder	Year	Type	Cyl.	Driver	Blr	Weight	TE	notes
1	Lima #2868	9-1916	3T Shay	12x15	36"		153,000	30,350	1
2	Lima #3057	1-1920	3T Shay	13½x15	36"		160,000	35,100	2
3	Lima #2765	5-1914	3T Shay	12x15	36"		146,000	30,350	3

Sound Timber also operated 5 MAC Rail Cars; three model 4-40's; one model 4-16 and one model 6-61.

NOTES
1. Built new for Sound Timber Co., Darrington WA;
   to Washington Veneer Co. in 1944, Darrington WA.
2. Built new for Sound Timber Co., Darrington WA;
   to Washington Veneer Co. in 1944, Darrington WA.
3. Built new for West Virginia Pulp & Paper Co. #10 (Greenbrier, Cheat & Elk RR #10), Cass WV;
   to Birmingham Rail & Loco (dealer), Birmingham AL;
   to R. E. Wood Lbr. Co., Hotchkiss VA in 1926;
   to Birmingham Rail & Loco;
   to Sound Timber Co. #3, Darrington WA in 1928;
   to Washington Veneer Co., Darington WA in 1944.

STANDARD RAILWAY & TIMBER COMPANY

(see Sultan Ry. & Timber Co.)

SULTAN RAILWAY & TIMBER COMPANY

LOCOMOTIVE SPECIFICATIONS

Road#	Builder	Year	Type	Cyl.	Driver	Blr	Weight	TE	notes
1	Heisler #1090	3-1906	2T	16¾x14	40"		52T	20,000	1
1	Lima #803	7-1903	2T Shay	11x12	32"		90,000	18,750	2
2	Heisler #1122	11-1907	2T	15x12	36"		37T	14,000	3
3	Lima #2653	7-1913	3T Shay	12x15	36"		140,000	30,350	4
3	Lima #2945	2-1918	2T Shay	12x12	36"		120,000	23,890	5
4	Lima #3038	10-1919	3T Shay	14½x15	36"		180,000	40,400	6
5	Lima #3074	5-1920	3T Shay	13½x15	36"		160,000	35,100	7
21	Lima #1810	1-1907	3T Shay	12x15	36"		130,000	29,835	8
?	Lima #3055	2-1920	2T Shay	11x12	32"		100,000	22,580	9

Note that Sultan Ry. & Tbr. Co. and Standard Ry. & Tbr. Co. interchanged locomotives between themselves and, indeed, had common principals in ownership; hence both names are reflected in this roster. This is also the reason there is no distinction between locomotives that carried the same road numbers, ie. "first" or "second" (see text).

NOTES

1. Built new for Standard Ry. & Tbr. Co. #1, Hazel WA;
   to Sultan Ry. & Tbr. Co.;
   to N. & M. Lbr. Co., Rochester WA
2. Built new for Sultan Ry. & Tbr. Co. #1, Sultan WA;
   to Puget Sound Mills & Tbr. Co., Port Angeles WA
3. Built new for Standard Ry. & Tbr. Co. #2, Hazel WA;
   to Sultan Ry. & Tbr. Co. #2, Sultan WA;
   to Wood-Knight Log. Co., Bellingham WA
4. Built new for Sultan Ry. & Tbr. Co. #3, Sultan WA;
   to Monroe Log. Co. #3, Machias WA; scrapped 1939.
5. Built new for stock engine and used as plant switcher at Lima Locomotive Works #3; rebuilt with 32" drivers and sold
   to Sultan Ry. & Tbr. Co. #3, Oso WA;
   to Canadian Robert Dollar Co. #4, Union Bay BC;
   to Thurston & Flavelle #4, Port Coquitlam BC;
   to Hage Tbr. & Investment Co. #4 (leased), Port Coquitlam BC 1923; R-13
   to Alberni Pacific Lbr. Co. #3, Port Alberni BC 1926.
6. Built new for Sultan Ry. & Tbr. Co. #4, Oso WA;
   to Lyman Tbr. Co. #6, Hamilton WA 5-1930;
   to Soundview Pulp Co. #6, Hamilton WA 1945.
7. Built new for Sultan Ry. & Tbr. Co. #5, Oso WA;
   to Monroe Log. Co. #5, Lake Stevens WA 2-1940; scrapped 8-1946.
8. Built new for Sultan Ry. & Tbr. Co. #21, Oso WA;
   to Sauk River Lbr. Co., Darrington WA;
   to Willamette Iron & Steel (dealer), Portland OR;
   to Buffelin Lbr. & Mfg. Co., Eagle Gorge WA;
   to O. W. Brown Locomotive & Supply Co. (dealer), Seattle WA;
   to Alpine Lbr. Co. #21, Alpine WA;
   to Security Log. Co., Skykomish WA; scrapped 6-1936
9. Built new for Lake Riley Lbr. Co. #1, Hazel WA;
   to Security Log. Co., Tolt WA;
   to Cispus Log. Co. #2, Port Orchard WA;
   to Sultan Ry. & Tbr. Co., Oso WA; scrapped 12-1938.

From the publisher:

This has been an exciting project. Dennis Thompson has brought together the material collected in his lifetime search for the railroads and men that caused those slashes and scars and trails on the hillsides of Skagit County, many still quite visible as you drive the North Cascades Highway more than 50 years after the last steam locomotive struggled up with empties and carefully braked the loads of logs down them. There is a deep fascination in our history and in how men (and women) met the challenges and solved the problems of survival. They did not foresee or design to *build great cities* but merely to survive, and hopefully prosper, in the best manner they could achieve. And the tasks they undertook - and usually accomplished successfully - were mind boggling, even if we, in hindsight, are able to acknowledge them with only a passing curiosity. The marvel of their accomplishments is now and then brought forcefully to mind such as a recent story that reached us. It seems Simpson Timber Company was marking the close of the last railroad logging camp (Grisdale) by cutting a huge old growth tree like in the 'old days' depicted in this book....which the logging crew could then not handle and load because it was too large for any current logging equipment they had! You can see that last Simpson log train out of Camp Grisdale - in 1985 and in steam!- in our companion railroad logging history book on Mason County, LOGGING TO THE SALTCHUCK.

We have purposely made this book more than a 'train book' or a 'logging book', we have endeavored to make it a total human environment history surrounding the logging community; from the logging trains, to the camp dentist (page 231) who uses a wheelbarrow as his *operating chair*, to *your* back porch (page 104) overlooking a ten wheeler and a couple Heisler locomotives simmering away at the end of the day, to the forlorn serenity of a railroad switchback in the forest (page 176), to the huge and spindly trestles that carried the steam machines and logs and men over deep canyons. From the inelegant tarpaper camp car of Faber Logging Co. to the pristine new logging camp 18 of Lyman Timber Co. (page 85), you can immerse your thoughts in an age gone by - not better, not worse , but fascinating. Would we want to live these *good old days?*, probably not, but we can certainly enjoy them from here.

The maps, painstakingly researched and drawn by Dr. Jost, are a gold mine of information for perusing and for guidance if you *get to ground* in searching out those old rail trails. The model railroad hobby can be much more than *playing with trains*. Many modelers have developed their modeling skills to the level of historian in miniature, recreating their favorite historical pictures or scenes in an actual operating miniature railroad. And these craftsmen were strongly in mind when selecting photographs and drawings for this book to aid them in re-creating this old history. The rosters of locomotives and the complete logging camp equipment inventory, plus other bits and pieces, all aid you and the historian modeler in accurately visualizing and modeling this era.

We take you from oxen and horse powered logging of the late 1800s to truck logging that completely replaced the railroads by the end of the 1950s. And we hope to leave you with a better understanding of Skagit County logging railroads and most particularly with many pleasant memories.

And we extend our deep appreciation and thank you to the many persons who shared their stories and photograph collections to help make this history possible.

F. Raoul Martin
NorthWest Short Line
August 1989

INDEX

E

F

G

M

I-6

N

I-10

Note: Many of the above entries have been marked "town" for clarification purposes only. In fact they were in many instances merely places named to identify the particular location of the logging company or operation and disappeared when the logging activities moved on.

Photographers, Photo and Drawing Contributors

VANISHED RAILS

A man is old, I've heard them say,
  When his visions are all of yesterday
When his eyes are turned to scenes that are gone;
  He lives in the past while Life rolls on.

And that, perhaps, is why I dream
  Of roaring stacks that billowed steam,
Of two thin lines of silver light
  That led through thc forest aisles at night.

A crossing whistle long and clear
  Reminds me of the cheek so dear
That sometimes nestled close to mine
  When I busted fog on the logging line.

There are rails no more where we used to ride.
  For the trees are gone from the mountain side;
And teeming life, of which we were part,
  Is only an echo deep in my heart.

But I see in the night a water tank;
  I hear the side-rods' muffled clank,
Or the eerie whine of the dynamo,
  And I see a face in the firebox glow.

Oh, a man is old - I guess it's truth -
  When his thoughts are all of days of youth,
When visions are full of hours that have flown;
  He lives in memories and he lives alone.

But I wouldn't trade for youth nor gold
  Just two little dreams of those days of old;
The clank of side-rods drifting free -
  And the girl who rode in the cab with me.

-Frank Bennitt

Reprinted courtesy Railfan & Railroad

R7E
R8E
R9E
DEMPSEY LBR. CO.
Birdsview Unit
LYMAN TBR. CO.
[HAMILTON LOG'G. CO.]
LYMAN TBR. CO.
Grandy Creek Extension
(SOUNDVIEW PULP CO.)
[McNEILL-O'HEARNE]
(Second Unit)
FOREST MILL CO.
PUGET SOUND SAWMILLS & SHINGLE CO.
McNEILL-O'HEARNE
Camp 3 Unit
UNIDENTIFIED LOGGING R.R.
McNEILL-O'HEARNE
(First Unit)
SKAGIT RIVER LOG'G. CO.
PUGET SOUND & CASCADE RY.
BAKER RIVER & SHUKSAN R.R.
SEATTLE & NORTHERN R.R.
BURLINGTON NORTHERN
Concrete
Birdsview
Hamilton
UL-2
UNIDENTIFIED LOGGING R.R.
UL-3
GALBRAITH BROS.
CLEAR LAKE LBR. CO.
Finney Creek Unit
(PUGET SOUND PULP & TBR. CO.)
PUGET SOUND PULP & TBR. CO.
Mill Creek Unit
CLEAR LAKE LBR. CO.
Pressentin Creek Unit
FABER LOG'G. CO.
COWDEN LBR. CO.
Rockport
SKAGIT RIVER RY.
SOUND TIMBER CO.
Continued from Front Cover
PUGET SOUND PULP & TBR. CO.
Day Lake Extension
ENGLISH LBR. CO.
(PUGET SOUND PULP & TBR. CO.)
SULTAN RY. & TBR. CO.
SOUND TIMBER CO.
DANAHER LBR. CO.
STETSON-POST LBR. CO.
BUCKER BROS.
NELSON-NEAL LBR. CO.
UNIDENTIFIED LOGGING R.R.
See Inset MAP B (Lower Right)
Halterman
Oso
Rowan
Hazel
Fortson
STANDARD RY. & TBR. CO.
SEATTLE LAKE SHORE & EASTERN R.R.
SOUND TIMBER CO.